P9-EJS-683

MY WILDERNESS WILDCATS

Also by the author:

A WORLD OF MY OWN

MY WILDERNESS WILDCATS

Mike Tomkies

Doubleday & Company, Inc., Garden City, New York   1978

The photographs throughout the book were taken by
the Author and the picture on the jacket shows
Freddy at nine-and-a-half weeks old, confident
enough to give a juvenile imitation of his fierce
father's spit.

Library of Congress Cataloging in Publication Data

Tomkies, Mike.
  My wilderness wildcats.

  1. European wildcat—Legends and stories. 2. Natural history—
Scotland. I. Title.
QL795.C2T65 1978   599'.74428

Copyright © 1977 by Mike Tomkies
Library of Congress Card Catalog Number: 77-12879
ISBN: 0-385-13477-0

ALL RIGHTS RESERVED
PRINTED IN THE UNITED STATES OF AMERICA
FIRST EDITION IN THE UNITED STATES OF AMERICA

For Allan MacColl
and Geoffrey Kinns

MY WILDERNESS WILDCATS

Chapter 1

As Highlander Allan MacColl walked along a lonely track eight miles from my isolated waterfront cottage, a sudden flurry in a steep-sided ditch made him look down. What he saw there astonished him. Spitting and hissing, two wildcat kittens had backed into a corner, their mouths open, tiny fangs bared, claws out, ready to fight for their immature lives with all the ferocity that characterizes their kind. Allan caught a glimpse, a shadow of a big cat with long striped bushy tail slinking away with more kittens through the undergrowth above the ditch. Peeling off his jacket, he threw it over the two spitting kits and, after a struggle, caught them.

He put his angry captives onto soft sacking in a grocery box in his van and drove them home.

A few weeks later, as the last of the 570 miles from London slid away beneath my Land Rover, and the broad highways of the Scottish Lowlands gave way to the familiar single-track roads falling precipitously through the mountains or winding beside the wild wooded lochs, I looked forward to merging once more into the tranquillity of the remote Highland area which had then been my home for nearly five years.

My six-week return visit to Canada had been an extraordinary period. I had trekked with an Indian hunter after grazing boars and mother grizzlies with cubs—stalking close enough for photos but trying not to provoke a charge. I had also chased on foot behind a pack of trained hounds over miles of mountainous terrain to photograph and help tree and radio-collar mountain lions. After managing those hard, blistering days, I wanted little more to do with the world of wild felines.

When I walked into Allan MacColl's village shop after my long drive to stock up with supplies for the months that lay ahead in my remote outpost halfway up a roadless, eighteen-mile, fresh water loch, I was conscious of a feeling of anticlimax. All the excitement of the bear and cougar treks, the days with new and old friends in both Canada and London were over. Once again I had to face loneliness, and the solitude that had become my permanent mistress, which was the price I paid for the privilege of studying nature closely in all seasons in the real wilderness.

It was a fine but cloudy day, with a strong southerly breeze, and at the door I paused to look to where the loch waters vanished four-and-a-half miles away in a bend among the mountains. I hoped the good weather would last for I had to go twice that distance to reach home and even from the wood where I left my boat and parked the Land Rover, I still faced a six-mile walk if it cut up too rough for a laden boat. The way led through woods with many windfalls, high ledges, rocky foreshore, several bogs and large areas of two foot high tussocks whose grassy crowns hid the treacherous gullies between them. Although I had frequently made the double trek with full pack, tired as I now was, I didn't relish the idea of covering the route carrying eighty pounds of supplies.

As I checked last items against my list, Allan's brother, Ian, a field officer with the Red Deer Commission, came up. We exchanged greetings, and then he said, "By the way, Allan has found a couple of wildcat kittens. He'd probably let you have them." With my head still full of my exciting trip, I only expressed mild interest.

Wildcat kittens? I thought. What were they compared with the wild black bears, bald eagles, cougars and grizzlies I had just been seeing? The wildlife of Scotland appeared humdrum in comparison. Besides, I had never liked cats. At one childhood school, while other boys had been bitten by dogs, I'd had the dubious distinction of being the only boy in the form that had been bitten by a cat. Cats had always seemed to me to be faithless creatures whose "love" for their owners was of the cupboard variety, who only came home for food and warmth, and whose "affection" was only given because they wanted at that particular moment to have their heads tickled or to be stroked before going their own independent ways. I was more of a dog man myself, proof of which, all six feet, four-and-a-third inches nose-to-tail-tip of him, was now reposing lion-like outside the shop in the Land Rover.

I had bought Cantersend Ringleader Beowulf—to give Moobli his full pedigree name—in January as an eleven-week-old pup from a top breeder in Sussex who was renowned for her large, powerful, award-winning yet amiable Alsatians. Although during my first three-and-a-half years in the Scottish wilds—when I'd lived in an old patched-up wooden croft on the Atlantic end of a sea island—I'd had no companion at all, when I moved to Wildernesse, my current home, I'd felt the need for a really good dog. Not only as a companion but also to help me track the foxes, badgers, and the roe and red deer that passed through my woods, so I could record their exact movements for my studies. Moobli was so far proving ideal. I had no wish to show him, which was just as well because, although he had seventeen international and national grand champions in his past four generations, Moobli lacked one characteristic essential for a good show dog. Alsatians should have stiffly pricked-up ears but, despite my ministrations with chiropodists' felt, one of his huge ears—four inches across the base—simply refused to stiffen. Its tip drooped forward, so when he looked at you it appeared he was waving goodbye with his right ear.

But he was gentle, astonishingly so. He suffered various sheep-dogs and tiny terriers, who felt rightly territorial, to bark and "drive" him away from the specific little areas around their homes. A good big aristocratic dog who is well brought up and sure of his place, naturally recognizes the territorial rights of all other dogs, big or small, and will put up with this kind of behaviour without retaliation. But there was one snag to Moobli's apparent supine toleration—he was still a pup, only eight months old, and already strangers who knew the breed would stop and exclaim that he was the biggest young Alsatian they had ever seen—and I felt sure that when he was mature, from three onwards, he would have his own rigidly defined codes of behaviour as far as other dogs were concerned, but this almost certainly would not apply to cats.

So, when Ian MacColl told me about the wildcat kittens, I felt Moobli and wildcats would not be a wise mixture to have around my lonely home. In addition, I had an enormous amount of work ahead. Quite apart from outdoor chores and normal wildlife treks, for which there were never enough hours in the day or night, a New York publisher had commissioned a book on my Canadian experiences, and I had to write sixteen long chapters before March. I doubted, too, that Allan's kits could be true wildcats. I'd never heard of anyone catching even kits by hand, and I felt they were almost certainly the progeny of a domestic cat gone wild, a common occurrence in the Highlands.

I drove away with plenty of daylight left for the long boat trip home, but as I was nearing the turn-off to Allan MacColl's cottage, I suddenly felt churlish. To go straight home without even bothering to take a look at the kittens would have been downright rude.

Outside his seaside cottage, Allan, dark haired and burly, greeted me with a big affable grin. I already had much to thank him for, as it was he who had first told me about the wilderness dwelling that was now my home. As he took me to the shed where the kittens had their home in a large wooden box, he said, "They were truly wild when I picked them up. If they had been any older I would have needed thick gloves." He picked the kittens out of the box with both hands. They spat and hissed, saw me, a looming stranger, flared loudly, struggled, one bit his thumb and he let them go. Immediately they hit the ground they scattered in opposite directions into the undergrowth, disappearing completely, like wisps of smoke, as if they'd never been there.

But that one glance had told me these were not ordinary cats. They were beautiful with superbly dramatic markings—two light tawny tigers with striped legs, bright blue eyes turning to green, and thick black-tipped tails. Allan said the wildlife park a hundred miles to the east would gladly have them but the problem was taking them there. He, busy with his mobile grocery van during the tourist season, had not the time.

As we rounded them up, grabbing them firmly by the scruffs of their necks, so they couldn't twist their heads round to bite, they made an odd, loud squawking sound with wide-open mouths, rather like the noise ducks make when startled or seized. I was surprised for it seemed an odd coincidence that I'd heard young cougars make exactly the same noise, though louder, when first handled by man. As Allan replaced the wire mesh over their box, I had the feeling that I would be seeing these kittens again.

Nearby I saw a sleeping bag with an old mattress draped over a pile of wood chips. Allan grinned, "I slept with them the first few nights, trying to tame them a little. I heard you should do that. It was a wee bit of a task coaxing them to lap warm milk and eat meat at first. I don't think they were quite weaned." He scratched his head. "Well, I kept them for you anyway. But if you don't want them we can let them go again later."

Touched by his kindness, I thanked him and asked if I could have a good think about it. Taking on a pair of wildcats who might grow to anything between eight and sixteen pounds wasn't something to do lightly.

In the pine and larch wood where I parked my Land Rover, I heaved my boat right way up and after laying a track of branches over the rocky shore, hauled it into the water. It was a thirteen foot, six inch Norwegian style fibreglass boat with a deep keel. Although it was only four and a half years old, it had seen some rough years on the rocky coast of the sea island where I had first lived in the Highlands and was now heavily patched along the chines, and I only used it for rowing or to leave in the woods nearer civilization when I made my rare trips out of the wilds. My new fibreglass boat, double-hulled and semi-cabined, which was essential for long winter supply trips in gale-lashed waters, was at home, on its wooden runners beneath an alder tree where I had winched it high above any possible rise in the loch level from rainstorms.

Before I finished loading up, Moobli proved there was nothing wrong with his memory. He leaped into the boat and stood in the bow, his usual place, looking at me solemnly, anxious to please. I couldn't help smiling. Even as a pup, he'd had a sad solemn look, a really alert but oddly philosophical expression which was not only endearing but went with his quiet nature, for although his bark was already deep enough to scare a cougar, he seldom used it. He was the quietest dog I'd ever known.

After the first three miles and the easterly slopes of the 2,774-foot mountain had receded to our right, the stiff southerly wind forced its way down the valley before the next high saddle of hills, and sent curling waves slapping the side of the heavily laden boat, throwing high spumes of spray over us. I headed into the waves until I was abreast of Sandy Point, a forty-yard long spit of gravel that ran into the loch from the north bank, then went north-east with the waves until I reached the slight lee of a gravelly beach two miles from home. There, I throttled down the engine, drifting near the shore. Again Moobli remembered—when I did this it meant his exercise run. He put his huge paws on the side, peered in at the rising ground below the surface and, when he judged it shallow enough, leaped out with a huge splash. Then, shaking himself vigorously on shore like a small bear, he set off alongside the moving boat. Heavily built though he was, all his flesh was fluid muscle and he could cover that last two miles, over terrain in which no man could run, in about ten minutes. It never failed to thrill me, seeing him run like that, hurling his body over the deep tussocks in deep bounds like a charging cougar, threading his way through the big boulders with his light tan chest, shoulders and thrusting rear legs flashing like quicksilver between them, or breaking into a loping trot over the yielding gravel banks, his head low and vast, semi-webbed paws spread out like those of a wolf, so that he virtually drifted over places where a man would flounder.

I arrived a few minutes before him and in the now-calm waters I edged the boat gently against the grassy bank below the ash and alder trees and stepped ashore into the paradise I call Wildernesse. During the eight years I had by now spent in the wilds of both Canada and the Scottish Highlands I had always regarded my home as being in the wilderness. But the moment I had first seen this extraordinary place, after reading the name in one of Henry Williamson's magnificent works, *The Pathway*, I had added the final "e." No other name suited it better for I had never seen anywhere in my life that encompassed in so small an area such a variety of wild and varied beauty. As I looked at it again, after my longest absence from the wilds, it was like seeing it for the first time.

To the west stood a four-acre wood in full summer bloom. Behind its southern fringe of scaly red-barked Scots pines, the land rose upwards, its centre a rocky thirty-foot escarpment from whose ledges sprang birches, rowans and twisted oaks. Areas of mushy swamp, tussock grass and broad mossy tables cushioned thickly with needles lay between the profusion of larch, ash and silver and Douglas firs, some of which reared over 100 feet into the sky. And at the top was an open undulating area where pines competed with larch, and red deer had their winter rubbing posts.

Before the old, south-facing, gamekeeper's cottage, that I had renovated after hauling paint, lumber and other materials up the loch by boat and raft, lay a one-and-a-half acre patch that had been verdant pasture when I'd left, for I had cut away the early bracken. Now, I noted wryly, the bracken was again in complete control, some of it six feet high, almost engulfing the twin bushes of crimson and purple rhododendron to the south-east. To the east of the cottage and starting from right next to it, stood a larger triangular wood of oak, ash, holly, rowan, hazel bushes and birch trees, dominated by a huge Norway spruce that was a full fifteen feet round the butt. Next to these ran a broad belt of tall larch trees which crossed a small secondary burn and merged with a deep grove of beech trees which lined the main burn. Along my waterfront, sixty yards from the cottage, a screen of alder and ash trees fringed and framed the shimmering waters of the loch, which from my door stretched in a spectacular view for a full four miles before the first bend below the big mountain. Immediately behind the cottage the land began to rise to the first 400-foot ridges, which were but the prelude to the rolling hills behind them which rose to some 1,500 feet then dropped down into a misty glen and a river before rising almost sheer again to the 2,719-foot, four-mile-long saddle of Guardian Mountain. These hills protected my home from the worst northerly gales, stored and reflected the heat of the sun, and, with the two woods framing the area, gave Wildernesse a mini-climate of its own.

It was a lovely kingdom, one that really extended for fifteen miles, for mine was the only home along that length of roadless shore, and it stretched back to the north for a good six miles of glens and mountains before striking a road. It was, in fact, one of the largest uninhabited areas left in the British Isles—a kingdom of red deer stags that roared in the autumn as they rounded up their harems of hinds, of golden eagles, ravens, buzzards, kestrels and sparrowhawks, of foxes, badgers and otters, who had their holts along the rocky shores, of roe deer who sheltered in and shared my woods with a pair of red squirrels.

Many meadow brown butterflies and sooty-black sweep moths flitted about the grasses and, amid the profusion of buttercups, red and white clover lined the path up from my log archway entrance. From the largest ash on the shore, a just-hatched green emerald moth fluttered weakly, like a tiny green-winged angel, to rest awhile on a bracken frond. In the clearings speckled wood butterflies hopped and dropped through the humming summer air. A lone cormorant winged powerfully westwards over the loch surface, looking every moment as if it would hit into a wave.

As the silent peaceful spell of Wildernesse enveloped me once more, I was joined by Moobli, panting heavily after his run, and in that carefree moment I ran with him to the south-east corner of my land on the lochside. Then we walked beneath the stately beeches along the banks of the burn which was the main vein for the mountains for some eight miles. A hundred yards north-east of the cottage, we came to the place that embodies for me the living spirit of Wildernesse. The burn flows over four deeply-stepped pools, drops down a ten-foot waterfall into the pool from which I pipe my water, then cascades in three separate forks down thirty feet onto a tangle of great gnarled rocks. Tiny ferns spring from the many fairy grottos in the rocks and in the sunlight the splashing water forms myriad rainbows from the spray, while from the trees above hang wefts of moss and creepers. A magic place.

Over the next few days I slashed the bracken back from the front area for, where this weed flourishes, nothing else will grow. I tried to avoid the foxgloves where so many bees came for nectar, and also the birch, oak and hazel seedlings which I would thin out later when I'd decided *how* I wanted the forest to encroach. The midges were terrible, rising in dense clouds from the falling bracken and often flying straight into my eyes. These predatory little insects, who affect the movements of both men and animals throughout the Highlands up to 1,800 feet—one reason red deer go to the high tops in summer is to escape them—have a bite worse than two mosquitos, to take a mite of your blood that wouldn't cover half a pinhead, and have hard little bodies so they can bore their way through your clothes. After a time they'd become just too much to take, reducing me to a self-swatting, scratching maniac; then I would run with Moobli to the shore and throw broken tree branches out for him to fetch. He'd steam out like a tug boat, head and shoulders well clear, tail drifting in his four-knot wake, grab the branch and steam back with it, reminding me of a bear.

My vegetable garden, a twenty-one-foot-square patch which I had laboriously cleared of more than two tons of rocks, and had fertilized with seaweed brought up in the boats and last year's autumn leaf compost, was now a weed-covered wilderness of its own. All the radishes had grown and gone to seed, so had the lettuces but the cabbages, sprouts and kale—ideal for wilderness greens as they last all winter and can stand frost—were fine. So I weeded the whole patch. But all my carefully sown peas had gone and the tiny diggings along their rows proved mice and voles had had them. Mice too had gnawed their way through the doors and into the house—to eat and litter the kitchen floor with my last year's crop of hazelnuts. It was then I remembered the wildcat kittens.

Next morning, when, with the aid of Moobli's fine nose, I went on my thrice weekly inspection of the woods to note the movements of foxes, badgers and otters along the shore, I thought of the kittens again. I was in the west wood, an extraordinary place, for every time I went there I seemed to find something I hadn't noticed before, and was standing in a rush-filled marsh, about to climb the thirty-foot rock escarpment, when I looked at it again with fresh eyes. The east edge ended in a tumble of huge jagged boulders, forming a bridge with the marsh, and these merged into a tangle of criss-crossed windfall trunks of fir, larch and oak, through which brambles with new-forming blackberries and necklaces of honeysuckle competed for space. Beneath the trunks, under this screening foliage and in places inaccessible to man, were many dry rock ledges covered with moss. To a professional forester interested mainly in rows of close-stacked, fast-growing conifers, the whole of the west wood would have been a mess. Certainly, I intended to plant many new trees, mainly broadleaf, but the difficulty with this, added to the fact that young seedlings could not regenerate naturally in my woods, was not only that deer ate them but also mice and voles. I had far too many of these about the place, and I often saw voles scudding like brown bullets through their grass tunnels. These little creatures can multiply to plague proportions, five hundred to an acre, and do great damage in woods by eating seed and seedlings and stripping young trees of their bark, as well as competing with deer for green grass. Now, as I looked at the dry grottos between the boulders, and the astonishing array of small sheltered retreats in the wood, I made up my mind. Wildcats thrive on voles, among their other prey of mice, hares, rabbits and birds, but the one species whose tracks I had never found in the area were those of wildcats. Yet here seemed to be a perfect wildcat habitat. From that moment, I thought about Allan's kittens in earnest.

The main problem was to ascertain, if possible, that they were pure wildcats. Consulting my few reference books and some accounts garnered through helpful zoological contacts, I was astonished to discover that just about the only two things all the naturalists were agreed upon was that true Scottish wildcats,

Felis silvestris grampia, were still rare, surviving only in isolated pockets in remote parts of the Highlands, and had been near extinction in the early part of this century, and that they were, despite several attempts made by humans, totally untameable. The rest was a mass of contradictory evidence:

Wildcats are larger and stronger built than domestic cats; they are sometimes smaller and lighter.

Wildcats have short truncated striped tails; they have long bushy striped tails.

Wildcats never purr; they purr like domestics but louder.

Wildcats bury their droppings like domestics; they never do.

Wildcats are faithful to one mate for life and never mate with domestic cats turned feral; they readily do but the hybrids are infertile.

Wildcats have shorter small intestines than domestics; this theory is nonsense.

Wildcats eat no vegetable matter; they sometimes do.

Wildcats have two, occasionally three, breeding periods a year; they have only one.

Wildcat females rear their young away from the toms who are liable to kill and eat them; the toms sometimes help feed the family.

The more I read the more interesting they became.

Domestic cats are believed to have descended from either or both the North African cats *Felis lybica* and *Felis margarita,* for the first records of domesticated cats are by the early Egyptians and then later in other Mediterranean countries, and these would not be related to the European and Asian wildcats, *Felis silvestris silvestris.* There is an opposite view, however, which maintains that domestic cats are descended from crosses between *Felis s. s.* and species like *Felis lybica.*

It was surprising to learn that the precise origin of the domestic cat is still not known. They are believed to have been brought to Britain and western Europe by the Phoenician traders some 1,200 years B.C. to keep rats and mice down in corn stores, and the first mention of *cattus* in literature was by Palladius in A.D. 350 as being "useful in granaries." However, the pure wildcat of Scotland, Europe and Asia was an indigenous prehistoric animal, its bones being found in Pleistocene deposits up to two million years old, along with those of the mammoth, great cave bear and cave lion, and its form and structure today has not altered one whit since then.

Although not hitherto a cat lover, I now found myself fascinated. It seemed very little was known for sure about the true wildcat, especially about its behaviour. And yet here, in south Inverness-shire where I lived, was one of the last main strongholds of the species. One of the first wildlife photos I'd ever taken, by the kind of miraculous luck that occasionally comes to a beginner, had been a day time shot of a huge old tom wildcat full-length on a rock less than half a mile from Allan MacColl's home one dawn two years back. Later, using the photo as a guide, I had measured the image on the rock and had estimated the cat to be nearly four feet long. It was just possible these two kits might be his progeny.

On July 23, Moobli and I boated up the loch against strong westerlies and went to see Allan and the kittens again. Two gamekeepers and a local man, who had studied indigenous wild creatures all his life, were all convinced they were pure. We worked out how the two kits, now about seven weeks old, might have come to be in the ditch. The mother had perhaps been crossing the single-track road with her brood on their first outing. A couple of tourist cars had scared the family into a run and the two weakest kits had been temporarily left behind. By chance Allan had pulled up into an open space and gone for a brief walk down a track that ran close to the river side. Perhaps she had been a young cat and burdened with feeding a large family during the wet spring, had been forced to leave the weaker when danger she could not fight had threatened. Possibly she had meant to return for them later. But Allan, not wanting to leave the kits, weak and tottery on their feet in the cold rain and muddy ditch, had caught them.

As I looked at the two little monsters again, now healthy and flaring and spitting in their box at the two humans looking down at them, Allan echoed my own thoughts. "Not much is known about wildcats. If you could tame them a wee bit and get them to live around your wild place up the loch, you might find them rewarding to study." He had heard of an American naturalist who had offered £200 each for wildcat kittens on Skye last year.

I told him I was grateful that he'd kept them so long for me and would be happy to take them. After we had put them into a large wooden box with two wire netting sides that I used for small injured birds, I was reaching for my cheque book when Allan swiftly put out his hand to stay my arm. "Please, I don't want anything for them," he said. "If you can look after and study them, they're yours." I stammered my thanks.

I brought them home on the deck of my boat in light rain, riding the waves downhill all the way. As they stretched their little thirteen-inch bodies up against the wire netting and saw the lone larches of Green Isle, the great grey dead tree snags on Heron Island and the wild woods of sessile oak and birch passing by, I heard strange whistling sounds—*wheeou wheeou*—rather like weak buzzard calls. At first it sounded as if they came from the air above, though there was no bird there, and then from the nearby land. Then I realized the kits were making them, through barely opened mouths. They were eerie, high-pitched sounds, not piercing yet far-carrying, and distinctly ventriloquistic. I felt they were probably special calls young wildcats make to summon their mothers from a distance, yet at the same time not attract predators. I'd never heard kittens make such noises before.

At home, I carried them up and set their box-cage on a stand in the fourteen-foot-square kitchen. When my head went near they both reared high on their hind legs at the back of the box and spat, growling like two tiny whirring dynamos. Puny though their spits were, they were being as fierce as they knew how. I sorted out two plastic bowls for food and milk and opened a tin of the cat food Allan said they liked most. As soon as I prised up one corner of the netting and they scented the meat—instant attack! Yowling and growling in their high treble voices they jammed their heads against the stout wire and slashed out at the food with the claws on their unusually big feet. I just withdrew my hand in time.

Immediately the bigger kit with a slightly broader head ousted the other, chewing the meat while it growled and flared at the other's attempts to get a share. With the milk it was slightly different—the bigger wouldn't let the other near until it had some in its belly but then it did relinquish king position a *little*, and the smaller shoved its head in, and they both lapped away greedily with a noisy ticking sound. With both thus busy, I tried to push their heads away from the bowl but they, not spitting now as they were too engrossed in the milk, resisted with amazing strength for their size, forcing their skulls against my fingers as they continued drinking.

As soon as they had fed and drunk their fill, they relaxed a little, just flaring slightly as I passed to and fro stacking away supplies. After supper I checked them against the wildcat descriptions I had gathered—the light tawny rufous fur, the dark grey-black leg stripes, the dark lines down the back that would one day merge, the malformed "M" on the forehead, the twin stripes back from the eyes, the ringed tail ending in a black tip, the black furred feet and soles, horn coloured claws, large canid teeth—all seemed to fit.

When I stole in quietly several times at dusk and after dark, they were both curled round each other, keeping themselves warm on the hay in the darkest corner, but one was always facing outwards with its bright red tongue sticking out slightly and half an eye open. This was probably instinctive wildcat kitten behaviour for protection.

Chapter 2

As I dressed early next morning, anxious that my two spitfires were still alive, I had an idea. One of my sweaters was the same rusty brown hue as the one Allan usually wore, so hoping it would make a difference I put it on. When I opened the door I was greeted first with silence, then a loud cacophony of squawls and *maus*—a sound as in Mau Mau and without the preliminary *ee* of the domestic cat's *miaows*. They spat as I got close but not as loudly as yesterday—perhaps they associated the sweater colour with the strange creature who had been feeding them since losing their mother.

Again the smell of meat and milk sent them into a small frenzy, flattening their heads against the netting and reaching out with their claws. Again the bigger ousted the smaller until it had eaten its fill.

After breakfast I let them go in the big kitchen to see how Moobli reacted to them. I thought he would have to be trained into not chasing them. The kits crept instinctively towards the walls, then discovered the iron fender before the fireplace, scrambled clumsily over it and peeped at us from behind. Astonishingly, Moobli took them in his stride. I sat with one arm tightly round him so he wouldn't feel jealous and he was as fascinated with them as I was. He looked with his large brown

eyes, brows almost as furrowed as a bloodhound's, and from time
to time as they tottered weakly about, examining log chunks,
mistiming feeble leaps at each other, he looked up at me in
query as if asking, Are they all right? He showed no belligerence at all. And when he moved forward cautiously to sniff
them, and they spat and struck out at him with their claws, he
just looked pained and retreated with a whine of disappointment.

We stayed as still as we could and, as they investigated this
new world, sniffing everything and moving their heads up and
down as they peered at us, the sun came through the window
and I saw the bright blue of their eyes was being edged out from
the pupils by a light greeny-gold colour. These piebald eyes
gave them a comical look.

Right from the start the kittens showed totally different char-
acters. The smaller, weaker one was shy and secretive, yet more
fierce at human approach. She had a slinky, feminine look and
always flared and tried to bite when being picked up. The bigger
was more easy going, outward looking, always investigating
strange objects first and after a time only crouched down with
flattened ears when my hand went near. I soon realized one
could not dither about when picking them up because if they
saw the hand coming slowly both would retreat and spit. But if
I spoke soothingly first, then grasped them quickly, firmly, yet
gently by the scruff of the neck as close to the head as possible, I
could usually succeed without being bitten. Once grasped the
big one went limp but the smaller squawked loudly.

Inspired by their wild beauty, and wanting to call them something distinctive, I hit on the name Cleopatra. Cleo would be the
thinner wilder one, and the bigger, also a female, would be
Patra. So CleoPatra would be a good collective name for the two
in the diaries I intended to keep about them.

As they spent the whole morning asleep, curled round each
other again, I wondered if they liked comfort as much as domestic cats. I brought them into my bedroom and let them go on
the thick wool bedspread. To my surprise they instantly flattened themselves on the open exposed surface, crawled to the
edge keeping as close as two striped moles, dived clumsily for

the floor and shot for refuge beneath the bed. I had quite a tussle and wore gloves to get them back into their box—clearly they did not appreciate the offer of human home comforts!

At midday, to help strengthen their legs after being cooped up in boxes, I fed them with meat dangling from string. Both kits leaped up for it as best they could and I rewarded them after the first few jumps by letting it drop. Instantly they fell on the meat with loud whirring growls. Even at this age their fierceness told me they would never be household pets. Their bites and scratches were little worse than catching one's hand on barbed wire, and I doubted they weighed much more than a pound apiece, but mature wildcats usually vary between eight and sixteen pounds and are reputedly able to kill animals more than their own weight. I decided to bring them up as naturally as possible and let them run free in the perfect habitat around my home. Such rare wild creatures did not belong in a house.

In the afternoon I transferred them to an old woodshed that nestles away from the prevailing winds at the back of my L-shaped cottage. And at night I fed them by the light of a paraffin Tilly lamp. I had no electricity at the cottage, nor, apart from the plastic water pipe from the burn, any other modern conveniences whatever apart from calor gas which I used for cooking on a two burner camp stove. By feeding the kittens nightly by the lamp's light, I hoped when mature they would associate this light in my window with the food and protection I'd given them when young, and so be free to choose my company or stay in the wild.

As they again fought each other over food, I realized I would have to feed them separately—a good use for all the empty rustless pipe tobacco tins I'd hoarded in the workshop. After boiling and scrubbing several, I gave each a bowl for food and milk— four bowls in all. Immediately they stopped scrapping and went for different bowls.

It soon became clear that while they would fight to reach food first, they would not fight *over* it like dogs, or try to grab it from each other. The first cat to get at the food, owned it. They were not proprietary over particular bowls and even though I always tried to feed Cleo on the right, Patra on the left, if one left anything it would permit the other to sneak over and steal it. Once when Patra was filching Cleo's meat this way, I tried to push her head away. Immediately she attacked, slashed out with her claws, trying to pull my finger back for a bite. Momentarily peeved, I gave her behind a light flick to let her know who was boss. It only made her fiercer. There was clearly no canine masochism here, and punishment, however slight, from a superior force, only increased their natural savagery. It had been a foolish thing to do.

Although I made a bed of hay in a deep tea chest for them the kits jumped out of it and climbed up to some sacking that lay between three logs which accidentally formed an open ended square. There, they were three feet off the ground and could clearly see any approaching danger.

Oddly, over the first few days, as Moobli sat just outside the shed and watched them with me, only sniffing at them from a few feet away as if registering the scent in his mind, they seemed less scared of him than of me. I thought this strange because wild animal instincts reach back through the ages and Moobli resembled a huge wolf, which would have been one of the wildcat's traditional enemies when both were common in Britain and Europe. As he was the only other furred four-legged creature about I wondered if they mistook him for a creature like their mother grown big! Certainly, I hoped if they ran away from the woodshed and got lost, Moobli might be able to track them with his excellent nose.

It was proving to be a rainy summer and the kits were spending most of the daytime in the shed, but on the first sunny day after a week I took axe and saw to the west wood to top up my winter firewood, and to get some exercise after days of just writing. My woodland policy was vague, but I felt I'd clear the areas nearest the cottage first, so leaving the wilder parts for animals and bird shelter. I would cut no growing trees, only windfalls, and by cutting those that lay jammed across other trunks on the ground not only did I get drier and rotless firewood, but I left the decaying logs on the forest floor. These ground logs provided homes for over 200 species of insects and invertebrates which, along with fungi help break up the wood and leaf litter into the humus all plants need, and also provided food for woodpeckers, frogs, mice, shrews, voles, birds and other small mammals. On these creatures prey the owls, hawks, foxes, badgers and one day, I hoped, my wildcats.

It was when I came back with my second loaded pack and a log under each arm that I found the kittens had left the shed. Thinking they'd only been disturbed by my working, I carried on for five more hours and despite adding forty logs, by stacking old and new wood right up to roof level at the back, I actually made more room in the shed than before. I went back at dusk after an hour's writing and the kits were still not there. Worried that I may have scared them away for good, I held their bed sacking to Moobli's nose and told him to track the pussy coots—which, by the strange perverse osmosis and idea association that comes to folk living alone with animals, had now become their slang name.

To my delight Moobli immediately put his nose to the ground, zig-zagged about a few times, then began bulldozing through the bracken that dominated the north hill behind the cottage. It was then I found that, while the kits accepted Moobli watching them inside the shed, when he was outside, meeting him in the open was totally different. Almost immediately Cleo shot out of the bracken like a small striped rocket, paused when she reached the open, looked quickly about her, then in two long bounds reached a broken knothole at ground level on the shed corner and vanished inside. Then Moobli started whining. He had found Patra too, but she was standing her ground, at bay, amid thick bracken. With ears flattened, her eyes narrowed and pitch black with expanded pupils, tail fluffed up like a flue brush she was growling like a high pitched motor, ready to claw him if he came any closer. "No!" I commanded. "Get back!" And Moobli backed off a few feet. Again I realized his whining wasn't from anger or a prelude to attack—for he could have finished either kitten off with one swift chop if he wanted to—but from disappointment that they found him terrifying and didn't want to play! When we both retreated a few steps and Patra felt safe again, she too took off for the shed and also squeezed through the knothole.

I enlarged this hole as they were probably using it as a regular exit and entrance at night. The shed door was in two parts and although I usually only had the bottom half shut, it seemed both cats preferred to use the ground level hole rather than expose themselves, even briefly, on the high thin edge of the half door.

The early training of Moobli's attitude towards the kittens and theirs to him, was now most important. I didn't want to punish him when he caught up with them outside, for that might have made him jealous and induced him to seek revenge when I wasn't there. And his natural urge to track after them was worth cultivating—in case they stayed out too long before being able to take care of themselves. So I kept eyes and ears open when I was working indoors and he was outside.

It was fortunate Moobli was still young himself and had had no nasty experiences with adult cats as many town dogs have when pups, so there was no ingrained hatred. In a way he was growing up with them. And if the kits happened to be in the open when Moobli and I first went out in the mornings, I realized the best way to get them to accept our presence without undue alarm or dashing for cover, was not to call them or try to make friendly overtures but to carry on with whatever chore I was doing and totally ignore them. Slowly Moobli learned not to make quick sudden movements when the kits were close by, and sometimes, instead of flying into the shed, they just retreated behind a loose board or into a pile of lumber by the cottage's west wall, and watched our activities with interest.

Patra was the first to lose a little of her fear. Within two weeks she knew I was the regular food and watered-milk source, and that despite his size even in the open Moobli meant no harm and that he always backed away from them on my command. But Cleo remained far more wary. Once when they were back in the shed at dusk, Moobli put his nose to the knothole. Cleo, unseen, was crouching behind it and she snarled, spat and swiped out at him. The expression on Moobli's face was a picture, but he immediately forgot this insult to his pride and picked up a chunk of tree for me to throw.

One early August morning, jaded after working on the book, I walked to the far end of the east wood and cut three ten-foot logs from a larch that had fallen across the secondary burn and had jammed over a large rock, so that its forty-foot top reared upwards threateningly over the forest floor. In every high wind it swayed up and down like a giant rush in a river current and made a loud creaking groaning noise—which I felt probably scared the deer who came into the woods at night as much as it once had me! It was a good straight tree and the first three logs were ideal for the windbreak I was building to reduce the power of winter gales which sometimes blew open my front doors. Perspiring after carrying them up to the house, itching from midge bites, I went to cool off in the waterfalls. As I stood there, swiftly refreshed in the cold mountain waters, I noticed there were several natural holes under the banks. And beneath them, also out of sight from the high bank above, were slabs of moss covered rocks that lay unevenly on top of each other. It seemed a perfect area for wildcats to hunt.

I dressed, managed to get the kits into their box, carried them back to the waterfalls and put them on a large log near the bank. They hated it! The splashing noises, so soothing to human ears, and the rushing water scared them. They flattened their ears, jumped off the logs and scattered for cover under the bank, away from the awful noise. I recalled then how Moobli, who was now almost as much at home in water as an otter, had reacted when seeing his first swollen stream as a pup—he had leaped backwards and barked at it. Although wildcats are said to swim readily when mature, so as to reach small islets to hunt or when danger threatens, water was something the kits would have to be introduced to slowly, in their own good time.

On the way back, though, they quickly forgot the experience and looked at the passing woodland with great interest. To see if they could climb yet I held Patra, the most forward of the two, against a thick-barked larch trunk. Although she clung on instinctively with her claws, she didn't know how to move down and didn't yet have enough strength to haul herself upward to the first branch by climbing. So she just stayed there and *maued*. But when I set them both on top of a branch, nearly eight feet high, they showed no alarm whatever at the unaccustomed height. In fact, as the midges swirled about us and I clapped my hands about my exposed face and neck, Patra delicately scratched one from her own ear with her back leg. As both kits began raising and lowering their heads, peering at the oak trees halfway up the north hill, Cleo suddenly looked up into the sky, her elliptical pupils closing to mere slits. I followed her look. High overhead a young buzzard that had been hanging about the east wood for three days, was soaring westwards. There was nothing wrong with their eyesight.

By this time their attitudes at feeding time had begun to change. If I put one bowl of meat down a fraction before the second, the first kit to reach it no longer tried to claw the other as she came near but merely growled and shot out an accurate clawless paw, placing it firmly on the other kit's head, to just hold it down and stop it coming any further.

And when, three evenings after the waterfall visit, both kits jumped down from their bed to greet me when I went in with their food, I thought I was really making headway, until Cleo grabbed her meat and dashed between the logs with it with high whirring growls. Momentarily irked by what seemed her constant wild ingratitude, I decided to experiment. Pretending not to be looking at her and waiting until she'd dropped the main piece of meat and was chewing a morsel, I snatched the big chunk back. There was no retaliation. It was suddenly gone and she showed no anger. I then gave it to Patra who also took it between the logs. This time I was slower snatching it back. Patra, usually the tamer, went for me, spitting like a firecracker and lashing out with her claws, drawing blood.

They had stopped clawing each other now but were quite ready to claw me, their regular food provider. I was determined to find out if Patra's attack had been due to a different temperament, at least as far as this specific food situation was concerned. I gave her another piece and when she was chewing it with her carnassials, her side teeth, I made a light fast grab for the piece she had left on the log. This time, her eyes averted as she chewed, she didn't even see it go. And when she did notice it was gone, she behaved just as Cleo had. No animosity at all. Their reactions were defensive. They would try to stop the meat going if they saw the threat coming but once it was gone there was no thought of vengeance. Again it was unlike canine behav-

iour. Although I'd brought up Moobli always to let me take his
food away while he was eating, an untrained dog will certainly
attack during the taking and after it has gone. The revenge mo-
tive did not appear to exist in wildcat make-up at all, either towards me or each other, over food.

Cleo was the first to catch wild prey and I was lucky enough to
witness it. One August afternoon I was looking through the rear
bedroom window when I saw her stalking through the long grass
in front of the bracken on the north hill. Crouched low, her eyes
glaring like twin headlamps, black-pupilled despite the daylight,
she moved with deathly slowness towards a disturbance between
a mass of buttercup leaves below a bramble bush. Moving one
foot at a time, her front elbows protruding above her back, rolling forward on her long rear hocks as if they were the runners of
a slow motion rocking horse, she edged forward until some two
feet away. Then, gathering her rear legs beneath her carefully,
her tail not twitching like a domestic cat's, she sprang, hit the
unsuspecting field vole a terrific stunning whack with her right
paw, impaling it on her claws, brought her left paw up, then
brought the vole back to her mouth for the death bite. As she bit
she flicked her head right and left, the vole shot a foot away but
she was on it again as it landed. It was all over in a second. Then
with flattened ears she ran with it in her jaws to the gap between
the woodshed and the cottage wall and ate it, starting with the
head. There was no attempt to cripple the vole with a bite, then
to play with it while still alive, as a domestic cat will do. At ten
weeks old it was a deadly efficient kill. The smash with the paw
was certainly to stun the vole before the bite and the total absence of tail twitch was interesting. That night I gave a dead
woodmouse I'd trapped in the kitchen to Patra. She sniffed,
touched it with a paw, then walked away. She didn't appear to
know what it was or what to do with it. Although she was
bolder, bigger and could often bully her sister's head out of her
own milk tin, as far as wild hunting instincts were concerned she
was more backward than Cleo.

As the dull wet August continued and ominous drips on the
wooden ceilings of both the main rooms told me the corrugated
iron roof had sprung a couple of leaks, I decided to perform my

yearly blitz on repairs. I drove the forty-four miles to the nearest town and bought supplies and materials.

Next day dawned hot and sunny but, as I performed acrobatic contortions on the roof, fibre-glassing leaks, replacing rusted nails, I felt queasy. Having never been ill since cutting out into the wilds eight years before, I put it down to a bug caught while eating an unaccustomed meal out in civilization the day before. As I scrabbled about on the roof, painting, I found the previous year's weather had opened up cracks in the chimney stacks. They would both need cementing over again completely and painting too but I'd run out of fine sand. So next day I boated five miles up the loch to where a new family of badgers had heaved out almost a ton of golden sand from their sett fifty yards above the shore and filled up several sacks. My stomach still bad, I felt some exercise would cure it and rowed home. To make my load lighter and give him some exercise too, I dropped Moobli off for a two mile run.

To my surprise, seeing the boat moving so slowly, he rumbled into the water and started to swim. Further and further out he went, following the wake of my boat right out into the centre of the loch, and going almost as fast as I was rowing. As he huffed and puffed along, his broad head and ears high, he looked just like a small grizzly swimming. Occasionally I let him get near— his long toes were spread out like stars, the half webs between them were now like paddles, his legs were kicking in easy powerful trudgeon strokes, surging him forward at about four knots. He easily swam the whole distance.

During the next two days, as I cemented the chimney stacks and painted them, I caught occasional glimpses of the kits prowling through the north hill bracken forests. Moobli crept near and quietly sat down, watching me and them, panting contentedly in the warm sunshine, as if grinning at them in proffered friendship. They now seemed to be accepting he was not too much of a threat.

I was painting away the third afternoon on the roof when I noticed all had gone quiet, like the silence one suddenly notices among children, and one wonders what they're up to. I climbed down my scaffold-ladder device and sneaked round the cottage to peep in at the windows. They were all in the kitchen. Cleo and Patra were eating the scraps from Moobli's bowl and he was sitting on the bed, not angry but watching them with a fond paternal air, as if they were his cats, his pups!

When I stole through the back door Cleo panicked, darted this way and that and shot outside. But Patra crouched down low over the bowl, perhaps because Moobli had followed the fleeing Cleo and was now stationed at the door, and as I muttered the usual soothing pussy coot phrases, she allowed me to pick her up by the neck scruff for the first time since she was really small. I carried her outside and placed her against the unusually gnarled bark of an old ash tree. This time she climbed up a little way, jerkily, before I lifted her off again and put her into the woodshed with Cleo. That night, after feeding them and spending some time in soothing talk, I managed to pick Cleo up too, although she didn't like it and scratched me. I was surprised to find that though smaller and thinner, she felt heavier than Patra. Her flesh was all muscle and sinew whereas Patra had plenty of fat. Cleo also had thicker and bigger claws.

Two days later I woke with a fresh attack of stomach cramps. I'd noticed too that the kits seemed subdued, hadn't left the woodshed at all. Clearly something was wrong and as I mixed water with their milk, I had a sudden idea to check our water supply. I walked up past the waterfalls to the pool where my siphon pipe was wedged under rocks. The decomposing body of a large hind deer was lying athwart the brink of the pool and was wedged right on top of the pipe. We were all slowly being poisoned and it had nothing to do with any lunch out in civilization. I kicked myself, because checking one's water supply regularly was a lesson I'd learned years back in Canada and I should not have had to learn it twice. The body must have been there for over a week.

With a short rope I hauled it away over the rocks. The flesh was covered with maggots and sexton beetles were all over the inside. The amount of good these little black and red burying beetles do in the wilds is enormous, for they scent rotting carrion from many yards and they all come flying to the feast and to lay their eggs in and help bury carcasses which act as a food storehouse for their larvae. But the stench was terrible and as I hauled, the deer's cheeks fell off, exposing the teeth in an awful laugh. I barely got the corpse into a dry recess between the rocks before I had to give up. Later I disinfected the area and poured disinfectant down the pipe, then blocked it up to let the fluid do its work. For three days I carried my water supply in buckets from the loch, then let the tap run all night to clear out the disinfectant.

Next morning the flow had dried up completely. Now something was blocking the pipe. I undid the joints outside—and saw the distorted head of a dead eel. I felt a bit sorry for it as I dug it out of the pipe for, after surviving several years in the higher reaches of the burn, after it had probably negotiated my sheer thirty-foot waterfalls' cliff as an elver by filling its gills with water and wriggling like a snake through the grass up the steep rocky banks, it had now been on its way for a spell back in the loch before the final extraordinary eel migration across the Atlantic to spawn in the Sargasso Sea. It had travelled far, survived much, and it seemed a shame its life had to end this way, in an artificial creation of man. As it had swum about my pool looking for a way down the falls, it had followed the gentle flow of water down the luring round hole of my water pipe, only to be slowly drowned by the flowing water piling up behind it when it hit the restriction at the far end.

Well, I wouldn't waste it. As eels frequently travel overland at night in summer dew, I wondered if they ever provided food for the nocturnal prowling wildcats. I nailed the dead eel onto my chopping block near the woodshed, and retired to my workshop window to look.

Patra was the first to emerge. She pushed her head through the knothole entrance, sniffing the air. Then looking carefully about her, she stalked towards the eel, sniffed, then seized it in her teeth. She tried to pull it off the nail, to run into hiding with it, then, realizing it wouldn't budge, she started to chew it with her carnassials. Clearly she had instantly recognized it as food. Just then Cleo also came out, sniffing, but as she crept towards her sister Patra let go of the eel, flared, then stamped her right paw down hard a few inches away from the eel, a gesture that said unmistakably "Stay away!" And Cleo, following the wildcat law of first come, first served, did. I went out, scaring both cats back into the shed, cut the eel in half and shared it between them.

In fine weather, I usually left the back door ajar so Moobli was free to run around the house at night, for true to his breed he never showed any inclination to wander alone in the hills. One morning I found both cats had climbed into the old bath where I kept the animals' sterilized meat sausages and were busily guzzling away. This, their swift ability to find the eel and their reactions every time I neared them with food, helped me realize that wildcats, contrary to much zoological belief, have excellent scenting power, and in the wild probably rely on it to find carrion when times are hard in winter.

By the end of August both kits were spending more time out in the bracken jungles, and sometimes came back with dead shrews which they seldom ate because of the distasteful scent glands on the little insectivores' flanks. These active hunting days in the finer weather seemed to make them wilder and hungrier, so they now instantly went for my fingers with their claws the second I put their tins down. To stop this, I upturned the tea chest they'd spurned as a bed chamber, and, using it as a table, sorted out their four bowls on its surface. While I did this they stalked to and fro beneath, *mauing* their hunger, standing anxiously on their haunches at times like otters, milling their claws around in the air below me. Once, Patra, unable to wait a second longer, leaped up onto the chest and hissed my fingers as I mixed the meats. When I tried to brush her off with my thick sweatered elbow she resisted and went on the attack, knocking over the milk. I didn't mind them being fierce but I wasn't having them attack me directly so I seized her thick bushy tail and with a quick movement hauled her off the chest and downwards. She was on the floor before she'd had time to dig her claws in. But again, no revenge, she just kept milling with Cleo and *mauing* for the food which I put beside them quickly. If they were as fierce as this at feeding time now, when they were full grown in about a year, I'd need to put their food out behind a protecting screen.

During the past ten days my activities had varied between painting the cottage, working on my book, writing a story about cougar preservation, cutting away a small log jam higher up the burn—to prevent more deer being caught up—watching a male bullfinch feeding three youngsters on birch buds in the east wood, photographing a red-throated diver and her chick fresh down from their nest on a lochan in the high hills, and also the red squirrels who were now active in the ash trees and hazel bushes. Trying to push the button at just the right moment as these deft burly little creatures zip in and out of focus is as tantalizing as trying to photograph tiny wrens.

One Wednesday with a pile of mail to post, I boated up the loch in mist and heavy rain. Moobli hadn't had much exercise that week so coming back late I dropped him off at Sandy Point, to let him run home the full three miles for the first time. Although dusk was falling, I felt he knew the way well enough after the first mile and hearing the boat engine in the north-east wind, could easily follow along the shore. Darkness had never seemed any problem to him. So I went back fast, to have the boat unloaded and all supplies up to the cottage before he arrived panting and hungry, tail wagging as usual for his dinner.

After half an hour he hadn't turned up and as it was now dark I became worried. Had he perhaps picked some old poison left out for a fox, broken his leg charging over the tussock ruts? I put on my raingear again, hauled the boat down and hurtled back in the rain and dark to search. I went right back to the truck again, whistling, calling and shining a powerful torch at various places along the shore, but there was no sign. Upset, knowing I would have to be out at dawn to look for him again, I just hauled the boat up onto the grassy bank. I walked up the path again in the blackness cursing myself for having made him run so far in the dark, a third of the way over ground he had not covered alone before. Then I switched on the torch and went to check the kittens.

I was greeted at the shed door by Moobli, tongue out, grinning, quite unperturbed. He'd reached home, probably as I was picking my third load out of the boat, and had gone to check the kittens were all right before I had. I had charged all the way up the loch and back again for nothing. I was too relieved to be angry, but I don't think he could work out what the sudden hugs were all for. And when I went to feed the kits—three hours later than usual—I discovered how the word "caterwaul" probably first originated!

Next morning, the sun streaming down again, I pushed my typewriter away and went to lie out in the hot rays. Suddenly I heard a loud buzzing noise. Thinking it was just one of the big blue Aeshna dragonflies who often flew close with rattling wings, I opened an eye. It was a giant wood wasp, a thick-bodied, two-inch long yellow and black insect which was rare in my part of Scotland. I sat up hoping to catch it for a photo when suddenly Cleo came round the corner, leaped up into the air twice, batting out with her paws, and caught it. As I got up she ran away, so I took my photo and then put the big harmless wasp onto the bark of a pine tree that was dying after being used as a red deer rubbing post, and on which I hoped it would lay its eggs. Later the photo and sighting were recorded at the British Museum of Natural History in London. Wildcats, it seemed, had uses I'd never dreamed of!

As Cleo and Patra were now becoming more adventurous, I took them one calm day to my beach front and ran back into the house with Moobli. From the window I watched Patra steal up first. She crept through the undergrowth from wads of rushes to bramble bushes, behind bracken patches, keeping well away from the path and all open areas, taking nearly half an hour to cover the sixty yards of strange territory in the glare of daylight, and reach the safety of the shed.

But Cleo stayed on shore. Searching for her to feed at dusk, I found her nine feet up an ash tree, clinging to the trunk. Moobli was worried at seeing her there and whined—which started her *mauing* loudly as she found she could not turn round and as yet didn't know how to back down. We went a distance away and watched her work out how to do it. She relaxed one front foot at a time, lowering it a few inches, then reached lower for new footholds with her back feet.

When she was only two feet from the ground she decided it was safe to take a chance. She looked at the ground intently, put right foot over left and sprang down, landed awkwardly for a cat, then ran like a hare straight up the path and back to the shed which she had clearly spied from up the tree. Although Patra had proved she could climb a little nearly two weeks earlier, this was probably the first time Cleo had ventured to do so, hence her hesitant clumsiness.

Later that afternoon, I heard a slight noise in the kitchen. I crept slowly outside and peeked through the window. Patra was helping herself to the pickings from Moobli's bowl, and he was sitting on his bed with an intent but soft and doting look. To my further surprise, she walked up to him and they actually rubbed noses. I never saw it happen again and what had caused such an extraordinary temporary ambience between two such disparate animals I will never know. But several times when both kittens had been in the kitchen in the early morning, taking scraps from his bowl, they had let him step between them and lick up a few crumbs too. Yet neither would let either him or me take or go near food when it was in their bowls. But it seemed they both now knew Moobli would not hurt them, at least inside the house. So far, it appeared he had tamed them as much, if not more, than I.

Chapter 3

One Sunday, tired of rattling out personal letters on the heavy old upright typewriter I reserved for this purpose, I was abstractedly staring down the loch at the huge, hunched, brooding mountain whose peak, a short sprint under 3,000 feet, dominated my landscape to the south-west. I glanced at my diary—September 1. The summer had slipped by and, while I had explored many of the mountains behind my home, I had not yet stood upon the peak of this, the largest. It was windless on the loch, with a touch of rain in the air but, although the cloud cover was growing slowly from the south, the sky was fairly bright. I switched on the battery radio—useful for weather forecasts and time checks before supply trips, for I had long ago given up clocks and watches—and heard the 2 p.m. news.

"Come on lad," I said to the napping Moobli. "We're off up the Ben." He pranced about with delight as I changed into trekking clothes, packed raingear, a sandwich, cameras, lenses and notebook, and in half an hour we were hauling the boat onto three branches on the gravel shore below the mountain.

As we worked our way over the lower boggy fields, real "welly" country, I trod carefully on the few upraised tussocks between the dark green water-holding blanket of sphagnum moss. Plunging up to the knees in slushy peat seems worse at the start than when one is truly into the rhythm of a trek and really warmed up. Some of the brown spikes of bog asphodel still held yellow and orange flowers, and in the soil among rocky niches, the pale green starfish leaves of butterwort waited as traps for unwary insects. The lower slopes were clothed with a woodland swathe of twisted birch, rowan and small sessile oaks and in every clearing the yellow four-petalled heads of tormentil smiled upwards at the wan sky. This is probably the Highlands' commonest flower but, though its stems have a thread-like delicacy so it seems to lean against other vegetation for support, it flowers for at least five months of the year, dotting the landscape cheerfully with its tiny suns.

We climbed up through the woods, emerging into small meadows among the heather-covered rocky outcrops where the white flourishes of meadowsweet were turning yellowy brown among their leaves, dying now like the miniature stingless nettle-like plants of eyebright among them. Here the late purple-blue Devils bit scabious held sway, nodding on their stems in the breezes. As we passed a sheltered spot by a large rock I saw a few large, white flowers. It was a nice little discovery: a small, solitary patch of uncommon grass-of-Parnassus, whose five large white petals had delicate tracings of greeny-grey lines, as if an artist had sought to add to their allure.

Although I sometimes saw little wild animal life on treks, especially in summer when foliage was thickest and animals were resting in the day heat, there was usually a certain serendipity about them. I was just thinking I had never been out yet without finding something new when I noticed Moobli looking up into the sky. A huge golden eagle was soaring overhead, a mere two hundred yards above us.

She sailed easily, seemingly unconcerned by the dog and human below, and landed on the skyline rocks above an angled granite face, through the centre of which ran a chimney with heather and sword grass on its ledges. As she folded and shuffled her long wings together, a weak ray of sun struck her and for an instant she seemed made of golden copper. I shrank behind the rock, fumbling in the pack to put my twenty-eight-inch-long telephoto lens together. Too late. Only moments later she opened her great wings again, felt the updraught of a breeze and floated off as my camera clicked, wheeling away to the west and behind the crest of the mountain. As she disappeared, seven hinds, who had been grazing over the brow, and had been startled by her, came at a trot towards us. In the dull light I hadn't much chance, but film is expendable and I pressed the button anyway. The hinds heard the click at the same time as they got our scent; one barked loudly in alarm, and they turned off and vanished behind a lower ridge.

As the herbiage grew sparser, giving way to herbs, lichens, moss and short grass, we steadily zig-zagged up the green ledges between the sheer rock faces to what looked like the top, only to find, as one often does, another peak higher up. A small flock of ptarmigan flew off a ledge beside us, their snow white wings whirring in odd contrast to their mottled browny-grey bodies which were still in full summer plumage. Snorting like pigs, they dropped over the ledge and stayed low to keep it between us. Ptarmigan are the only British birds with the arctic ability to grow all-white plumage in winter, as camouflage against the snow on the high tops. They seldom venture below 2,000 feet; only in blizzards or in the early morning do they descend to near the tree line. These were the first I'd seen near my home and I wished we'd gone slower, so that I could have tried to get some photos; though these birds, who crouch like just another stone among the rocks, are always hard to see before they take flight.

Certain that we were near the top now, we climbed the next ridge, only to find a small plateau with a lochan and more ridges of a mini mountain ahead with mists wisping over the top. Not quite 3,000 feet? I asked myself. We trudged upwards as the wind increased from the south and a light drizzle began to fall. We were now heading westwards and had just surmounted two more ridges when I saw yet another ragged looking peak ahead. "We turn back after this one," I muttered, heaving myself up through the jagged grey outcrops.

Suddenly we were on a huge broken pile of rocks and five steps later were on the mountain's highest peak. The wind, colder now, was blowing mist about us in wefts but through occasional gaps I saw the broad sea loch to the south-west like a

slate grey mirror wending its way through the hills, while to the
north-west my own fresh water loch ribboned snakily, ending at
the village where I picked up my supplies, and beyond that lay
the grey expanse of the Atlantic. As I took a couple of photos in
the short gaps, I could just see the sea island where I'd spent my
first three-and-a-half years in Scotland. I don't know how long I
stood there, entranced, wishing I'd made the climb on a summer
day of pure blue sky, but when I looked again to the left I saw a
great mass of grey mist heading towards us.

Within seconds we were totally enveloped. It swirled about,
thick, heavy, almost tangible, with just occasional glimpses of the
rocky route we'd taken. This was clearly no time to hang about.
A night out at this unsheltered height in the Highlands, even in
September, was not to be undertaken lightly though one could
survive well enough if wrapped in thick uprooted heather. But if
the mist lasted two nights, without food and extra clothing, we
could have been in trouble. And as the mist grew thicker and as
I'd forgotten my compass, it seemed for a few moments as if this
might be a possibility.

We scrambled back down, using the wind as a direction in-
dicator, occasionally sighting the small lochan to get our bear-
ings through the mist. But once we were 400 feet lower we were
leaving the mist behind. Surprisingly the ptarmigan were back
on the same ledge and once again they took off with loud snorts.
Going down was harder than going up because we took what
was a shorter route to the east and kept coming out onto open
scree faces, where one has to step short and steep between the
loose stones in a way that is tough on the knee caps. The rain
was now falling steadily and, by the time we reached the boat, I
was soaked through the shower suit.

As soon as we reached home we went to check the kits. Patra
was in the woodshed alone, not in their bed but high up on the
firewood logs looking badly scared. As I entered she leaped up
behind some corrugated iron screening my paraffin drum,
crouching there with huge black eyes, her ears flat. Of Cleo
there was no sign at all, which was odd at evening feed time, especially as both kits must have heard us coming.

Suddenly Moobli growled and ran off to the north corner of

the west wood. Every few steps he leaped high, like a gigantic jack rabbit, well clear of the high bracken as he tried to look over it. I caught the pungent ammoniac whiff of fox. Within seconds Moobli was in the wood, giving vent to a baying noise, deeper and louder than a bloodhound, a sound I'd never heard him make before. It made the hairs rise on my neck and would have scared off any wild creature.

I finally found Cleo crouching beneath an old tree stump. I tried to pick her up but she growled and spat and batted out with her claws. I called Moobli back and together we rounded her back into the shed where I closed the doors and blocked up the exit hole. I felt sure it was a big fox that had been after them and this must be a normal danger for wildcat kittens straying in the wild. Certainly Cleo and Patra seemed to have had a near miss but for our lucky arrival and Moobli's keen senses.

Before taking out their food, I switched on the radio—just before 6 P.M. Leaving aside the boat trips and the time with the kits, we'd been up and down that mountain in under three hours. A pretty good five-and-a-half-mile trek, I reflected as Moobli subsided on his bed with a tired groan after what had been his biggest climb to date and I washed my hair and had a flannel bath in the kitchen. Like many of the good days in a wilderness life, none of it had been previously planned.

For the next two weeks, wet or fine, I left the back door open every night, so Moobli could keep an eye, or rather nose, on his charges. While it was clear the fox had not been put off earlier by Moobli's scent, it was probably a fly beast who watched and scented from downhill or from the hill above, choosing a safe moment before making a move towards wherever the kittens were. I felt, however, that if it was brave or hungry enough to come again, Moobli would either scent or sense its presence. It didn't seem likely at this time of year a fox would be that hungry but I was taking no risks. But by mid-September the kits were able to scoot up trees easily, so were then reasonably safe.

One day after two nights of lashing rain, I saw that two windfall larches were causing a blockage in the small run-off burn along the east side of the west wood, flooding a small bed where two uncommon water avens had found a foothold. I rather liked my little water avens with their beautiful, nodding, red, bell-like heads for they added a fine dash of colour to the woodside in summer. Dead larches aren't much use, even for insect larvae. So even though the sky overhead was filled with thunderous looking rainclouds, blue cauldrons with pink inside, reminding me of the winter to come, I cut the trees up for firewood. The young cats were away all afternoon as I stacked the logs in the shed but when I went out at dusk with their meal and gave the usual food call, "*Mau*, the pussy coots!" and banged the tin lids together, they both came streaking in from the bracken like striped missiles. Although they didn't approach close or walk about with tails up rubbing against me, like domestic cats, it was wonderful to see them come to my call for the first time.

But as often happened with them, just as I thought I was making progress, I received a setback. One night after Cleo had eaten her food out of her tin like Patra, without as usual seizing a piece and retreating into the woodpile with it, I stroked her and she seemed to accept it. So I picked her up. Instantly she scratched and bit my forefinger, and I put her down fast. A few minutes later I went back with more food and she was quite amiable again. It had been purely instinctive action and she bore no grudges. By now my fingers were lacerated all over from their claws and I wore sticking plaster in several places. Would they never be hand tame?

Both kits began to stay out at night more and sleep in the shed by day. Often first thing in the morning Moobli would find Patra in the big rhododendron bush by the path, crouching below the protective, twisted tangle of brown stems. It seemed she was establishing her first small territory, using the bush as headquarters from which to stalk during the dark.

Once, when Moobli and I were indoors and Patra was sitting on some logs, I saw her ears prick up and she looked west. I could see and hear nothing but sure enough, a few minutes later a boat came up the loch. She had heard it long before I could. Good sight is usually the main sense attributed to wildcats but it seemed their hearing is equally keen—of great value when hunting and they are trying to pinpoint the position of prey rustling about in thick herbiage.

In late September the first autumn gales and driving rain began roaring in from the west, whipping the loch surface into a froth and stripping the first leaves from the trees. Alder leaves began to fill my boats and litter the shore and, when the first hailstones fell, whole twigs of ash, made heavy by the wet, were torn away. Hazel leaves flapped against the windows and their nuts also began to fall. In fine periods the pair of red squirrels, who had a high drey in a silver fir in the west wood, worked through the bushes, snatching down the branches with their tough little forepaws to nip off ripe nuts and race off with them in their mouths to stash them away for the winter. At times the feathery needles of the larch trees, now turning yellow, floated thickly through the air like dry rain. The small-leafed birch and willow trees, together with the stout oaks and stately beech, held onto their leaves the longest. Occasionally the old ash trees behind the cottage shed small branches which thumped to the ground or fell with a clang on the iron roof.

One wild night I heard Moobli whining in the kitchen. He was at the closed back door from behind which came loud *maus*. When I opened it Patra was outside. It seemed that, bewildered by all the new noises of the storm, she had come to seek shelter in the kitchen. She had probably been coming more at night than Cleo when the door was left open to raid the bowl of the monstrous but soft-hearted creature who, from long periods of just sitting nearby and watching her, she now knew meant her no harm. On impulse I picked her up with my boat gauntlets, brought her in and set her on the bed. This time after nervous glances around, she felt the soft warmth beneath her and settled down. Moobli passed the next twenty minutes with his chin resting on her bed, gazing at her dozing form with what looked like adoration. But the moment I moved at the desk, she dived off the bed and defecated beneath it. I decided wildcats and human beds was not a good idea after all and transferred her back to the shed, where she and Cleo promptly began licking each other. Their faces were now changing with growing maturity: Cleo's slimmer and thoroughly feline with oval eyes, Patra's fatter, rounder, and the tops of her eyelids almost straight, so that her eyes were like full moons with a slice taken off the top.

Returning from a supply trip one fine day, I found a rabbit that had been freshly killed by traffic on the road. As rabbits are among the favourite larger prey of wildcats and there were many past a wood up the loch where I intended to release the cats, I decided to start training Cleo and Patra to hunt. I fixed a pulley onto a fence post thirty-five yards from the window of my workshop, and put the butt of an old sea fishing rod into the vice on my heavy workbench. Then I wrapped cellulose tape round the line already on the reel and wound a double line of sixty-six-pound breaking strain nylon fishing line round both reel and pulley. By tying either a dead mouse or the rabbit on the bottom line I could, by reeling in and out, make the prey dance, run and bounce through the grass and bracken most realistically.

For three afternoons towards dusk at their normal feeding time, I tried to teach the kittens to stalk in true wildcat style. Fast or slow, sudden jerky or smooth movements—all could be controlled by the speed of the reel. Naturally, it worked best with the mouse for I could make it move and dart about faster.

At first the kits chased the mouse for all they were worth and on the third run Cleo, far keener and with her eyes jet black from fully distended pupils, caught the mouse with both sets of claws, snatched it back to her mouth and with two heavy tugs pulled it from the line and ran into the bracken to eat it.

But hunting the rabbit proved vastly different although I had fed them short rations the night before. At first both chased it with swiping claws but ran off again as soon as it stopped. On the second day they attacked it but later ignored it and went to investigate the squeaking pulley. So I oiled it. Then they played games but not hunting games. They stood in the path of the moving rabbit, leaping out of the way at the last second and giving it a playful swipe as it went past. I tried letting the rabbit lie until they made a move towards it, then making it leap off. This brought a few more half attacks, mostly by Patra. She crouched behind tufts of grass and bracken, curled her feet beneath her, quivered, and made sudden dashes but seldom made contact.

By the third evening they had lost all interest so I took the rabbit off the line. Although I'd gutted it to preserve it longer, it was beginning to smell. While I felt it likely that wildcats do eat carrion, their instincts would tell them that dead, slightly off meat would not get up and run! I also realized by watching them that for a wildcat every kill would be different from the last because of minute differences in terrain and individual behaviour of the prey itself.

Even though I'd moved the pulley site about, the sight of the same rabbit always heading to the workshop window, the sight of the fishing line fore and aft, the moving pulley, all became associated in their minds. And they soon had it worked out as an artificial contrivance. It was interesting that Patra made five attacks the first day, three on the second and two on the third. But Cleo made five attacks the first day, only two on the second and none at all on the third. Although slightly smaller and skinnier, Cleo was the shrewder. I finally gave up teaching them to hunt when hordes of bluebottle flies chased the rabbit far harder than the cats ever had.

Two evenings later Cleo brought a dead common shrew back to the shed, as if to tell me "We do know how to hunt, you know!" It had been slashed in the neck, almost surely killed by claw stroke alone.

Nevertheless, I was disappointed at what I felt to be a poor showing towards the rabbit prey. The kits were reaching the age when they needed more roughage in fur and feather than I was able to give them, and I doubted if voles, mice and shrews, which only Cleo seemed to be catching though she never ate the shrews, would be enough when they were mature. Perhaps my easy upbringing had spoiled them and they would not be able to hunt large prey. Something else happened one late afternoon that also had me wondering about the wisdom of having two growing wildcats loose around the home. I have a bird table a couple of yards from my study window and while few birds used it in summer, they were now, with insects and vegetable food harder to find, coming to it regularly—mainly chaffinches, great tits, blue tits, blackbirds and robins. I was sitting at my desk when Cleo came stalking round the corner, looked fixedly at the tail of a chaffinch protruding over the edge as it pecked into a hunk of brown bread, made a clumsy leap—from which the bird escaped easily—and hung for a moment from the table by her front claws. I opened the window and shooed her away. I hadn't thought about this danger to the birds around the table before.

When I was on a seven-mile trek to a long valley to the east and found the remains of a deer calf in a wood, my doubts increased. All round it the ground had been worn and stamped down to bare mud but on the edge were the unmistakable four-toed prints of a large wildcat. One of the legends surrounding these creatures is that the big toms will often eat young kittens.

Although wildcats are said to have a territory of roughly 150 acres, such generalizations on a solitary, largely nocturnal, predatory animal seemed arbitrary, for a rough hunting area would depend entirely on the kind of terrain and available prey. A wildcat with a den in a wooded rocky ravine flanked on each side by desolate bog and tussock country might hunt nearly all its life in the ravine. Although these tracks were a mile and a half from the cottage, and I'd never found prints or droppings nearer, much of the route back was flanked by cliffs close to the shore. It seemed to me quite possible that a big cat could make spasmodic raids from that far away.

During another spell of bad weather, as if to further confirm my doubts, both cats came into the back door at night and broke into a new sterilized meat carton, ripping it open with their claws. While they were often out in light rain, the autumn winds and swirling leaves certainly scared them, and they were now more belligerent at feeding times. On the day the first snow fell on the top of the big mountain, Cleo tried to bite my hand as I put the food down. I pushed her off with the toe of my boot, which she also swatted and clawed. She also became enraged when Moobli sniffed towards her, though he had been nearer to her on other occasions. She slashed out and flared until he backed off, whining with hurt pride.

Next night Cleo again attacked before I could remove my hand, growled and bit my right forefinger again. Without thinking, I tapped her backside with the hand she wasn't biting. She let go, dropped to the floor, spat, and as I sucked my again bleeding finger, she squeezed her flattened broad head sideways and slid between crevices in the logs, her body with its pliable ribs able to go anywhere her head could fit.

I was sorry then and felt I had finally learned my lesson. Never, ever, get angry with a wild animal, no matter what it does to you, short of serious injuries, of course. A wildcat acts instantly, upon pure instinct, does not pause to reason first. It was foolish of me to have taken Cleo's latest attacks personally. And because I, too, had acted on mere instinct, I had undone weeks of work. There would clearly be many problems as they grew bigger, and from then onwards I wore the thick gauntlets with more leather gloves beneath when I fed them.

This latest belligerence plus all the doubts that were now accumulating, as well as the thought that maybe they would not survive the winter in the wild after my soft upbringing, prompted me to write to London Zoo.

I was by no means sure yet that I wanted to part with the wildcats but when I found in the Zoo's annual report an *individual* I could write to—Dr Michael Brambell, MA, PhD, MRCVS, FLS—I thought I'd just write a preliminary enquiry. I knew the Zoo was now moving away from the old policy of keeping animals singly in cages and was re-creating larger habitats with natural conditions where breeding pairs or groups could live. I suggested that if I felt later that my two females wouldn't survive healthily in the wilds, might the Zoo care to have them, or just one, to breed from?

"I don't want to keep them as pets," I wrote. "I feel if they have to be captive they might well serve as inspiration and education to thousands of kids who know little of our wildlife heritage and thus might want to know more . . ." I knew too that the cats would be well cared for by professionals.

Next day both cats were absent at feeding time and only by working round the land in decreasing circles with Moobli could I herd them back into the shed area. Patra took one mouthful of food and ran between the logs. Cleo flatly refused to come in until I went away.

In front of the cottage, on the bank before the land dropped down to the vegetable garden and the trees on the shore, grew two long thickets of brambles. I'd intended to clear them but as they gave a slight crop of blackberries the first year, I decided instead to stake and train the growth sideways, cutting off the probing leaders so all the strength went into the fruit bearing stems. After all, blackberries were as good a fruit as any, full of Vitamin C, and could be made into jelly, jam, tasty compôte with apples, and wine. At dawn on the fifth day after my contretemps with Cleo, I spied her working through the thickets and the tangles of grass, soft rush and hogweed around them. She had found a vole colony in the rocky tunnels below the topsoil.

That day I worked quietly outside peeling logs, ignoring her completely, and at night feed time she brought a vole into the shed as I stood outside, dropped it, ate her food, then picked up the vole again and took it into the logs to eat. At least she had returned while I was near but it took several more days, by putting titbits of steak and liver in her bowl on the logs, to win back her trust even to the low level it had been at before.

Living alone in the wilds, one unconsciously plans ahead as winter approaches so that apart from wildlife studies, there is plenty of work piled up to take the edge off loneliness in the long cold dark wet days ahead. My fifth lonely winter in the Scottish Highlands was now looming and my panacea for this one was to finish the book about my Canadian experiences on which I'd worked sporadically for the past four years. But the confirmatory letter promised by the New York publisher in early July had not yet arrived, and I was worried they had changed their minds. Back in late July while walking in the west wood, the date September 27 had kept coming into my mind. With the odd insights that occasionally come to one alone, I had written in my diary, another alleviator of loneliness: "This will be a good day. Something significant will happen now." But apart from being the sunniest day for nearly three months and Cleo biting me really badly, nothing at all had happened.

On Saturday, October 5, I boated up the loch for mail. As I noted with both relief and fear that there was a letter from New York, and also one from London Zoo, the postmistress asked me how my wildcats were faring. She had heard that a young man had come to live in a glen a few miles to the south and that he had been given a university grant to study—wildcats.

Back home, fortifying myself with a few drams, I opened the New York letter—the book deal was at last really confirmed.

When I returned from capering in mad delight around the cottage like an ageing centaur, I opened Dr Brambell's letter in euphoric mood.

"We cannot take your two wildcats. I have a male and really feel we should be finding somewhere with better accommodation for it." He added that he knew of a Yorkshire gamekeeper who wanted to keep a species of wildcat, that he'd written to him suggesting the possibility of the Zoo's old male and also my two females, and could he put the man in direct touch with me?

I looked at the date on Dr Brambell's letter—September 27. It seemed more than an extraordinary coincidence.

It was at that moment, when I realized there genuinely was an increasing interest in this rare member of our fauna, that my serious wildcat project was really born. If my females did become too belligerent as they grew bigger, I could always build a large natural pen for them after all. Immediately I wrote back that I'd only thought of the Zoo so my wildcats could have been an inspiration to young people seeking to understand the last of our wilds. But perhaps I could achieve something from the educational view by writing about them myself, so if they had to be looked after by just one individual I'd carry on with their care myself. Then I added:

"In fact, if the gamekeeper doesn't want the wildcat tom you have, and it is capable of reproducing, perhaps I could take him too." The thought of actually breeding wildcats intrigued me. And what better home could the Zoo's old wildcat tom have than here in the wild woods at Wildernesse? Little did I realize the events that lay ahead.

Chapter 4

In early October, the hills and ridges behind my home resound with the roaring of red deer stags in the rut. The big master stags in their prime come first, leaving the high tops where they have spent the summer in their bachelor herds, covering many miles as they seek for harems of hinds which they try to keep together and defend from other stags. The roars are eerie, almost frightening to one hearing them for the first time. Something like the bellowing of a bull and loud, low groans, filled alternately with lust and the despair of frustration.

They are now in top condition after their summer feeding and are at their most aggressive. While fatal attacks on man have occurred, they are rare, and it is an invigorating experience to be behind a rock alone in the hills with several stags trotting ponderously around their smaller females, pausing to roar occasionally or to come up onto a knoll and stare aggressively towards the source of any small disturbance.

One Sunday afternoon after a heavy overnight rainfall, with the sun sinking towards the west, Moobli and I were stalking towards a 1,771-foot peak along high heather-filled ledges when we heard a stag roaring from behind a small hill up ahead. Cursing that I'd run out of colour film and only had a last roll of black and white in the camera, with Moobli obeying my hissed command to keep back, I crept upwards.

As I slipped past small rock faces and crawled up the small knoll, using every tuft of heather as cover, it was comical to see Moobli also sensing the need for caution. He kept his head low and set one foot in front of the other with great care like a huge stalking dog-eared cat. The situation was perfect, the golden sun behind us would dazzle anything looking our way, and the cool, east breeze took away both sound and scent. Pulling my camouflaged bush hat low to hide as much face as possible, I peeped through the heather.

There, only fifty yards ahead and slightly below was a fine young ten-pointer stag with nine hinds. None had heard us approach and as I watched he lowered his head, walked towards a hind and reared as if to mount her but she slipped smartly away as my shutter clicked loud enough to rouse the dead. But they had heard nothing and for a full half hour I took pictures of him scratching his right ear with his right back leg, being nuzzled by a hind, sitting down dozing, running round his harem, but he made no more attempts to mate. Occasionally I sneaked a slow look behind—Moobli was five yards back, sitting down and he too was peering through the heather, fascinated by the deer and what he now clearly realized was part of my work. This was the closest we had so far been to a wild stag and his hinds together and I was surprised Moobli had learned to keep back and stay still for so long with such little training—apart from a few rump whacks for running ahead as a pup.

That evening, as if to put the cap on our successful day, Cleo once more came to my feet with Patra at feed time, the fire and anger flashes gone again from her eyes.

During the next few days, the sun still shining during the short Indian summer, the two cats took to sunning themselves in front of the two corrugated iron pyramids I'd erected to keep my spare lumber dry. Whenever Moobli or I came round the corner they dived for cover beneath these sheets. And when Moobli put his nose too close, Cleo growled and swiped out with her claws. By now Moobli was so used to this, he could anticipate it and did a swift little Muhammad Ali shuffle out of the way. But once as he gazed at Patra in the sun, lying still several yards away so she would not panic, Cleo came up from the rhododendron bush by the path and out of the long grass right in front of him. Surprised, he got to his feet. Neither cat would face Moobli in the open if there was time to run, so Cleo ran and when she did he naturally followed. She scooted up an old fence post where she balanced precariously on top, growling and flaring as Moobli whined and twice reared upwards from below. He was playing, she was not. I called him away, put on the thick gauntlets and gloves and when I went near instead of spitting she just crouched down with jet black eyes and depressed ears. Reckoning she couldn't claw me without losing her balance, I seized her neck scruff without much protest and carried her inside the shed where Patra too had fled after Moobli had jumped up. Oddly Cleo didn't dive into the logpile but merely crouched there, looking at me as if knowing I had "saved" her from danger.

That evening as they lay in their bed together after their feed both cats started licking each other as I stayed quietly nearby. Suddenly I heard an odd clattering almost purring sound, louder and slower than a domestic cat's and with a faint whistling note to it. It was Cleo, sounding as if her voice box had broken loose. I'd never heard either cat purr before and taking advantage of her sudden good mood, I gingerly put my gloved hand out and for only the second time, Cleo let me stroke her. What odd creatures they are, I thought. I hoped such progress would continue because if they stayed wild, the day would come when I couldn't handle them even with gloves, for they were as yet only a little over five months old.

One evening after a seven-mile trek along the shore which had yielded only the sight of some ravens performing aerobatics in the north-west winds, plus a small bagful of honey fungus—delicious when fried in butter—I was having a flannel bath when I noticed black specks floating past the windows.

It seemed the entire colony of little pipistrelle bats who had their home in the woodshed eaves were flying around the house with shrill squeaky cries. I counted nine, flitting to and fro on their skinny web wings. A mist had come down from the hills and a light drizzle was falling but this didn't seem to bother them at all. It seemed the continued presence of the cats below had made them decide to come out and find a new home before winter set in. As I watched, individuals hovered before the eaves of the cottage and the small gaps in the lead cladding below my west chimney. Suddenly one of them landed below it, folded its wings with a snap and scuttled upwards under the cladding like a tiny mouse. As soon as one had gone in, the rest began to follow until as dark fell there were only two left. It appeared a somewhat cold and cheerless new home, I thought.

In late October, after a rough boat trip up the loch on a day with less gales than were now usual, I received Dr Brambell's reply.

"I do not know if our wildcat is capable of reproducing. I have no reason to believe that it is not. If you have a cage to keep ours in beside yours but not with them until they have become familiar, I should think it might well work. I'd be very happy to get our wildcat rehoused and would only ask that you give him a good home."

Now I had a long journey ahead for I felt it wiser to go down to London and fetch the cat back by Land Rover rather than have him sent up in the noisy cold guards van of a train. As I wrote my reply next day, there was a blurred streak outside the window. Patra, like Cleo earlier, had stalked round the cottage corner and had made a leap for the birds on the table. They escaped easily and as she swung to and fro on her front claws like a gymnast I scared her away again, but I realized this almost certainly would be a problem in the hard months. I had hoped as they grew older the wildcats would wander widely for prey, only returning at night to their familiar home in the woodshed. Cleo was now roaming alone and foraging further afield—we once surprised her in the west wood—but Patra seemed more inclined to stay around the cottage area.

A few nights later Patra leaped onto the lighted window sill, catching moths that were attracted by the bright paraffin lamp. She munched them up, wings and all, as if they were cornflakes. Later, with the light out, I saw Cleo also catching moths by moonlight. It seemed these insects were a part of their natural diet, at least while young.

During early November, I rowed down the loch for new stag treks, wrote, picked blackberries, raked leaves from the woods for compost, watched a badger digging for roots and beetles by moonlight, cut and hauled firewood, and made a small temporary run for the tomcat.

Realizing this wildcat would be a little bigger and stronger than the females, I constructed it with ash poles and one-inch wire netting, with the strong box I had used for bringing the kittens home fixed on one end for bed and shelter. This would hold him until I'd made a large natural enclosure among the rocks, bushes and wild plants in what seemed a perfect spot—where the kits normally played in good weather—just west of the cottage.

As bad luck would have it, the day before the trip to London produced the worst weather for weeks. The south-west gales that had been blowing for three days veered to the north-west, collected huge lowering clouds of rain, and, as if actively trying to prevent my visit to the capital, started hurling millions of gallons down. While on a map it might appear I could huddle along in the lee of the north bank, in practice the north-west gales hit the mountains on the south side and roared back north-eastwards up the loch, the waves almost as bad as those from the sou'westerlies.

I had long ago worked out a plan for leaving the cats in the woodshed. Six pints of sterilized milk were mixed with water and put into a slightly tipped bowl, then covered partly with a plank so the cats could drink but not spill or foul it. Nearby was another bowl of pure water. I hung half cooked sheep's hearts and liver on the walls at varying heights so they'd have to work for their food, and put beef and eight fifteen-ounce sterilized meat sausages around the logs. I'd only be away for a week but they had enough food for a month, and in the cold weather the half cooked meat would keep fresh a long time. Then I locked the doors and widened their exit hole.

Next day the winds and steady rain had turned to squalls of hail. With the box for the wildcat, sleeping bag, food and all the other gear and clothes I needed for various work and contacts I had to make in London covered with a thick plastic sheet held down by rocks, we waited until one heavy squall had passed. Then in the pocket of relative peace that followed, we set off. We covered three miles before the next squall hit us but even so I was soaked when we reached the Land Rover in the wood six-and-a-half miles away. The long drive to London seemed a welcome period of luxurious ease after such a boat trip.

Moobli was fascinated by his first visit to the big city. As befitted his aristocratic pedigree, he took readily to the carpeted luxury of the small Hampstead hotel. He discovered doggy smells on the plane trees of the lovely avenue where I had once lived in a bed sitter and had to be constantly watched when off the lead as he showed an alarming propinquity to dash into the road if he saw another large dog on the other side. Small dogs he largely ignored. I was surprised at the number of pedestrians who, seeing an abnormally large Alsatian heading in their direction, instantly stuffed their hands into their pockets or behind their backs, terror on their faces. Some even foolishly stamped and said "Go away!" or begged me to hold his collar as we drew near. Patiently to each I tried to explain that bad dogs, like children, were the result of bad upbringing, that a German shepherd that had a good, fully exercised life and knew his place, who wasn't tied up all day in a garden while its owner was away at work, or ill-treated, or was spoilt to death, was the best tempered dog alive. But in the public eye, Alsatians, seen as the tools of crooks in films and on TV, or as vicious police dogs catching criminals, seem to have a bad name. If a small dog bites anyone little is heard, but if an Alsatian does it makes the papers. But I had to admit Moobli did look frightening. He was now six feet, four-and-a-third inches long including his tail, and his head was one foot, nine inches round and eleven inches from nose tip to ear base—not a bad *bear's* skull in fact.

But within three days, as I travelled about London buying equipment, having my backlog of films developed and printed, met magazine contacts and publishers, he was taking London in his stride and knew pavements were for walkers and the black and white stripes were for crossing the road.

On the fourth day I kept my appointment with Dr Michael Brambell at the Zoo. The Curator of Mammals turned out to be a tall, broad-shouldered, progressive character, full of enthusiastic plans for his new breeding units at the Zoo and the new gorilla and lion houses; he was a few years younger than myself and often spent holidays camping and boating in Scotland a few miles south of my home. After we talked about animals for a while, he seemed satisfied I would take good care of the Zoo's only wildcat, and took me to meet the youngest head keeper, Nobby Clarke, a tall, dark-haired Cockney who was in charge of small mammals.

Both men said the wildcat was getting along in age. He had been caught in the Highlands as a kitten, had spent two-and-a-half years at the Welsh Mountain Zoo in Colwyn Bay, Wales, and had been taken in by London Zoo in April 1968. So he had been in captivity for nearly all his ten years.

I said I'd pick him up the following Monday and put down the stout wooden box I had brought for him. The two men looked at each other. "Er, I don't think that box will be suitable," said Clarke. "But we could perhaps let you have one of our special boxes, if you'll send it back to us." As I agreed he added, "Would you like to see him first? I could show him to you now?"

I was anxious to see the tom I hoped to breed from and one day introduce back to the wild.

As we passed the glass front of the pen, I peered in eagerly but the cat wasn't there. He was in his den at the back.

"We always get him in there first, then shut the door while we clean out his cage or put his food in," said Nobby Clarke. I thought his tone of voice a trifle odd.

We went down a corridor along the back of the cage block and he stopped by a black door. "He's in here."

Chapter 5

As Nobby Clarke raised the trapdoor of the cubicle where the wildcat tom was, I bent down expecting to see a rather large type of tabby cat with a fine bushy tail. First I heard a growl that sounded as if it came from a small lion, then as my eyes came level *"PAAAH!"* a blast of hot steamy air shot past my face and I was looking into the great, mad, gold eyes of the Devil incarnate. The cat was well over three feet long, thick-bodied, broad-headed and was standing at full stretch on braced powerful forepaws, one of which he had just smashed down in front of him to accompany what Dr Brambell called his spit. Spit? it sounded more like a small charge of dynamite going off! As I stared at the open mouth, the curled rasping red tongue, the fearsome array of brownish teeth and sabre-like canines, the flattened ears, I could have sworn I saw flames flickering behind those huge malevolent eyes. Flames of hatred towards all humankind. "Holy crow!" I heard myself say in a far-off voice.

"I suppose you'll not be back for him on Monday," said Nobby Clarke seeing the shock on my face. I managed to recover.

"I'll be here," I said, trying to look more confident than I felt. "He'll be more of a handful than I expected but I've come all this way. I'll take him."

"It will be interesting," said Clarke with masterly understatement when I said I hoped to breed him with one of my two females.

Later, as we discussed the wildcat's diet, care and the sort of draught-proof den I should make him, both men agreed that pound for pound the wildcat tom was probably the fiercest animal in the Zoo. Never once, in all the years of his captivity, had he shown the slightest liking or even momentary toleration towards those who cared for or fed him. *

Clearly, the small temporary run I'd made back home would be hopelessly inadequate. Such an animal, as powerfully muscled as a small cougar, could have torn his way out of it with ease. While he was similar in colouring and shape to my ungrown females, there was a great difference in size for he was an exceptionally big and magnificent specimen. Over the next three days I searched for and bought nearly £50-worth of thick, green, plastic-covered Rylock fencing for the tom's enclosure, and had a roof rack fitted to the Land Rover so I could keep the inside clear of ropes, boat engine, tank, all my new supplies, and gear, and the fencing itself. On the Monday I went to pick up the wildcat.

It had been put into one of the Zoo's big barred black animal boxes, complete with galvanized water and food containers. Both men wished me luck with the venture, and as I left I thought I heard one of the under-keepers say, "Is that b . . . really going?"

As I struggled over the asphalt with my unused box under one arm and the sixteen-pound cat hissing and growling in the other, a stocky under-keeper who'd worked with the tom, offered to carry it for me. "We called him Sylvester—after the cartoon cat," he said. "You'll need to be very careful. I went into his pen once and he was up high on a tree branch. He dived at my head, would probably have half scalped me but I just got out fast enough and shut the door as he struck it."

---

* In later correspondence (spring 1977) Nick Jackson, Curator of the Welsh Mountain Zoo informed me: "He came to Colwyn Bay in an attempt to commence breeding, but as great difficulty was found in obtaining a female, and as his presence could not be justified from an exhibition point of view, it was decided to send him to a collection where he could be paired. He arrived in Colwyn Bay certainly not as a kitten but probably between one and two years old. During his stay here he proved to be a ferocious and highly secretive animal . . ."

I knew then I'd call him Sylvesturr—because of the awful low growl he was making . . . *Urrr urrr,* like a dynamo throbbing deep in the bowels of the earth. I put him on the floor at the back of my vehicle, covered his box with a cloth, instructed Moobli not to bother him, and managed to make the 570-mile journey back in fourteen hours. It was hard driving in a loaded Land Rover because of foggy patches north of Preston which worsened around Glasgow. When we stopped on the big hill overlooking Loch Tulla, Argyllshire, sleet was falling in the silent darkness. Sylvesturr clawed some liver from my gloved hands and ate with great relish despite his growls. The journey did not seem to be upsetting him too much but we pressed on through desolate Rannoch Moor and Glencoe in case snow was on the way, headed round Loch Leven, turned west at Fort William and arrived at a quiet lonely spot by the sea at 2 A.M. After heating a can of soup, I put the bed down in the back and with Moobli's vast snoring form cramming me against the wall, and to the sound of Sylvesturr's low growls every time I moved, managed some brief sleep.

Next day dawned with cloudless blue skies and but for the cold it could have been summer. On the beach below, oyster catchers ran in and out with the tide ripples, tapping shellfish with their bright orange beaks, curlews prodded the sand and herring gulls turned over seaweed looking for sand eels and hoppers. When I approached with his breakfast Sylvesturr gave a loud hate hiss and made his low growl—like distant thunder or the start of a minor earthquake. But he was already proving to be a cunning old cat for he hadn't once dashed about inside the box trying to force a way out, nor had he fouled himself by disturbing the sawdust.

As we boated up the loch later in the sunlight, the somnolent, belligerent gloom that seemed to be his dominant expression lifted slightly. His great golden eyes glared between the bars as he watched the passing oaks, firs and alders. His face registered the fact that he knew he was somewhere different and perhaps the idyllic mountain landscape evoked memories of his long-ago kittenhood.

As I walked up the path, carrying Sylvesturr, Patra, fat, sat at the top as if to greet us, while the pink nose and long white whiskers of Cleo peeped from the edge of the rhododendron bush. They ran for cover as we approached. They still had some milk and water and there was red blood on the bone of the meat that was left. We couldn't have timed it finer.

I swiftly made a temporary run from the stout wooden two-foot-square box, the aluminium frame of an old deck chair and stout half-inch wire netting. Then, wearing three sweaters, an old jacket and the thick gauntlets and gloves and making sure all gaps were blocked with spare netting, tipped him into it. He landed with a loud hiss, went straight onto the attack, spat, then huddled in the back of the box. I put a large beach towel over the sides of the netting, to darken it so he'd feel more secure, then heaved the whole run into the wintry sunlight for warmth.

A few minutes later, from below, I saw Patra walk to investigate this strange new cage but a sudden spit, *PAAAH!*, sent her fleeing. Then Cleo, sniffing gingerly, moved close, gazed in with eyes like dark lamps and began moving very slowly. Apparently Sylvesturr tolerated her approach because he didn't spit at her, though I couldn't see what he did do because of the towel. I thought this extraordinary as he had never seen another cat since his mother while he was a kitten in his whole life, yet he appeared not to find the approach of Cleo, the wilder one, disturbing.

But when Moobli went towards the cage, curious, he went instantly on the attack, *PAAAH!*, slamming his right paw down on the ground, then clawing the netting with his left. Moobli leaped back several paces and as Sylvesturr repeated the performance at my approach, and I noticed in the sunlight with a slight jump of the heart that his horn-coloured talons were almost an inch long, Moobli started to bark. But the big cat stood his ground, braced at full height, glaring from me to the dog and I had no doubt if the cage had not been there and he'd gone too close, as big as he was, Moobli would have lost at least an eye. Unlike a truly wild wildcat which, if it can, will flee and hide, Sylvesturr was well used to humans, had found they were afraid of him, so he was more dangerous to them or any dog he knew to be with them. I had to get things right from the start. Hating myself, knowing he was probably only trying to protect me, I whacked Moobli hard with my hand, told him to stop barking and spent some time explaining to him that Sylvesturr was now one of us.

From that moment on, Moobli never again acknowledged Sylvesturr's presence. He looked through the big cat as if it were just not there, yet his fascination for the two young females, especially Patra, remained as strong as ever.

For four days, mostly in the rain, I slaved to make a fine natural roofed enclosure for Syl in the sunny area west of the cottage. There was a big natural rockery there with small hazel bushes, ferns, bracken, brambles and entwining honeysuckle. To give him both flat ground and the rocky habitat wildcats like, I cut right through the high rockery, heaving the boulders out with a crowbar, then drove in the side and end posts to a height of five feet.

The den, some 3½ feet long by 1½ feet wide, was made with big smooth rocks. Inside, I lined the floor with polyurethane chips to repel any moisture that might seep up, put gravel on top of that, then covered this with brown dry bracken and finally masses of hay cut from the front pasture. The den's roof was made of larch slabs, lined with hay, covered with perspex sheets, lined again with hay, then topped with a sheet of aluminium, tipped slightly for draining, and the whole den was then covered with armfuls of loose bracken. I made a stout wooden door with a curved entrance hole and slung it from the cats' "hunter training" pulley so I could raise or lower it from outside the pen, and built wooden draught excluders from the prevailing winds.

Right from the start Syl acted as if I had been appointed by the Creator for the sole purpose of feeding him and catering to his needs. No familiarity, however, was tolerated. After the first sunny day, his feet now back on terra firma, the long noisy trip over, he was back in full vigour, and a frightening creature I felt him to be. I could never move near him without seeing those great eyes upon me, watching every move. During fine spells I placed his cage so he could watch me making his enclosure, watch me working with hammer, saw, pliers, sledgehammer, skinning my hands heaving rocks out, and stretching and digging the fencing into the ground. My slender hope was that after the drive, the boat trip and all this building work for him, he might recognize me as different from other humans whom he was prepared to attack. Here was one working very hard to make him a superb natural enclosure and den back in his homeland, who fed him well, protected him from the dog and so forth. A slender hope. He kept his eyes on me but the moment I walked near, or our eyes met, he stood up with a growl. I had never seen such a glance as his, not even from an eagle. It was most disconcerting. He seemed even more wary of Moobli, spitting the moment he came into view. This was surely a hereditary fear dating from when wolves and more wildcats inhabited Britain.

Just putting his meat into the cage was tricky for, the moment he scented it, he came out on the attack to get it, and one had to withdraw one's hand back fast through the roof flap. But I found if I growled back at him in exactly the same way, he would eventually retreat into the box portion, so I could quickly set the food and drink down.

He seemed almost too independent for his own good for if ever he became sick, how on earth was I to treat him? Never, since he had been a small kitten torn away from these wild hills, had he permitted a single human hand to touch him. But at least he had one good point—I knew exactly how I always stood with him—total inviolate hatred!

North-west gales with intermittent hail began blowing on the last working day so to make the den totally draught proof, I lined it with a thick cardboard box, springing the sides open from the top with a hazel twig. I felt it could rain and blow till doomsday and the den would stay dry, the box a final comfort.

Transferring Syl from the heavy box-cage to the pen was tricky and I don't mind admitting I muttered a silent prayer. I had to hold the whole contraption three feet off the ground, with the box end thrust into the triangular flap in the fencing. There was a gap below the box which meant if Syl tried to escape back through it he'd emerge in the region of my groin! And I had little faith in the flimsy wire netting I'd arranged there, especially as it fell away slightly when I moved to shake Syl out. Calling Moobli for support, I shook and shook and he growled and hissed with rage, then finally landed on the ground. Instantly he

The wild kingdom of Wildernesse, viewed from the first of the 500-foot ridges above it, showing *(right)* the largely conifer west wood, the cottage, wildcat pens and the mainly deciduous and larch forest flanked by the far burn to the east *(left)*.

Moobli, one year and a quarter old, atop a mountain five miles to the north of Wildernesse.

Patra putting paw on Cleo's ear to keep her away from food, shortly after arrival July 23, 1974.

At eight weeks, Cleo and Patra hated being touched, and hissed and spat as a hand went near. But once grasped, they sometimes went limp and docile—as Cleo here.

Proving their scenting powers at eleven weeks, Patra *(right)* and Cleo raced to a sausage pinned on an old stump. The first to reach the food "owned" it and stamped a foot to keep the other kit away.

Further proof of scenting powers. Cleo gnaws at a dead eel placed near the woodshed exit hole at age of three months.

"Teaching" the kits to hunt at four months proved an hilarious failure. Patra chases halfheartedly at a dead rabbit I was winding back and forth on a fishing line *(left)*. Cleo surprised me by having two magnificent eight-and-a-half-inch-long kits on my birthday, May 25. Here they are just two days old. She was an excellent mother and, strangely, her wildness lessened after the birth *(right)*.

Although only eleven days old, their eyes not yet open, Freddy and Mia try hard to hiss and spit at any outside disturbance.

Cleo spent long periods while sitting, lying or even eating, encouraging Mia (shown here) and Freddy to "hunt" the black tip of her tail which she constantly flicked about. It was an excellent way of exercising them while expending little energy herself.

glared round, saw me, spat loudly and launched a direct attack. I growled back even louder, from defensive fear, then he saw Moobli and went at him through the fencing as I desperately struggled to retrieve the box-cage from the pen door and shut it all up before he escaped.

Moobli didn't bark but bounced about, facing down the cat who suddenly turned and with glowering eyes seeking a refuge, spied the entrance to the den and shot quietly into it, his long bushy black and buff striped tail following like a snake. It was a success, without injury to any party.

Two hours later I went out and Syl had gone. I checked the entire pen outside but there was no sign of him. By torchlight I found my latest addition had been a foolish mistake. Seeing me approach, Syl had forced his way onto the top of the cardboard box. In time his weight would crush it. I now had to get that box out again.

Hastily, from an idea learnt with cougars in Canada, I turned the box-cage into a cat trap—with a falling door at the back held up by a nail which would be whipped away by a mousetrap spring when anything took the bait. Poling a piece of plywood against Syl's entrance hole, to keep him in, I set the box-cage cum trap inside the pen and at midnight he was safely caught in it. I carried him to the porch, intending next day to remove the cardboard box and make his den smaller and cosier.

But next morning Syl had escaped. In the dark I hadn't hooked the flap down properly and he had forced his way out between the roof and wall netting despite a five-inch overlap. Now what? Thrusting Moobli's head into the trap so he could get a good strong scent, I pointed to the ground and gave the usual command when making him follow animal trails in the woods and hills. Track it Moobli. Track the pussy coots! This was only the second time I'd asked him to track cats and I was afraid his dislike of Sylvesturr would make him refuse. But instantly he took off, zig-zagged, nose down, round the pens, through the front pasture, back up from the shore, and headed past some hazel clumps into the west wood. Within minutes he was by the big rocky cairn east of the rock escarpment—exactly the spot I'd thought a wildcat would choose. When I caught up he was whining and pacing over the rocks by a hole, from which came the unmistakable growls and flares. But he wouldn't put his nose into the entrance itself. Nor was Syl, now he was safe, going to come out. Hoping he'd emerge at night and prowl for food, I deemed it more sensible to set the trap between the wood and his pen.

Next day after a night of gales and hail showers, I hurried anxiously out. Cleo was in the trap. She had obviously scented the meat from the woodshed, a good forty yards. Worried about Syl being out foodless in such weather after his sheltered Zoo years, I blocked Cleo and Patra in the shed and set the trap again, near the dark shelter of the rhododendron bush by the path where I reckoned he might pass if he came back to the area where he'd been fed the first few days.

Dozing next morning, I heard a slight thud. I rushed out half dressed—there was Syl, perfectly caught, all the meat gone. So he *had* come back around the area when he was hungry. That was a small victory in itself. When he saw me coming he raged up and down, then fled into the box part again. Long soft hairs caught in the roof netting proved the cunning old cat had remembered how he'd escaped before and had tried to do it again, but he had eaten all the bait meat. I quickly made his den cosier by lowering the roof, putting wood at the back and stuffing all crevices with thick hay and bracken. Then I put Syl back into the pen. This time he ran straight into his den without even looking round, the second example of what I found out later was an extraordinary memory.

Happier with the smaller den, he soon made a bowl in the hay in which he sat, long bushy tail curved under and its thick black tip peeping from beneath his chin. I watched him carefully through early December, worried about how he would adjust to the cold outdoors. Luckily the weather co-operated for at first there were more sunny calm days than gale-ridden ones, the latter coming only occasionally as if to serve as brief toughen-up courses. Syl's appetite increased and he usually ate just after sunset, taking the liver first then returning for the rest about an hour later. I weaned him to life outside as gently as possible, erecting a screen in front of his den in the worst winds, cutting a hole in his food pan so rain water would drain out, or moving it under his den roof if rain was heavy.

Several times after dark I found him exploring his new territory, sniffing delicately at the posts, his long white whiskers twitching like feelers. Although I'd put heavy wire liner along the fencing bottom and dug it six inches into the ground, setting rocks and logs round the outsides too, he never once tried to dig out. At first he darted back into his den when he heard us coming but after a week he was more confident and, as his body stocked up against the cold and for the winter, and his tawny grey-striped coat grew thicker, he became more hungry. He, oddly, was not as afraid of the hissing paraffin lamp as he was of human or dog forms looming up in the dusk. His eyes proclaimed his age for they flashed with a dull yellow against the light and the sides of his pupils were pitted in two places with black spots—quite different from the brilliant green flashes of Cleo and Patra's youthful eyes.

I never knew quite how he would react when I went out with his food. For several nights he advanced out of his den the moment he smelled the meat. First a huge muscled foreleg emerged, next his broad head, then he looked about him with a hiss and slow, mad, fierce looks. He had a crazy, sideways glance that seemed a prelude to possible swift attack. I can only describe it as like the look the fine Indian actor Jack Palance uses when he plays parts like the classic gunfighter in the film *Shane*, a look suggestive of hatred, caution and suppressed explosive power. Then as I put the food through the fencing into his pan, he looked at it then rushed out in a furious attack, stopped an inch or two away from the fencing, slammed down his foot with a blasting *PAAAH!*, glared straight into my eyes for a second or two, then seized a piece of meat and ran back with it. But at other times he flew out, *PAAAHED* and stood his ground, guarding his meat with a big outstretched paw between it and myself, and carried on eating, growling all the while. Once he came out, stalked the lamp and after one bouncing bound, flew straight at the fencing, spat and hit it a hard blow with extended claws that had a spread of almost two-and-a-half inches. I finally decided that while I didn't want to cow him, these attacks should not be encouraged as he might, if I kept flinching as I did, continue them when I'd released him to the wild. So I took to standing my ground, knowing the fencing would hold him, and growling back while waving the light, which kept him back from my fingers.

Although it became clear over the first few weeks that Sylvesturr would never, in any sense, became even half tame, I felt a strong empathy with him. Now, at forty-six, I was living totally alone six-and-a-half miles from my nearest neighbour up a lonely loch, where except in the fair weather days of summer I didn't even see another boat for eight months of the year. I lived in the wilds now because after many big city years in countries half across the world, understanding the last wilderness areas, the natural world and its wildlife, had become all that really interested me. And in matters of love I had long lost any abilities at the useful art of compromise. So, in some ways, Sylvesturr seemed almost a soul mate. This old, fierce wildcat who was set in his ways, who would never, could never, give even the cupboard love of a normal cat, who would sooner have died than compromise his instincts, seemed a symbol of independence. Unloved, unlovable, he would be a loner to the end. There were lessons to be learned from him. While to many it may seem odd to feel any affection for so choleric a creature, for so intransigent a species—for my females, after being personally reared by me, were only a little less wild than Syl—I *liked* him. I admired his cussed pre-historic magnificence and, as I believe man must now act totally as custodian, not merely the user of the natural world and its last great animals, it seemed increasingly important I try to breed from him and, if it could be done safely, release him and his progeny back to the wild.

But it appeared at times his irascibility was largely confined to humans and dogs. One afternoon I saw a feathered thorn moth fluttering over the grass before his den. He watched it for a few seconds then came out and put his paw on it. But he did it softly, not killing it, as if he just wanted to slow it down so he could see it better. There was an odd, almost kindly expression in his big eyes as he looked at it, and presently it fluttered up and away. It was probably the first moth he had ever seen—and he didn't seem to regard it as food as did young Cleo and Patra. Although the two females occasionally walked outside his pen, looking in at him with huge eyes, he showed little interest. His eyes followed their movements but he didn't come out on the attack or even move. I felt he possibly regarded them as mere attachments of man and that they were prowling there after smelling the extra food. Certainly, after four days of heavy south-westerly gales and lashing rain, which scared the females, all the cats became hungrier, were eating almost two pounds of meat and cat food daily. One night the wind blew in the front door as I lay abed. In the morning Patra was curled up on a kitchen chair. And Moobli was regarding her dolefully with his head on his paws. His pack of meat sausages had been broken into again, one half-eaten by Patra.

Cleo never came into the house now, but Patra would when I was not there, taking advantage of Moobli's liking for her. She once even deceived him into thinking he was about to give her a lick but her eyes were darting about for food and as soon as she located the half-sausage on the sink, she was off and up after it so fast, Moobli hardly saw her go. Patra was much more cunning about the house area, ate like a horse even when her stomach was distended, and I felt could possibly be at least half tamed in time, but Cleo never.

It had become my habit after putting out Syl's food, to sneak a look round the cottage corner an hour later to make sure he had eaten it. One evening, a little calmer than the last few, I did this—and saw Patra stealing along by his front fencing. She stopped in front of his half-full pan and as he watched her through the curved hole of his door, she stretched in a paw and tried to scoop some food out with her claws. Instantly he shot out of the den but instead of a loud *PAAAH!* and enraged foot stamp, he put his head close to hers, delivered a discreet small spit. However, it was more than enough to terrify her. She may not have seen him coming because he moved like silent lightning, but the sight of the great head more than his spit scared her back to the woodshed as fast as her legs would carry her. Syl then ate the rest of his food, between growls, out in the open. It seemed he wasn't taking any more chances.

One morning after a night of gales in which I'd heard a loud thump above the pounding of waves upon the shore, I went out early. My boat had been blown bodily from its trolley. Luckily the loch had risen two feet in the previous day and it had landed in shallow water, keel out towards the waves, on a grassy patch between rocks. In winter the loch, swelled by rain and fed by the burns that drain the mountainsides like seething white veins, could easily rise eight feet above its summer level. I'd been lucky this time but had to spend the morning crowbarring the winch off the old ash trunk and setting it higher on a post in the garden, so I could now haul the boat up between my log archway out of the pounding water's reach.

Next day, needing cat and dog food, with much mail to post and my book contract well overdue, we fought our way up the loch. The waves were so bad I had to sit at the back, constantly adjusting the engine throttle, slowing down through the worst and speeding up through the smaller ones. As the prow tended to fly up and almost fall back on us as it was hit by the wind after the big waves, I yelled at Moobli to keep up front as a counter balance. He hated it, bracing his feet against the sides, looking as scared as when he was a pup in the boat for the first time. The contract had arrived but the publisher wanted it back, signed and witnessed, as soon as possible. At the store I forgot an item, set my pack down by the rear wheel, went back for the extra purchase, came out, forgot about the pack—and reversed over it. Now I had to buy a new pack. As I also wanted a flash unit for my camera to photograph Sylvesturr who seldom came out before dusk, have the contract witnessed by a lawyer, I now had three good reasons for making a trip to the town over forty miles inland—a rare chore I usually put off as long as possible.

On the way back, after putting Moobli off for his usual run, I was riding home with the waves when I saw him stop by a rocky lair where he had once found an otter. His tail was waving agitatedly—there was clearly something in the holt—but I couldn't turn the boat. Suddenly above the noise of the wind I heard two high-pitched screeches. I shouted to Moobli to come away. He looked towards me briefly, there was a sudden brown blur and an otter shot between his legs. Moobli gave a loud yipe but before he could turn, the otter had vanished into the water. As he ran home he limped slightly. I had just managed to haul the boat out before the waves swamped it when Moobli joined me, jumping up with unusually enthusiastic greeting. I soon found the cause of his limp—a one-inch open gash right across the knee joint of his rear left leg. The otter, in the moment my call had distracted him, had seized its chance and on the way through Moobli's legs had delivered a slashing bite. Now I had a fourth reason for visiting the town—the wound was too large to heal naturally on a constantly flexed part of the leg and would need to be sewn up by a vet. We seemed to have run into a spell of bad luck.

We didn't go next day, however, as the first heavy snowfall of winter had arrived, and before breakfast we went out to do some tracking. As we emerged two deer hinds who had been grazing between the hazel trees near the west wood, trotted into the wood, joining five others who had sheltered there overnight. The cold and snow had finally driven them down from the hills and from now on, providing they weren't disturbed, they would be using our woods as a dormitory most nights.

I was surprised as we followed our wildcats' four-toed tracks in the snow by how much ground they had covered in the night. One set went right down along the edge of the path, around the boats, and along the shore for about one hundred yards before turning back to the garden. From the shed more tracks led into the east wood, and one set went over a fallen tree that bridged the burn and covered fifty yards of the far shore. In front of the house the tracks criss-crossed and they had clearly hunted a long time in the bramble banks. Between them, although they had both hunted alone, they had covered over half a mile in the cold crisp snow. But I found no trace of a kill. Both had walked round Syl's pen too, and inside it his larger tracks proved that he too had been much on the move. I had read somewhere that wildcats mainly laid up in rain and snow, except when driven out by hunger, yet the three had been extremely active despite being well fed. There was still food left in Syl's pan.

Two days later, with drizzle melting the snow, we made it to the town. After my contract was signed, witnessed, copied and

posted, I took Moobli to the vet, a visit that was not overly im-
pressive. First the young man in charge that day said he'd never
treated a dog Moobli's size before and he hoped he did not bite.
To stop him biting he produced a piece of cord and tied it so
tightly round Moobli's muzzle that it wrinkled his skin up and he
whined. When I asked if he hadn't a proper dog muzzle, he
replied aye, they had one but as they usually only treated collies
or terriers it wouldn't fit a dog as big as Moobli. As I held
Moobli's head down on a tiny bench and re-assured him with
soothing words, the young man put on some liquid he said
would numb it a bit, scraped the wound open, then put in a single stitch as I held the poor dog down by force, and gave me a
bill for £1.40. When I said I had wildcats and asked if ever one
became ill would he be able to treat it, the young man registered
more surprise. "A wildcat! I've never treated a wildcat. We'd
need several days' notice if you were bringing one in." As I
wouldn't be bringing in a wildcat unless it was really sick and
several days' notice would probably be too late anyway, and to
give such notice I'd have to go by boat to reach a phone box
and would thus be halfway to the clinic already, I made a men-
tal note that if any of my cats ever did get sick I would be treating them strictly on my own.

We were walking back through the town after our purchases
when we were hailed by a voice. "Ah, 'tis yourself, the man with
the fine dog!" It was Willie, a Council worker whose unabashed
admiration of Moobli had once brought us into a street conver-
sation and who I'd since been told owned two pet foxes. As we
talked I asked if he would show them to me. "To be sure, come
on down." We went to the lochside where he lived in an old caravan below the railway line. The foxes, sister and brother, were in
a small run nearby from which he took them for walks as if they
were pet dogs. They were beautiful creatures with thick red
coats, black ears and feet, and they moved with the cat-like
grace of raccoons. The bigger dog fox had lovely bright orange
eyes and when I put the back of my hand down, he nuzzled it
gently with his wet nose. But when Moobli went near, sniffing,
he spat at him like a cat. I coveted them immediately but

when I said he was lucky to have them, Willie told me a sad story.

He had just retired and, as a new by-pass road was about to be constructed beside the loch, he had to leave and was now living on a caravan site in a village some eleven miles to the north. He was coming back to the town each day to feed the foxes and take them for runs before deciding what to do with them.

"There's nowhere for me to keep them up there," he said, running his hands through his thick greying auburn hair. "Ah'll just have te have them destroyed if ah canna find a guid home for them." I found myself gabbling—I would be glad to take them, I had the ideal place, studying wildlife was my work, I'd make a big natural run for them between two up-ended stumps in my east wood, they would be in a perfect wild environment away from the towns. I'd gladly pay him for them, look after them well, let him know how they were faring . . . and, at the end of my peroration, Willie said he would be happy for me to take them. He would let me have their run plus some thirty yards of fencing. We agreed I would come to collect them on the Thursday or Friday of the following week, depending on gales, but somehow or other I'd be there on one of those days.

Two tame foxes, I thought, as we boated home in high winds. What a windfall. It seemed our little run of petty bad luck was at an end. And, when I went to feed Sylvesturr, three hours later, for the first time he didn't spit, flare or growl. Instead, he just watched quietly as I put his food down. Maybe the deathly silence around the house had worried him and now he was actually grateful he was to be fed after all. Only Moobli seemed a little unhappy, limping a little and licking the stitch on his sore leg, after his most traumatic experience to date.

Over the next few days I alternated writing work with building a twelve-foot temporary run for the foxes from spare lumber and fencing. It was bitterly cold work amid gales and hail showers but it had to be done well, totally enclosed with the fencing and stapled all along its length on every strut so the foxes couldn't dig out, and with an upward hinged gate at one end. With Willie's two wooden hutches at either end for male and female to have separate quarters they could live just as they did in his smaller pen, until I could make a really large run in the east wood. I built it on fourteen-foot-long runners with handles at one end and curved sledge runners at the other, so I could drag it about to wherever I wanted it.

The late December day we went back to the town to fetch the foxes was a disaster from the start. After a calm dawn, the southwest gales started again half an hour before I hauled the boat down. Holding it against the waves with one hand while I loaded an empty calor gas container, fuel tank and pack in with the other I badly pulled a back muscle. We fought our way up the loch—and got the anchor stuck under a tree root at the other end. Complicated prodding with a larch pole freed it, but resulted in icy water filling both my boots.

At the town Willie looked pale and drawn—his brother, near whom he now lived, had been killed in a car crash. I went with him to his butcher and bought nearly £7 worth of meat for the foxes and cats. Then, as it was my last day out before Christmas and was half-closing day, I asked him if he'd mind waiting till I'd posted important mail, bought last-minute supplies, then we'd devote all our time to transferring the foxes to my Land Rover and discuss their future care. The post office refused to accept for registration a kind of envelope I had registered many times before. An argument with the manager, who quoted regulations about signatures and sealing wax, ended in a long double walk through town to a stationer's who kindly gave me the requisite wrappings.

When I got back to Willie rain was pouring down and someone had stolen my driving windscreen wiper. As I struggled to transfer the other over with a pair of pliers, Willie came up with the vixen in his arms. "Where shall I put her?" I said I thought he was going to let me have the hutches in his run. But no, he needed them himself now, also the fencing. I said I couldn't put two foxes loose in the Land Rover with Moobli. "Well," he said, "you'll not be taking them now, you come back when it's better weather and you have the run." I said I *had* the run at home, had spent three days making it, and had battled my way up the loch, come all that way, to keep the appointment to take the foxes. But as the rain teemed down, and the vixen shivered in his arms, I realized that now the actual moment had come, he couldn't bear to part with his beloved foxes after all. I could see it all in his haggard face.

"Oh dear," I said despite my keen disappointment. "You can't bear to let them go, eh?" Suddenly, he seemed confused and half shouting that I could pick them up some other time, he ran away through the rain like a gawky two-legged giraffe, with the vixen in his arms, not towards the pen where the dog fox was pacing alone but back towards the town.

I stood there drenched, miserable, furious about the stolen wiper, and at myself for not having taken the foxes first and so giving Willie time to think. But as I saw the poor man vanishing between the buildings I knew I couldn't take the foxes anyway, not if it meant his unhappiness. I drove back.

The gales, now southerly, had dragged the anchor and we just arrived in time, as the boat stern was beginning to bang up and down on the gravelly shore. Coming back was the worst boat trip of the year, in almost pitch black darkness; we could only make our way by following the lie of the hills against the sky. And we had to hug the south shore then ride the alarmingly deep and fast-running waves across the loch. The only way I could land was to put all the gear onto the starboard and landward side of the boat, then twist it at the last moment so keel and bow were to the waves, leap off, rapidly heave everything ashore, then haul it up the grass bank, one end at a time, before the crashing waves filled it completely. Boat and engine weighed some 600 pounds so this frantic activity did nothing for my hurt back.

As I walked up the muddy path in the wind and rain, drenched and trembling, I felt depressed—all those risks to return home foxless and to yet another lonesome Christmas in the wilds. And to cap this odd day, when I went out with Sylvesturr's food an hour later than usual it seemed this time his normal belligerence had not turned to worry for he came straight out on the warpath with a foot stamp and a loud *PAAAH!* I looked at him for a second. I couldn't help it. "And *PAAAH* to you too!" I yelled back, stamping my booted foot so hard the ground about us shook. His ferocious glare turned to astonishment and for the first time ever he turned tail and shot back into his den like a tawny furry express train.

But I had one consolation. The new fox run was a blessing in disguise. Not only could I use it to keep the females away from the bird table at my own discretion but also to force a close introduction between them and Sylvesturr. By setting the pen endways to his in early spring—when I hoped the mating urge would come upon them all—I could have all the cats close together yet still keep the girls safe from any possible attack. It would be a tricky operation, needing great care, but I had plenty of time to work out the details.

Although it was more than eight years since I had embraced the wilderness life, starting in Canada where I'd really dreaded the first Christmas alone, I still found the whole end-of-year season slightly traumatic. One is never more aware of loneliness than when one knows most other folk are back with wives, children or loved ones, enjoying the traditional parties, music and general social goodwill. My usual method of coping with this period in the years in the Scottish wilds was to dig out old photos, diaries, letters and personal memorabilia and indulge myself in a great sentimental wallow of nostalgia. This would last an hour or two, then I'd reach for the typewriter and in a great creative burst, from heightened awareness through my lonely plight, furiously pound out thousands of words on little personal philosophies.

This ninth Christmas started out as no exception but after a couple of hours I suddenly realized I wasn't feeling any great emotions, that I was now actually enjoying my loneliness, not only because it was a useful state for a man studying the natural world but because of the perverse feeling of strength it gave me. Then as I caught a glimpse of Moobli sitting outside, gazing at me with a sorrowful look in his brown eyes, I realized that for the first time I was not really alone anyway. This was his and my first Christmas together, and I also had three other oddly assorted companions—Sylvesturr, Cleo and Patra.

I put all the writing materials away again, made a rich dough for four pounds of wholemeal bread, prepared my small turkey and shoved them both in the calor gas oven together. Then I took Moobli for a quick two mile trek in the hills despite the constant drizzle and cold south-east wind. After my own royal feast of turkey, I fed the animals like fighting cocks with it and usual meats, then tried to make friends with Syl.

Always before I had put all his food down at once and he, depending on how hungry he was, either came out on the attack to get it, or stayed glaring from the den door and growling until I'd gone away. I wondered if this was because after putting all his food down and then standing nearby, he regarded my continued presence as a threat—in that I might take it all away again. So I tried a new method. For over an hour in the rain I sat hunched in my grass-green oilskins on a small log and just dropped small tidbits into his pan. At first he growled from the den door but as I didn't move he came out, grabbed the small portion and took it back inside. I persisted, with very small bits, and finally he realized I was only staying there to feed him. He suddenly associated me with a constant food supply and he relaxed enough to actually come and feed near me, munching away with his side teeth. Occasionally his great golden eyes would switch onto me warningly, and his old teeth grated together as he chewed, and he went *noine, noine, noine* deep in his throat. So, in an affectionate voice, I imitated him back "noine, noine, noine." The fact that he soon stopped doing it was worth his first look of disgust. Although it was gratifying to see him feed in the open near me for the first time without foot stamps or spits, I had no real wish to tame him as I eventually intended to let him go, so I didn't do it again.

In the early dusk, although they'd eaten far more than usual, both Cleo and Patra leaped onto the bird table and consumed some bread and biscuit crumbs. Each cat had eaten almost as much as a man today and I realized it was time to get them used to the new run. Moobli simply refused to keep either cat from the bird table.

On Boxing Day I put the two females into the fox pen with a thick wooden rubber-roofed den box I had made. Cleo accepted the fact that she couldn't escape after a careful look round and went to sleep in the box, but Patra got her head stuck three times in the fencing squares as I watched hidden from the bedroom window. The last time she couldn't get back again and started bawling like a squawking duck. With gloved hands I managed to get her head back through again but she sank her teeth into the gloves, luckily missing my fingers. After feeding them in the run I let them out again two hours later.

Chapter 6

New Year opened on a sad note. We were walking along below the rocky escarpment in the west wood when Moobli suddenly got a strong scent and bounded over two piles of tangled windfalls as I hastily followed. We found a newly dead red deer hind, and right behind her, as if they'd both fallen while running in echelon, their legs stretched out as if still pacing, a deer calf. At first I thought both were dead but as Moobli sniffed the calf it tried to lift its head, found the effort too much and let it fall again. Its eyes were blinking slowly because the normal wet mucus of the eyeball was almost dry. Telling Moobli to sit back, I lifted the calf's head and tried to get it on its feet but even after putting its legs under it in the sitting position, it couldn't even hold its head upright let alone stand. Its mother seemed to have been dead for about two days, the upper eye turning opaque already, which happens quicker in rainfall than in dry weather.

I hurried back to the cottage to put some warm milk into a baby's bottle with a sheep feeder teat which I kept for such emergencies, though I felt we were probably too late. Such occurrences aren't rare where I live in winter. Red deer were originally woodland animals until the march of man's civilization and agricultural and forestry fencings forced them into the bare Scottish hills. In cold wet winters, their strength sapped by poor food, warble fly holes in their coats, the oldest and youngest animals with severe infections of lung worms and nasal bot fly grubs, rapidly weaken. They return to whatever woods they can find for shelter, finally dying from pneumonia. But there was no blood from the hind's nose which is frequent in such cases.

By the time we got back, the calf was also dead. It was sad but there was no point wasting the meat. The wildcats and Moobli would eat a great deal between them and at least the death of the deer would save me long trips up the stormy loch. Making doubly sure the calf was dead I hauled it onto a downward slope and bled it while I skinned the hind, taking a shoulder and one haunch for dog and cats. The cause of her death was soon clear —the other haunch held four shotgun pellets, the flesh around them contused and black. Poachers were known to have been in the area, working from their vehicles on the roads, blinding the deer with lights then shooting indiscriminately. The nearest road was over seven miles from me so this hind had probably limped all this way before succumbing.

Her calf was very young, probably late-born in September or even early October, after its mother had perhaps come into a second season and mated with one of the young stags who take over when the master stags have left. Hinds and young deer live in strictly matriarchal herds but when this sick mother had wandered off alone into the woods, the calf had naturally followed, her milk had dried up, and it too had died, from a combination of shock, cold, loneliness and starvation. I just took the two haunches of the calf and left the rest for the wild predators. The two carcasses would provide much needed winter food for ravens, buzzards, crows, foxes and even badgers who occasionally eat carrion, plus the useful burying beetles and other small scavengers.

Although its strong gamey smell wasn't at all like the beef and mutton flank he'd been used to, Moobli wolfed his first venison half haunch with relish, and Cleo and Patra rushed off with their pieces to separate corners. Syl just sniffed his, glared with a "What trick is this?" look and went back into his den. But it was all gone, and some bone too, by morning. Within days he developed a strong appetite for venison. It seemed to make him fiercer too, for once again he started coming out on the attack at feed times. But I found by dropping a large lump down first, he made off with it while I put the rest down without risk to my hands.

I now studied his habits in more detail. He showed no tendency to bury droppings, preferring to leave them on piles of old bracken than on earth or grass—once in every two days seemed the regular pattern. He could chew and swallow quite large pieces of bone without harm, like a dog. If there wasn't enough roughage in his food or I couldn't catch a weekly mouse—the two females had virtually eradicated them from around the house area—he chewed bracken and rush stalks and grass to provide his own. Vegetation, I noticed from his droppings, was an important part of his diet. I felt sure wildcats subsisting largely on carrion in the depths of winter would also supplement their diet in this way. They would also need it to help clear through any pieces of bone.

For several days, to help them regard it as a second home for the time when I'd use it to help introduce them to Syl, I fed Cleo and Patra in the fox pen. Eventually Patra gave up her attempts to escape, sharing the sleeping box with Cleo as amicably as they both shared their sacking bed on the logpile most nights.

One early January evening I saw one of the females stealing along the front of Syl's pen. Now it was Cleo who was after his left-overs. But instead of shooting out as he had done to repel Patra weeks earlier, he was now more discreet. He walked out very slowly, head low, eyes hypnotically fixed on hers, sneaked up to her and when their heads were close made a mere light *phutt*. She pulled her head back only slightly but didn't run. For all the world, it seemed he didn't want to scare such a lady as Cleo with so crude a gesture as *PAAAH* or a foot stamp. He ate a morsel himself then trotted back into his den, leaving her to help herself through the fencing.

For the next few nights I went out after dark, waited till my eyes were accustomed to it and sneaked round the corner to see if it was a regular occurrence. Each time Syl was out and prowling round the edges of his pen, which was most unusual. One mid-January morning his heavy outer door was flat on the ground—he had clearly kicked it outwards which seemed foolish as it made his den draughty. By now, his coat had grown very thick, so he looked even larger than when I'd first taken him from the Zoo. It was also darker and greyer than its former tawny brown, which would give him better camouflage for hunting in the greyer landscape of winter.

I wondered if the deer meat was making him stronger or whether he might be coming into a male oestrus. If some naturalists were right about wildcats having two litters a year, it seemed possible. I had, from extensive correspondence, now traced an isolated record of a wildcat in Berne Zoo having kittens on March 29, which, allowing for an average sixty-eight days' gestation, placed conception in mid-January. Although this was the only evidence I had that such early breeding was biologically possible, it had happened under artificial conditions, and I felt it unlikely to happen in the cold winter conditions of the wild. I hauled Syl's door up and poled it back into place.

Later that night, well after feeding time, I heard a loud ruckus from the woodshed. I rushed out with Moobli and a torch. Both Cleo and Patra were up high on the logpile and some of the logs had been knocked down. They were unharmed but scared. I shut both doors and hurried round to Syl's pen, as Moobli suddenly dashed off into the east wood with a low growl. Once again Syl had kicked his door over but was safe in his den, and none of the fencing had been disturbed. I replaced his door as a heavily panting Moobli returned and went back indoors. I decided it was probably a prowling fox and the two females, quite capable of taking care of themselves now, had either knocked the logs down when launching a defensive attack or while scattering to safety after being disturbed from sleep. Either way, the fox wasn't likely to come around for a long time, certainly not if it found the deer carcasses.

South-west gales sprang up during the night and heavy hail showers rattled on the tin roof. In the morning I went out to find Syl's door a full yard away from the den which was now empty. I checked all round the pen, the rocks and tangled undergrowth but there was no sign of him. What on earth had happened? Then I found some of his hairs, far longer and softer than a domestic cat's, on the triangular swing door I had made in the fencing. He had climbed the five-foot fence and then found the strength, while braced high on the wire, to force his way between the top lumber strut and the flat wood lining the swing part of the fencing. And on a kink the heavy binding wire that held the door tight had snapped. A man using both hands would have found it hard to force such a gap. What strength he possessed!

Why had he forced his way out now after being used to confinement all his long adult life, when he had never tried to escape before from the roomy pen? I recalled how he had been searching its perimeter for several nights after dark after eating his food, but now he had left half last night's sausage and cat food in his dish. Maybe the sight of the wild woods all around him, now he was used to the territory by sight, had finally aroused his long suppressed instincts. Or perhaps he had come to like the half raw venison so much he had decided to go and search for more.

I tried to get Moobli to track him but he had never liked Sylvesturr in the way he regarded the females as his personal property; in fact he always acted as if he couldn't even see the big tom, and he now proved maddeningly obtuse. Every time I said "Track the pussy coots," he put his nose to the ground and tracked the night movements of Cleo and Patra which kept leading him back to the shed. Naturally I checked they were still there, entering carefully in case Syl was lurking with them. But both were on their sacking bed as usual, Cleo fleeing into the logs as I went in. Neither gave any sign of knowng Syl was free. I checked the deer carcasses which had started to decay slightly but they had not been touched, and Moobli could get no scent near the rock cairn where Syl had hidden once before. There was too much grass and too many twigs and leaves around the deer to see any tracks at all, never mind sort out wildcat from fox.

I checked them again by torchlight but could still find no sign. Suddenly, as I stood there in the eerie darkness, the firs and larches soughing in the wind above, I remembered the wildcat tracks in the autumn on the path a mile and a half away to the east. Could the disturbance last night, and Syl's breaking out, have been caused by the presence of another wildcat? If so and Syl was now in oestrus, it would probably be a female, also in oestrus, and he had broken out to be with her. I had been out in wild Canadian woods where bears roamed free but the thought that fierce, intractable Syl and a mate might now be lurking in the dark nearby was still a little scary. Well, to heck with him, I thought, let him spend the night out. He had come back when he'd escaped after only being here a few days and surely he would do so again when he was really hungry. I put some food in his pen and tied the swing door open, then blocked the females in the woodshed.

Throughout the night and all next day the gales, sleet and rain showers continued. It had turned bitterly cold and as the food in his pen was untouched, I began to worry. Searching carefully I found some mixed-up scuffs among the mud and spruce needles by a rhododendron bush south-east of the cottage which could have been made by a wildcat. Fortifying the box-cage trap, oiling the moving parts with butter, I carried it down and set it with strong smelling venison between the bush and the spruce glade. Again I shut the females in the shed so they could not take the bait.

Next day, the hail having turned to rain overnight, I was woken by the cronking of ravens. Four were perched in the west wood trees—they had found the deer carcasses. I went out, saw the trapdoor was down. It had been sprung, the meat had all gone, yet it was empty. And there were no hairs on the bottom of the door. I didn't think Syl would have had the sense to keep the door open on his back while taking the meat, but a big sly fox could have done it. But it would have to be a hungry old fox with bad teeth to risk such a trap on its first day out. Sometimes if I set the trip nail too far into its hold in the trapdoor, the mousetrap spring would go off but would not be strong enough to pull the nail out. It was always a delicate operation. It was just possible Syl had managed to get the meat out before the door fell and after being loosened by his vibrations, it had dropped later in the wind. I checked the deer again. They had been well chewed, apart from raven peckings and Moobli followed fox scent for some yards—shown by his occasional leg cocking on tufts—but didn't seem able to find any cat scent at all.

For weeks now, apart from occasional treks, I had been forced to spend the few daylight hours—it was dark before 10 A.M. and after 3:30 P.M.—working indoors on my Canada book, racing against time to get it finished by the due date in March. My only heating was the wood fire and an old paraffin stove. The fumes from this and smoke blown back down the chimney were bad for the lungs, and the shimmering light from the paraffin lamp did nothing for my eyesight. I'd go out in the mornings and find it took some time to focus on detail in the distant hills. Living in the wilds isn't easy in winter and I'd spent most of the last eight winters this way. But I stubbornly refused to have a generator thudding away in my woods, generating more fumes than electricity and scaring the wildlife.

On the fourth day, the wind now cold again from the north, I shut Moobli in the house and went to the trap. The door was down again and as I approached, the whole trap started to shake violently. There was a large dark brown animal in it. Thinking it must be Syl, his coat made darker by the wet, I ran towards it but suddenly the door edged up and a thick-bodied chocolate brown animal with a thick pointed blackish tail shot out, ran heavily like a huge weasel through the next rhododendron bush to the south-east and disappeared towards the loch. It could only have been an otter and it had managed to hook the door up with its claws in desperation at my approach. I drove slanting nails into the sides of the door so next time it fell the nails would go past the wooden slide grooves, and the caps would dig in like a rough lock if anything tried to force the door back up again. Then needing supplies and to post some chapters, I made a rough trip up the loch.

Next day the meat was still untouched and I began to lose hope. After a day spell in the fox run, I blocked the females in the shed overnight and moved the trap nearer to Syl's pen and also put sausage meat in the pen itself. For two more cold rainy days I did this, hope being slightly restored once when some of the meat in the pen had gone. I felt no completely wild animal would actually climb into the pen but it hadn't all gone—and I realized it could well have been chewed by hungry shrews or taken by birds. I was then thoroughly depressed. Syl had been gone for eight days and nights now and for a cat totally unused to catching his own wild prey, combined with a dearth of prey anyway in the height of winter, I felt I had truly lost him. I had let the Zoo down but even worse I had let Sylvesturr himself down. That night, with fresh venison and wearing gloves soaked in boiled spruce needle juice—a trick I'd learned in Canada for reducing man scent—I set the trap as delicately as I knew how.

January 18 dawned calm with cold clear blue sky, the first rainless day for over two weeks. I went out, the trapdoor was down. I hurried round to the front and there he was! He saw me coming and raged up and down with ferocious snarls and spits, giving those mad sideways Palance glares as he looked for ways to get out. He leaped up, as loose hairs showed he had repeatedly done, at the top of the netting where he had escaped before but I'd now sewn it all up with stout wire.

There was a little blood on the wooden floor of the box portion and at first I thought it had come from the raw venison. But as I got close and he slammed down his huge foot and *PAAHED* at me, I was terrified to see a thin trickle of blood from his nostrils. Had some sharp deer bone cut the sides of his throat? But he wasn't choking. Perhaps it was only blood from recently eaten meat, coughed up in the act of spitting. He was wet through and much thinner and had clearly lost a good deal of weight, but he was still full of life and all his old ferocity.

I struggled to carry him up to the pen and although his den was still perfectly dry, I was just renewing all the hay and bracken when I heard a strange whimper and a watery sneeze. Now there was more blood coming from his nose. There was something terribly wrong and my heart sank for this was no mere nose bleed. Sylvesturr had clearly developed pneumonia, or at the very least inflamed lungs, from being out in the cold and wet so long without proper food.

I thought only briefly of the inland vet who hadn't even had a dog muzzle. It was a Saturday and he had wanted several days' notice before treating a wildcat. In that state, hating humans as he did, I doubted Syl would have survived the boat journeys, the long jolting eighty-eight-mile drives, the complicated anaesthetic operations necessary to examine or treat such a fierce creature. No, my only hope was to try to nurse him through it, in a heated room in my cottage. Racing indoors, knowing he was probably too ill to keep himself clean, I stacked sheets of newspaper on the bedroom table, put in a paraffin heater, and set the box-cage with its hissing, flaring bundle of gold-eyed hatred onto two two-inch-square blocks so I could extract his droppings without disturbing him too much. There was no time for fear. I gathered an armful of dry hay, opened the trapdoor, foiled his furious attack with a blunt hazel stick and pushed the hay in with it. Draping the huge beach towel over the cage so he would have some darkness and also as a shield so he couldn't see what I was up to, I managed to fix his drinking bowl to the netting with wire so he couldn't tip it over.

Searching through a box of useful items sent to me by a kind young veterinary nurse down south who'd read in a magazine that I treated sick animals, I found some blue aureomycin, a broad spectrum antibiotic, and some mild penicillin tablets, both of which I could sprinkle in light doses on his food. When I went in to feed him at night the blood had stopped but he arched up at full stretch, spitting, and it began to flow again. Yet he pounced on the meat, eating avidly, and drinking the milk as if he hadn't drunk anything at all in the whole eight days he had been free. I left him alone then but as I went to bed I couldn't help mouthing a silent prayer that he would live. Next morning I went in quietly and he was lying at full stretch on his side. At first I thought he was dead for I'd never known him do that before, but as I put my head round the edge of the towel he shot to his feet, slammed down his foot and spat. Then he coughed, sneezed, and more blood came from his nose. It was awful to see and I quickly went out, knowing I'd have to leave him alone as much as possible to prevent exciting him.

I found it hard to work that day as I felt sick, sad and terribly guilty, for I could blame no-one but myself for not ensuring his pen was escape proof. Whether another wildcat had come around, inducing him to suddenly decide to get out, I would now never know. He had clearly found nowhere snug and dry while he'd been free and the rain and wind together had caused constant loss of heat, allied to lack of food. A cat always knows instinctively how to catch small prey but after his years in zoos, inexperienced and with so little prey abroad in winter, he had been in real trouble.

The fight to nurse Sylvesturr through the first crisis, until the blood stopped completely, took a full five days, and at times he was clearly battling for his life. At the end of the second day he was so weak he couldn't get up and I felt the end was near. He lay on his stomach, his back legs, thighs inwards, stretched out towards the window. His left front leg was splayed out at right angles to his body, while his right was tucked beneath his chin—as if he had collapsed in that position. But he still tried to spit when he heard me come in, growling as I pushed the food right up to his mouth. Then he pushed his big head weakly over the edge of the dish and managed to eat a few mouthfuls. After a short rest, as I sat quietly hidden in the shadows, after shutting the door so he thought I'd gone out, I saw him pull his legs beneath him one by one and stagger weakly to his feet. He stood there swaying but he could still lap up his milk. Naturally, with the loss of blood he was very thirsty but as his bowl held over a pint I didn't have to keep going in to fill it.

I'd never thought of myself as acting nursemaid to a wildcat but during his weakest period I had to quietly extract his droppings with little sticks through the bottom of the netting and hay as soon as he released them or he would have fouled himself completely. At his weakest he seemed to be in a semi-conscious stupor but at times he whimpered faintly, like a child, and it was poignant to see him occasionally try to clean himself with his long tongue. As I sat beside him at times I found myself willing him on. *Live, live, live,* I breathed silently. I felt strangely moved by his courage, and slowly he began to respond, knowing after the third day, I think, that I was really trying to get him through. This magnificent, unchangeable creature, so inviolate in his pride that he would rather die than submit, once so fierce he would have tackled anything, man or beast, that challenged him, was now reduced to total dependence on a human. In some ways I saw myself in this old cat and, strangely, he was teaching me a lesson too—to learn to love that which hated me, a lesson we

must perhaps all learn if rare wild creatures and the last wild
beautiful places of this earth are to survive. I had never felt any
strong emotions towards him before but now I found myself loving him and it became extremely important to me to make sure
he lived and that his ultimate freedom would not come too late,
that he should fulfil his wild destiny, his birthright, next summer
whether he mated with one of the females or not.

Some oddly rewarding experiences came at this time. When I
went in on the third evening he didn't try to spit but just looked
at me quietly. By now I had found a way of talking to him that
seemed to soothe him, calm him down, and as he lay on his side
he actually let me stroke his long soft hair several times without
protest. Taking advantage of one such moment, I measured him
with a ruler outside the cage. To my surprise, including his tail,
he was three feet, six and a half inches long. He was not quite a
foot longer than the females but was more heavily built, more
like a small puma than a cat.

On the fourth day an extraordinary thing happened. Patra
stationed herself on the window ledge outside, a mere two feet
from his box-cage, and gazed in at him with a look that could
only be described as adoration for at least an hour. He seemed to
take little notice of her, however, but in the evening he was back
on his feet and eating hungrily from the selection of mutton,
liver, venison, cat food and conditioner and eggs that I now
varied in his diet. By now there was no more blood flow from his
nose, just a slight green discharge.

Next day Patra spent the whole morning on the window ledge
and by midday he was staring back at her with rapt attention too.
On an impulse, I caught her with the gloves and brought her
into the room, setting her on the inside window ledge, by the
light side of his cage. She stayed there and the two gazed at
each other with such unwavering intensity that I felt an in-
terloper and quietly left the room. Two hours later I sneaked
round the back and they were still doing it, neither having
moved an inch. Her presence seemed to calm him down even
more.

By now, despite all my ministrations with newspaper and
cloths, the bedroom was really smelling of tomcat urine, so next

day I moved Syl and his box-cage onto my workshop bench from where he could also have a full view of the females' woodshed. Being smaller, the room was easier to heat. To my astonishment, Patra jumped down from the window and followed us like a dog.

I had a sudden thought—perhaps these long periods of staring at each other, Patra's enormous interest in the tom, meant she was ready to mate? If Syl's apparent recovery was merely a temporary upturn before a final relapse, maybe I should try and give him a chance to mate right now, if he wanted to and if she was also ready. At least I would have given him that. If he pulled through, he was already, by wildcat standards, an old man, and for all I knew his chances of being able to mate could well be running out. The two had now been gazing at each other for most of two and a half days and it was surely something more than mere toleration on Syl's part.

At dusk, I decided to take the chance. After feeding both, I fixed his door so the gap was large enough to let her in but not, I hoped, to allow him out. If she chose to go in, maybe it would work. Then dressed in three thick sweaters and with gauntlets and under gloves, I held Patra near the opening. To my surprise, she looked in at where he was standing, watching us intently, then she struggled and clawed to get in. I moved her nearer and she reached out with her claws, dug them in and hauled herself through the opening. I winced, expecting an awful fracas but nothing of the sort happened. Patra sneaked, very slowly, up close to him and he seemed to take no notice of her whatever. I propped the door up so she could get out if and when she so chose but as I left, Syl by-passed Patra and went on the attack again—at me! Now he had a companion, it seemed our truce was over. Sylvesturr could not have ever seen or been close to a single female cat in his entire adult life yet it had come naturally to him not to attack her. To me that was astonishing. When I peeped in later they were gazing at each other, their noses only inches apart.

In the morning Patra was still with him although she could have walked out any time she wished. She was unharmed but her ears and neck were all wet as if they had been well chewed.

It seemed there had been an attempt at copulation. She was still gazing at him with half closed eyes, while he seemed to be glaring at her with his huge eyes wide open. Was it possible in these long staring sessions he was actually hypnotizing her? At times he came close to hypnotizing me! When I went in and he made his usual *PAAH!*, Patra stood up beside him and spat too. She didn't emerge until 4:30 P.M. when she was hungry. I fed them separately, noting Syl was drinking far less now, having made up his lost blood.

Two hours later Patra wanted to get back with him. As I opened the door and she clawed to get in, Syl, thinking it was my rake coming in, immediately went on the attack. After that noise, I thought this time he would kill her, but she *maued* slightly as she went in, then she flared loudly herself, and to my surprise he immediately subsided. Whenever Patra moved in his cage she did so very slowly as though not wanting to trigger off any violent reaction from him. And she had an innocent expression on her face, as if saying "Don't worry. I'm not up to anything." Next day there were no signs that Syl had tried to mate with her again. When she came out at night she seemed oddly shy, big-eyed and wary and wouldn't let me anywhere near. As she looked round for somewhere to hide, I herded her out through the front door and fed her with Cleo in the woodshed as usual.

Syl was standing up and peering intently outside when I went into the workshop next morning. Now Cleo was sitting on the window ledge gazing at him with loving eyes. Maybe she felt it was her turn. But she was wilder than Patra and would be hard to get into the house. Although Syl now seemed back to his ferocious old self again, with just a little phlegm from his left nostril, I felt he'd be better left alone for a while. But as Cleo sat there most of the day and all the following morning, I decided two chances were better than one. By now I was really obsessed with the idea of reproducing such a magnificent beast if possible and I was by no means sure he *had* mated with Patra successfully.

Again, I would let Cleo choose. When I went out with sweaters, jacket and double gloves, Cleo was surprisingly easy to catch, as if she knew what was happening. I put her on the bench and she remained by the cage all afternoon, gazing at him with inscrutable smiles while he appeared to be staring past her, surveying the outside scene with a lordly unconcerned look. At night, after feeding both, I held Cleo near the gap. Like Patra, she clawed to get in—this time he didn't hiss or flare at all. But when I checked the end larch slab was secure, Syl, thinking my hand was coming in, hissed and growled, Cleo growled at me too.

Two hours later Cleo was still inside but both cats were facing opposite ways. I had the odd feeling that while Cleo might have fancied him, Syl's feelings were not reciprocal. Cleo had wild yellow eyes and a thin, muscular body and perhaps Syl preferred the plumper, floppier figure of Patra! But it seemed he was too much of a gentleman to be rude to Cleo or hurt her, for he could have killed either female if he'd really wanted to. Perhaps the belief that wildcats are monogamous, are faithful to a single mate for life, was true. This would help explain their poor reproductive rate and their rarity, for a town tom domestic cat will mate with any willing female in heat that it can find. Another explanation, though, was that it was really too early for either Cleo or Patra to be in heat. I had looked at both females' rear parts afterwards but had seen no evidence of what might be described as penetrative activity! By 10 P.M. Cleo had left the cage and although she was sitting on top of its covering towel next morning I felt sure she had not been inside it again. I put her back in the woodshed.

By now the entire house reeked of tomcat and as the weather had improved, I cut down on Syl's heating to prepare him for life outside again. After three sunny days, I hauled the fox pen down to a windless spot in the L-shaped corner at the back of the cottage, filled the thick wooden box with hay, covered part of the ground with sand and shingle, which had been the kind of flooring he'd had in London Zoo, and transferred Sylvesturr.

But it was quite an operation. After I'd pushed the box end of his cage into the run and blocked all holes with wire netting, so he couldn't escape or attack me *en route*, he simply refused to leave the cage. And when I tried to shoo him out with the blunt hazel stick, he bit deep holes in it with a force that would have severed a man's finger. I felt sorry, and would have loved to free him but it was clear he couldn't survive in the wild in winter, and he was getting no exercise at all in the box-cage. When he did finally jump out, he ran with a low crouch and mad glares, refused to enter the new den box at the far end, stood on it for a few seconds, then ran straight back at me.

He leaped for the dark patch where the top of the box-cage was still covered with the towel, thinking it was an exit, as I struggled to hold onto the box with tiring arms. Then he tried to force his way out where the wire netting was stapled against the box with loud growls, a mere six inches from my face. My own growls deterred him not at all, one staple tore free and he was actually forcing his way out against my hand, towards me. Only when I banged loudly on the box right in front of his nose with my other hand did he finally turn and, seeing its dark entrance at last, leap into the new den box. As I quickly hauled the box-cage out and hastily shut down the pen door and fastened it, I found I was trembling all over.

Surprisingly, the fracas which had unnerved me didn't appear to have bothered him too much for an hour after dusk he was out again, tucking into a meal of mutton, venison and liver. No wonder he was so strong, I thought, as I watched him from the bedroom window. And so he should be on a protein diet better than my own. But at least he was now well and safely outside again.

Chapter 7

After his recovery, despite the disruption of his move outside, Sylvesturr seemed more placid and never again went on the attack when I took him his food. Whether he now regarded me as a strange superior being who could produce female companions at will, or his feline consciousness told him I had nursed him back to health, I couldn't know. But he was, if not grateful, at least prepared to tolerate my occasional presence.

Now I tried some experiments with the wildcats. The general belief is they rely mainly on sight when hunting, with hearing second and their ability to scent one of their least important senses. One night I quitely took Syl's meat out but instead of putting it into the fox pen, I just stood in silence. After about ten seconds, I saw the white flashes of his mouth, jaw and neck appear in the dark entrance hole—wildcats probably evolved these white patches on their otherwise tawny, grey-striped bodies, to help see each other in the dark—and as his face came further out, I noticed his down curved whiskers were twitching, his pink nose wrinkling. He could clearly smell the meat in my bowl. I repeated the experiment on other evenings and found he could scent meat from a good twenty-five yards away.

Later I also made trials with the females. With Moobli shut in the house, I walked into the woodshed with their food, held it as they *maued* hungrily on the logpile, then walked a distance away and set the meat down in a small thicket of grass and brambles. Patra always found it. Once I watched her walk round the front of the house, pausing every so often to sniff the air with one paw upraised like a pointer, then locate the meat hidden in vegetation a full forty-five yards away. When hard pressed in winter, wildcats are probably able to scent carrion at fairly large distances. Cleo would not co-operate in the experiments, perhaps because she feared being caught in the open while it was light, but months later she was to surprise me even further with her scenting powers.

Some accounts say wildcats bury their scats—which are usually twisted, double ended, joined narrowly in the middle like a dumb-bell, and have tapering tips. Other accounts say they never do. I discovered that Syl, who had never made any effort to bury his droppings on dried bracken or grass, now always buried them in the sand or gravel in the fox pen. From the bedroom window, I twice saw him standing close beside them and raking a foot high mound over them with his right paw. The females never buried theirs on earth or short grass, usually did in long grass and on dried bracken, and always did on sand, gravel or snow. Usually all the cats defecated after dark, within an hour or so of eating. Although adult wildcats have no natural enemies in Britain apart from man, this could have been a hereditary instinct from the days when bigger predators like wolves and lynx inhabited the country. They would not then be caught napping, so to speak, in broad daylight.

In early February came one of those superb winter days that seem almost unique in the northern hemisphere to the Scottish Highlands. The sun shone in a brilliant azure sky, shimmering a silver path across the loch surface, and it was so hot through the window, I had to give up work on my book. What better day for putting Syl back into his old pen? I re-made his den completely, re-lining it with larch slabs, insulating it with two sackfuls of dry bracken, and made a big bed of dry hay he could rake round into a bowl. I no longer felt afraid of him and, when I tacked a plywood sheet over his box hole, he didn't even growl, as if he knew he was going home.

When I held the box in the pen he dropped to the ground and without a single pause to look round, ran straight into his old den. Yet another example of perfect memory.

Next day, as Moobli had made deep muddy tracks round the back of the cottage on his eternal inspections of the females in the woodshed, and they had been at the bird table again, I decided it was time to pen all the wildcats up together. If they had not been already, they would surely be coming into full oestrus in the next few weeks, and the sooner they were free to mate with Syl the better. I wouldn't introduce any particular cat to him—just let them make their own arrangements!

I dragged the fox pen to the west side of Syl's pen, so the two made an L-shape, then, so the females wouldn't be treading on the uncomfortable bottom fencing squares, filled its floor up with sand, gravel and earth. The big problem was how to fix it so that the females could be with Sylvesturr when they actually chose to be. Then I had a brainwave. I made a connecting hole between the two pens, big enough to allow them access to his larger area, but small enough to stop him from getting into theirs. It was fortunate he was such a large specimen. Now, if he objected to their company, they could easily escape from any possible attack or sudden bad mood. Then, with a small square of wood on a long hazel pole, I made a gate that I could operate myself from outside, which would seal the two pens and the cats from each other when I chose. I filled the den box Syl had recently been using with hay and set it at the north end of the females' pen on some logs, to keep it from ground damp, and left them all to it while I went on a supply trip in the welcome sunshine.

On my return, I dropped Moobli off on the first sandy beach for his two-mile exercise over the rough ground, and sped back to the cats. Then I pulled aside the gate, lifted Syl's den door on the pulley and hid myself behind the bramble tangle south of the pens. Cleo was the first to venture through into Syl's pen, pausing with upraised paw, her head going up and down as she sniffed the air, she slowly went through the gap then padded straight to his drink and feed dishes, licking up the bits he'd left.

As she passed his now-open den, he lifted his head up from the hay, and stared as if he couldn't believe his eyes. He blinked, once, twice, then over that old curmudgeonly gloomy face there came a soft expression, a positively tender look, and a patriarchal twitching of the whiskers. I could almost have sworn he smiled. As I let his den door slip down again, Moobli came up panting.

For the next few days I kept careful watch on their mixings, making sure they were separated at night until they really knew each other well. Cleo usurped the coveted inner position inside the females' den box, in spite of Patra's bigger size, and was the first to find her way back from Syl's pen. Patra forgot and walked up and down three times before rediscovering the gate hole. It seemed Syl liked both girls in his pen for he made no aggressive moves nor treated either with special favouritism.

On the fourth brilliantly blue day, with the females sunning themselves in Syl's pen, it was clear they were now all far happier. The girls had over 200 square feet of rocks, bushes, hazel trees, brambles and grass, with groups of daffodils and bluebell shoots peeping through here and there, to sport around in. And Syl, sedentary in his old age, had them for permanent company. I was sure he would not try to escape again. He even looked happier. One morning, Cleo sat for two hours on top of his den but Patra was more brazen. She sunned herself on a rounded rock right in front of Syl's door, occasionally looking in at him. But he just sat, with his eyes peeping above the hay bowl he'd made for himself. Apparently no invitations into the inner sanctum were issued!

At night both females came rushing in when I fed Syl, and promptly, without the slightest protest from him, gobbled up all his food. Far from attacking them, his patriarchal, gloomy face again took on a benign look. He actually watched them steal his food and squabble over it without doing a thing to defend it from them! I decided to shut them in their pen until he had finished eating—which was now often near midnight.

One odd thing now was that although I put the occasional hen's egg with their food, neither Cleo nor Patra seemed to know what to do with it, yet Syl, after leaving the first one alone for twenty-four hours, recognized it as food. I watched from a few yards away on the second night, wondering if I should remove it, when he came out, sniffed it all over, put one spread paw on the big end then bit the other open with his teeth. As they crunched through the shell, his head shot back in surprise at finding the liquid contents. Then he sniffed again and lapped all white and yolk up with gusto. It seemed possible wildcats would include birds' eggs in their diet, which they could find in ground nests or by climbing trees.

In the mornings now, both Cleo and Patra, smelling his leftovers, would be milling about by the small gate. The moment I lifted it, they raced in to polish them off. Thinner Cleo was now developing into the more cunning of the two. She was usually the first to reach the food and to slam her foot down or stick a clawless paw straight onto Patra's eyebrow whiskers, to stop her reaching the choicest morsel. But on the few occasions Patra got there first, Cleo respected her ownership and turned off at her snarl. Again the wildcats were practising first come, first served. There were no grudges or taking things personally and I had never yet seen one cat drive another off food. Yet the girls were now becoming more hungry and had taken to hissing and flaring at me again when I set their food down on a special feed plank in their own pen at dusk.

By February 20, Syl had gone off his food almost completely, only taking the fresh raw meat. I had been told by the Zoo this would probably happen in late February and early March. It seemed to be connected with the onset of a possible male oestrus, just as animals like red deer stags eat little during the rut. I hoped the fact that the females were becoming wilder and hungrier meant they too were coming into oestrus—it made sense, as females would need to build up reserves if about to start carrying kittens. What worried me was that I never saw Cleo or Patra in Syl's den with him. Well, I'd just have to wait and see.

Now the small birds around my cottage seemed to know the cats were not free and began coming to the bird table in droves. For two winters I'd been watching their apparent pecking order —blue tits could be faced down by great tits, which would be faced down by rare-visiting hedge sparrows, which could also drive chaffinches and robins from the food. But then a determined little blue tit would dive down and put a hedge sparrow to flight! There was so much individual varying aggression between the different species, my bird table was a constant source of amusing entertainment as they chased each other round. At times the hazel and larch twigs I'd put around the table looked like a giant flashing catherine wheel.

At least once a week I shoved typewriter aside and trekked through the winter hills—often seeing so little that the trek became nothing more than hard exercise. One five-miler, over a 1,800-foot hill and back along the deep river valley to the east, yielded nothing more interesting than a few meadow pipits, their white outer tail feathers flashing in flight, a huge furry brown fox moth caterpillar that had emerged from hibernation to gnaw on new ling heather, and a dead hind. But a six-miler over two tussock-filled hills up to 1,600 feet to the north produced the sight of sixty-three hinds, straggling across the face of the next hill like a small herd of antlerless caribou, and the harsh *chek* cry of a peregrine falcon, but it was too misty to catch more than a glimpse of it flashing overhead.

The day after I finished my book dawned bright and sunny so I took Moobli for a twelve-mile trek westwards along the loch shore. As we crossed the first burn in the oak and birch wood which began a mile from Wildernesse, Moobli got a strong scent from the north, went to where some dwarf alders screened a rocky drop to a small gorge, and peered over. There was a young sheep, a last year's tup lamb, standing on a broad ledge below us. Its fleecy coat had been caught by a thick briar in a bramble patch and although it had turned round many times, embedding the bramble deep into its wool, it hadn't the sense to gnaw through it, and now stood head down, almost all in, resigned to its fate. After a bit of a struggle I managed to free it and lifted it back to the top of the bank, where it tottered off weakly a few yards and began to graze. But for Moobli's scenting powers, it would have starved to death. Three miles further on, clouds now obscuring the sun, we saw a disturbance in the water. It was too early for fish to be rising, so I took the camera from my pack, clipped on the long telephoto lens and crouched down. A few seconds later a huge otter climbed onto a flat rock with a fish in its jaws. No sooner had I focussed on it than it dived off again just as I pressed the button!

By the end of February the first of the thousand daffodils around the cottage were flowering in its lee, shaking their heads wildly as if wishing they could change their minds when the first three days of sun were interrupted by one of south-west gales and rain. Twining honeysuckle stems were sprouting new velvet green leaves, holding out bright jewelled cups of water, and the first bluebells were poking their dark green leaves like stars amid the patches of sodden winter grass. A roe buck and his doe were now sleeping in the west wood, and a few red deer hinds were using the mossy ledges of the rocky escarpment above the wood as their night time beds. Two huge eagles flew together over the cottage from their winter quarters on the white hare moors, their white tail rings and under wing patches showing they were first or second year birds, probably too young to breed this spring. A tribe of bullfinches invaded my garden as I dug over and manured my vegetable patch and trimmed back and mulched my four gooseberry bushes. As they pulled at the new leaf buds on the oak, birch and my two cherry trees, they gave their plaintive little *phui* calls.

As the sun gained strength, even cranky old Sylvesturr seemed to be feeling the stirrings of spring—I caught him outside the den once, stretched out fully in the sun, his whiskered head tucked between his front paws and his long hind legs extended behind him at full stretch. I was rewarded for my unintentional interruption of his warm siesta by a loud *PAAAH!* as he dashed indoors again.

If the females were to come into breeding condition at all this year, this was surely the most critical time. So I now poked Syl's food and drink dishes right into his den and closed the door down. This way I could leave the gate open all night as the girls were hardly likely to push their way right into his den and steal his food a few inches from his nose. They would thus all be free to make their own arrangements as regards a little love making under the cloak of night without poor old Syl at the same time being half starved to death.

One afternoon I came out to find Cleo racing round the pens, swiping out at something white flying in front of her. As I came up she knocked it to the ground but with a loud "PAAH!," a trick I'd learned from Syl, I scared her off it and she dashed into her den box. It was an oak beauty moth, rare for my part of Scotland, and luckily undamaged. As it didn't recover, I preserved it and it is now in the collection of the Natural History Museum in South Kensington. Cleo's ability to move with lightning precision a fighter would envy certainly had some unlikely uses.

Two more oak beauties came to my lighted window that night as cold rain was falling. I left them putting up a natural fight against the new cold. In nature, especially in the insect world, there is much waste and the early-hatched, that can not find shelter or food, are killed by sudden patches of bitter weather, leaving only the fittest to breed later on.

For weeks now I had been putting off a trip south to do urgent zoological research, buy equipment, visit relatives and try to line up enough writing work to earn our few civilized needs for the next six months. In mid-March, with sparrowhawks, tawny owls and other birds showing nesting activities in my woods, I decided to go—to leave them all to settle down for a while without disturbance.

As heavy rains had caused the loch to rise several feet, I hauled the big boat up to between the log archway, then fenced off half the woodshed so Syl would have the whole rear logpile and some eighty square feet as a warm sheltered home while we were away. I hung up cooked and half-cooked meats and hearts, sterilized meat sausages, and covered large bowls of long-life milk and water with pine sheets so he could drink from but not foul them. Then I made a hole in the fencing so the females could get in to him, the same system as with the outdoor pens.

Now all I had to do was trap Sylvesturr. I didn't think he would attack me now but just in case I dressed in sweaters, old jacket and gloves. As I carried the box-cage trap into Syl's pen, Moobli, who'd been watching from outside, started bouncing up and down, playing. But this action scared Cleo who flared and spat at him, then suddenly shot through the gate and straight into Syl's den! To my surprise Syl barely blinked at her sudden intrusion and she crouched down quietly beside him. But the instant I came into view in front of his den and he realized I was actually inside, he reared up, *PAAAH!*, and stamped his right foot, flinging out a small pile of hay. There was a definite protective air about his action, as if he was saying "Leave her alone. She's mine!" I climbed out quickly and went to shut Moobli in the cottage. But when I got back Cleo was still in Syl's den and her huge eyes were glowing with what 1 hoped was love. She was gazing up at his profile like a fan suddenly close to a favourite movie star, and he too had changed position so his shaggy old head was close to hers. I left them for an hour but when dusk was falling and I still had to set the trap with bait, I managed to chase Cleo out with the blunt hazel stick and back into the female pen, where Patra was watching these goings-on with a supercilious smile, then I baited the trap.

Now I had to entice the females into the woodshed and to do it I relied on their sense of smell. Instead of feeding them in the pen as usual I set out food and drink in the front part of the shed in the same way I had for Syl, and left their pen door open. Within half an hour both girls were guzzling away in the shed and I shut their pen door so they couldn't get back.

Next day Syl was safely in the trap. I carried his heavy growling form into the shed, set him up in the rear portion and as I shut the doors, leaving the females' exit hole open, he came out and *PAAHED* an "affectionate" goodbye. After closing up the cottage I made a rough trip up the loch and hauled the small boat into the wood at the far end. By midnight Moobli and I were well over the Scottish border.

In London my anxiety about the wildcats' welfare was only one spur that made me dash about my business affairs like a scalded cat. The other was the vastly increased cost of living; so high were hotel bills, that I spent three nights sleeping in the Land Rover in the noisy streets, though it was once embarrassing trying to dress behind a flimsy curtain as a traffic warden stuck a ticket on my windscreen! For some weeks I'd been having a desultory correspondence with a television producer who'd written that he wanted to film my way of life for a BBC 2 programme called *Look, Stranger*, of which, having had no electricity or TV set for years, I'd never heard. One evening, with three hours to kill before a friend arrived on a train from Sussex, I found his last half-forgotten letter on my "Attention" clip board. I rang his office; there was, indeed, a comma between "Look" and "Stranger," I was assured, and why didn't I meet him and his assistant for a drink in Mayfair? We met and the producer, Colin Morris, turned out to be a large, cheerful, affably intelligent man who had written the successful play *Reluctant Heroes*, had helped originate *Z Cars*, directed five films and had just written and produced *A Walk with Destiny* with Richard Burton. He had also directed several *Look, Stranger* programmes, including one on the great fell runner Joss Naylor, and had worked with Christopher Brasher, both of whose reputations I greatly admired. I felt highly flattered that Colin Morris should find my odd isolated life of interest and, when he said my home would not be identified, I agreed to think about it.

In little more than a week, all business completed, I was on my way with Moobli back to the wilds.

Chapter 8

When I hauled the boat down over the pine roots and we set off up the loch, it seemed the whole of nature was welcoming our return. The north-west gales and snow showers that had greeted our arrival in the darkness now abated completely, the sun shone bright as a diamond in the kind of aquamarine blue sky one seldom sees in the yellow-pale mists of the Highland summers, and the mirror surface of the dark blue waters reflected the snow-capped peaks around us as we slid gently along. As Moobli stood proudly in the bow, surveying the scene we had both come to love, I saw the drab grey and tawny hills of winter were gradually changing colour, patches of light green springing as the tussock grass and heather sent up their new spring shoots. Although April was still four days away and the new leaves were as yet buds on the waterfront trees, it seemed as we covered the six-and-a-half miles in an unhurried hour that we were being given a preview glimpse of spring on its way.

A glimpse was all it proved to be, for within minutes after we had landed and I'd carried the first load of gear up the path, the sky darkened and we were in the midst of whirling snow.

I hastened to the woodshed—all the cats were fine, the two females as fat as butter, with Patra hesitantly half tame while Cleo, as usual, raced behind some logs with a slight growl.

Sylvesturr seemed strangely subdued, as if total isolation from humans had not agreed with him. Perhaps he missed having someone to spit at each day. His milk had gone but he had plenty of water and the cooked beef flank I'd hung beneath the woodshed window hadn't been touched. I'd nailed it there hoping he would take exercise to feed from it. A domestic cat and young cougars will leap onto hanging meat, take a few bites while clinging to it with their claws, but apparently this wildcat would not; perhaps he distrusted its hanging in such an unnatural position. Maybe such pernickety inability to adapt to anything new was one reason why pure wildcats had become rare, and begun to die out when faced with the onslaught of man's encroaching civilization, whereas domestic cats gone wild or the cunning foxes had learned not only to adapt to man but how to use his food stores, wastes, unhoused poultry and specially reared game birds to their own benefit.

Before doing anything else I put fresh liver steak and milk in Syl's dish, shut the door then peeped quietly in at the woodshed window. His huge old face glared round his den box hole, saw mine outlined against the window, snarled and drew back into his box. Immediately Patra sneaked in through the hole and started tucking into his food, followed in a few seconds by Cleo. As they squabbled and spat at each other, Cleo leaping up onto the logpile with her first mouthful of meat, Syl, gentleman as usual with them, made no protest. I realized then they had maybe eaten much of his food too. Perhaps I should have shut just Patra in with him, for it seemed he preferred her, and let Cleo stay alone on the other side. I had to wait till they'd eaten everything, entice them out with more food later, then shut the hole up while I put his food and milk out again. Within an hour of dusk he had eaten the liver and drunk half a pint of milk.

For the next two days Syl remained very quiet, just crouching in his box, barely even flaring when I went in, and he still wasn't eating all his food. Yet he was not thin and his few droppings seemed quite firm and normal. I felt he was probably psychologically "down." He had been lonely. Cleo and Patra, despite the snow showers, were spending little time in the woodshed now and while we had been away, with the threat of being caught out in the open removed, they had clearly been increasing the range of their foragings. Apart from raiding his food stores, they'd possibly spent almost no time with him at all. So, cooped up in the silent woodshed, when even the stimulation of a human to spit at had been removed, he had lacked all stimulation and also exercise—for he certainly hadn't the sense to take exercise for its own sake. It seemed he was now, though it may seem foolish to apply it to a wildcat, in some form of spiritual depression.

I couldn't let him free, in weather like this, bearing in mind what had happened before.

Somehow or other, he simply had to be jollied out of it, re-stimulated to full activity again, even if it meant the stimulation of anger. I fitted pine sheet over his entrance and put him back in the box-cage in my slightly heated workshop. Then I visited him several times a day, feeding him tidbits of best food, and within three days of frequent visits and tomcat fight games, plus the kind of soothing sounds I'd made to him when he was ill, he was his old ferocious self again. As he again launched the furious frontal display, stamped his foot and *PAAAHED!*, and his bright red tongue curled contemptuously inwards as he glared with a challenging look, it was odd to reflect that the ferocity that once had seemed frightening was now actually endearing to his reluctant jailer.

As Cleo and Patra now spent so little of their time in the woodshed, I wondered just where they were going all the time. When, on the fifth day after my return, they hadn't returned for their previous night's food, I took it away and set Moobli to track them. He hurried several times around the cottage, zig-zagged over the front pasture, then took off for the west wood but ran out of scent. Hoping they were now there, I shut him indoors, then went to sit on a mossy rock below a broken old rowan tree, leeward of the wood and the north-west winds so the wildcats wouldn't get my scent and might show themselves.

It sounds easy, just sitting down for an hour or two waiting for things to happen, but it requires a deal of patience in the cold winter wind when you feel certain after half an hour nothing will happen, but you force yourself to stay motionless until you feel you've turned to rock yourself. After about an hour, with my hands and feet numb with cold, I saw a sudden movement. Patra emerged from a weed and grass thicket and leaped onto the trunk of a large fallen silver fir which was still in full leaf. Half hidden by this foliage, she crept upwards, then made a quick bound onto the moss and heather covered side of a five-foot tall root tangle at the base of another fallen tree. Immediately a small brown blur shot out past her, and as it perched a few yards away on a high spray of the fir, making loud ticking alarm notes, I saw it was a robin. For a moment Patra clung there, claws embedded in the moss and heather, then looked around foolishly, sprang back onto the fir trunk, jumped down again and vanished in the undergrowth.

I went to the upended roots—there was a robin's nest where Patra had landed, with one white and red-brown blotched egg in it. The robin was laying her first clutch, and now she knew where the nest was, Patra would undoubtedly return. As they had already proved, there was nothing wrong with wildcats' memories.

I had feared this might happen in the spring. While there was an abundance of robins in my woods this year—they had been hotly disputing territories for several weeks—I didn't want any of the wildcats preying on actual nesting birds. The time had come to put them back in their pens again. Also, I dared not keep the females and Sylvesturr apart too long if I hoped to mate them this year. Some naturalists believe wildcats have a breeding period in May so, as I feared neither of the females had yet bred with Syl, I decided that the sooner I had them all back into the runs the better.

But I had no chance of catching Cleo and Patra before nightfall when, as I'd removed their last night's food, I hoped they would be especially hungry. Meanwhile, I had to guard the robin's nest—so that afternoon I crept out again to keep watch.

It was the same as before, the cold huddled vigil. But this time it was not Patra I saw but Cleo. Just before dusk she came up from the area of the rocky cairn and crept slowly over the marshy area between the old tangles of windfall trees. Where she was going I never found out for there was a sudden movement above

—a large female sparrowhawk floated downwards like a huge
cuckoo from two pine trees that grew from a small knoll. After
landing in several trees as she descended lower and lower, investigating the strange moving object below, she made a sudden
downward dash, clearly thought better of it when she saw Cleo,
and shot upwards and away out of the wood to the west like an
arrow. As Cleo padded over the fir needles and vanished, not
one whit put out by the hawk's close flight, I went over to the
pine trees. There was a fresh nest at the top of the largest and a
few white droppings below indicated it was the hawk's.

That night I put the females' food in their pen, blocked up the
woodshed entrance and when, an hour or so later, having located
the food by scent, both girls were inside, I let down the door.

Next morning, with bright sunshine melting a small overnight
snowfall, I had even more cause to be glad the females were
now secure. I was sitting at my desk, only half conscious of the
robins, chaffinches and tits that were squabbling over the crumbs
and seeds on my bird table when everything went strangely still.
I looked out—a blue tit had frozen in a crouched attitude on the
surround twigs, one chaffinch was squatting in the lee of the nest
box on the west edge of the table, and the most dominant cock
of the chaffinches was perched, also in a prone position, on top
of the box itself. I was just thinking that it was probably a kestrel hovering over the house, when there was a sudden rush of
air and something hurtled past the window. I caught a brief
glimpse of barred feathers, and as the other two birds flew for
their lives, the uppermost cock chaffinch vanished. I jumped up
just in time to see the sparrowhawk carrying it away to the west
wood in its talons.

Natural though it was for the hawk to prey on small unwary
birds, I didn't want it happening on my own bird table with its
hungry congregations. That had not been my purpose at all! I
felt, illogically, that the hawk was cheating. Yet it seemed an
ironical rough justice that the less wary bird here had been the
cock-of-the-walk chaffinch who had been so largely because he
was intent on driving other birds off the food. It appeared the
birds had enough trouble with the hawk about, so I was more
glad Cleo and Patra were now back in the pens.

On the third sunny day in succession, worried at Sylvesturr's lack of real exercise, I moved him out onto the front grass in the warmth before preparing his den for his return to the outdoors. As I put the cage down, the bottom of the trapdoor caught on my knee and Syl immediately shot at the slight gap, growling loudly as he scraped and tried to heave his way out. I had a hard task forcing his feet back without having my gauntlets torn to shreds by his powerful inch-long talons.

Later, as I struggled to hold Syl's cage up to his pen door and once again he dropped out with a hiss and padded straight into his den without looking around, I said aloud, "You can go free in the summer if you really want. But first you have a duty to perform, you ungrateful old sod!" As he ran, I noticed he had small, half-naked patches between his rear thighs and stomach. And that he had left some buff hairs around the box-cage. He had started a spring moult.

In these few sunny, lengthening days of early spring the wildlife was busying itself around us. This is the best time of year for the naturalist for much can be seen before the leaves are out making a foliage screen on the trees and bushes. A roe buck and his doe were regularly in the east wood at dawn, browsing on the bramble leaves, putting back their lost winter fat. The common gull colony had now returned to the small islet just off my south-east land spit and made the days raucous with their clamouring as they conducted their courtships and disputed over nest sites. Dippers bobbed their white chests on high rocks in the flowing burn as they established their small territories, thrushes called from the highest twigs in the woods, blackbirds *bink-binked* in the rhododendron bushes, robins sang their little silvery songs in the thickets, and, from stubs of old brown bracken, tiny wrens sang strident refrains in voices four times their size.

This is a time for trekking and, on a long hike up the river valley below the great mountains to the east, Moobli and I found a tawny owl on three white eggs on wood chips in a hole only eight feet from the ground in a lone dead old oak. At the end of the valley, a wintering sanctuary for stags, we found a bachelor herd of fourteen. Some had already shed both antlers, others still had the full set while two walked about looking comically off balance, having only shed one antler each. Like many deer at this time of year, they were weak from cold, wet and poor winter diet, so were easier to stalk, being loath to run unless sure danger lurked. We found three dead hind carcasses coming over the hills on the way back and, on the loch side, two greater black backed gulls, ten miles from the seashore, rose from a dead carcass they had located from their high buzzard-like cruisings, and began rocking on the surface as if they'd only happened to be there by accident.

Abruptly the weather changed again, as it often does in the Highland spring, and we were suddenly plunged back into the depths of winter. North-west gales ripped over the mountains for a day, sending the corrugated iron sheets on the spare lumber flying, one wafting past the window and landing on the edge of the east wood. Then the winds slowed down, to carry snow blizzards so thick at times I couldn't see the loch shore at all. After two days of this, with drifts piled three feet high, fearing Syl would not stand up to this new cold, I decided to forget all about mating him and put him back in the woodshed with a heater—at least that would also provide me with a place to dry out my washing!

But Syl simply refused to go for the meat in the trap. Next morning, feeling desperate as he had not eaten in twenty-four hours, I decided the only way to get him back to the shed was to haul him out bodily. I wrapped up in three sweaters, old jacket, treble gloves and with a piece of wire netting resting on my arms, to foil any possible damage to my face, I screwed up my courage and, lifting up his wooden door, thrust in a sack, hoping I could tangle him up in it. I also very much wanted to hold him, just once, to know if I did manage to hold him tight by his neck scruff whether he would accept it and go limp. I expected him to attack at first, but far from attacking, although he growled, spat horribly and slashed out with his great claws, he retreated as far back into the den as he could, just beyond my reach. It was as if he were psychic and knew I would not put up with his nonsense. I tried to drag him out when his claws were sunk deep into the sacking but he always let go at the last moment, pulling his feet, with claws in, out of my grasp. He literally fought off all my attempts to get him out of his den and at last, with the sun coming out again and melting the snow, I thought he'd better stay in after all and just hoped the weather would continue to improve. He certainly seemed in fine spitting shape after the long tussle —and again I felt occasional excitement did him more good than harm, as if it was an antidote to long hours of sitting down—yet I didn't want to upset the old cat too much. "Syl, old boy," I said. "You're on your own," and retired defeated. That night when I put his food in, he came out for the first time since the Autumn and ate part of it in front of me, glaring and growling as he chewed away. What a baffling creature he was.

Later I went out in the dark with a torch. Then I had a clue why he wanted so much to remain where he was—in the bright beam I saw what looked like Patra's big tawny backside blocking up his entrance hole. And Cleo's was blocking the female's den box. If they were not courting then Patra was just helping herself to the remains of his food behind the door, but at least one male at Wildernesse was having female company.

On a briefly sunny morning in mid-April I saw what seemed to be an example of wildcat mating behaviour. Patra walked into Syl's pen, peered in at him as he lay in his den, then plumped on her left haunch right outside his door, virtually blocking it. Then she slowly lifted her right rear leg, as if capriciously exposing her soft seductive curving furry thighs where the grey stripes faded into the delicious buff and tan of her under belly, then started to lick in the area of her private parts. If that wasn't calculated to turn him on, heaven knows what it was! Sylvesturr merely watched her with interest, deep in his raked hay bowl, his eyes peeping just above the rim with the silly soft look he sometimes had when the females were near him, but he did not move.

One morning Moobli whined to be let outside early. We had only taken a few steps towards the shore when there was a great flurry of big wings and a flock of white front geese took off from the grass on the shoreline where they had been grazing below the trees, and rose almost vertically into the air. I was surprised for, although the small flock wintered at the west end of the loch, it was the first time I'd seen them on my own shore. White fronts nest in Greenland and Iceland and it seemed they were raiding such a small but possibly dangerous area for some last untouched rich pickings for the energy they would need on the long flight north.

Although I waited hidden in the woods in the pre-dawn dark on the next two mornings they did not return, but I did see small groups of whooper swans cruising up and down the loch, their great white wings singing like harps as they passed by overhead. By now the woods were carpeted with primroses lifting their bright yellow faces to the occasional sun; bluebell spikes were pushing up too, taking advantage of the light before the budding leaves on the trees made the woods dark. Both flowers now added a decorative touch to the wildcat pens. I counted 973 daffodils and fifty-eight narcissi now out around the cottage, hanging their heads bleakly in the snow showers.

On our next mail and supply trip a telegram awaited me at the post office—TV producer Colin Morris wanted me to telephone urgently. I did so and he said the BBC were most anxious to make the film on my isolated wildlife work and he would like to start the week's filming, with a crew of five, on May 13. The show, he said, was already slotted to go out in early July. After he again guaranteed my exact locality would be kept secret and that I'd receive a copy of all footage for my own use, I reluctantly agreed. What an ironic twist, I reflected as I boated back again. After leaving the big city world of journalism in Europe and America, where I'd finally specialized in film and TV personalities, that world was now seeking me out. Well, it would be an interesting experience. And if I didn't like the material the BBC chose I could at least have fun making up my own film during the long winters.

Towards the end of April, on the first sunny day after five of sleet and rain, the big black slugs began emerging from hibernation and scenting carrion, fungi or plant food with their moist tentacles from a few yards away, they converged upon it. Syl's food bowl proved specially attractive to the slugs and, on the first day they were out, I removed five as they slid towards his meat. But on the second night I discovered Syl had raked a great mound of twigs, leaves and earth over his bowl. And he continued to do it every night throughout the summer.

It was an extraordinary example of inherited instinct for he could not have seen a slug before in his entire adult life. In the wild, like cougars, it seemed wildcats protect their food kills in this way, not only from slugs but also from ravens, crows and other predators who would scent or see it. The females began to do it too but not so often because they usually ate most of their food as soon as it was put down. Greedy Patra often sneaked in to take some of Syl's food but I dared not shut them apart now for clearly the time for wildcat breeding, by any standards or beliefs, was coming to an end. I just hoped Syl under cover of darkness was receiving other favours in return!

As luck would have it, no sooner had I committed myself to making the BBC film than wildlife activity in the woods and hills began to flourish in a way I hadn't experienced before. A male woodcock started its "roding" flight at dusk over the east wood with eerie high-pitched *kwik-kwik* cries, and I found he and his mate were nesting in the lower end of the wood. A pair of rare black throated divers had decided to nest amid the common gull colony on the island—so filming on the island was now out of the question. Not only tawny owls and sparrowhawks were nesting in the west wood, but a pair of kestrels had also set up home in an old crow's nest a mere 100 yards from the hawks— which was most unusual. Greater spotted woodpeckers were drumming on resonant dead snags, pied wagtails, chaffinches and coal tits began gathering Moobli's loose hairs from the patch outside the cottage for their nests, and to top it all, ignoring my other nest boxes in the woods, a pair of great tits began breeding in the nest box actually on the bird table right outside my window.

There was no question of cancelling the film unit's visit now, not only had I contracted to do it but five people were committed to the long journey from London with all their equipment, plus a lighting man from Glasgow for two days. As the date drew nearer I admit I panicked. What on earth was I going to say and do? Morris had said they'd want to know why I'd left the big city life, about the hardships and loneliness of wilderness

living, the birds and animals I studied. There would be sequences on woodland, trekking, campfires, boating, fishing, gar-
dening, wood cutting, cooking free wilderness foods, and a special visit to the sea island where I'd spent my first Highland
years, plus a sequence with the wildcats.

As if to confirm my fears about disturbance, when the crew arrived on May 13, Patra was actually inside Syl's den in daylight
for the first time ever. I could have wept. This *could* be the true
wildcat mating period, I thought, at least for first-year females,
who perhaps don't come into oestrus for the first time until May.

But my worries on wildlife disturbance proved largely ground-
less. The sun shone throughout the filming, the crew turned up
in their own boats each day, and brought not only all their own
food but mine too. They were quiet, creative, hard working and
respected all my wishes that we keep out of certain areas. In fact
not a single nest was deserted and the great tits incubated their
eggs with the male feeding the female with green winter moth
caterpillars even when we were only yards away.

On the third day, with Patra still in with Syl, the shooting
schedule demanded we do the wildcat shots. Well, she had now
had three days and nights with him and if they hadn't mated by
now, they probably never would. Syl was due for a change of
bedding anyway, so the crew shot this taking place. The old
tomcat proved a real ham, spitting and growling superbly on
cue. He was now in magnificent shape, his fur all grown back,
though a lighter colour, from the moulting areas around his
flanks and stomach, and seemed almost half as big again as when
I'd first taken him from the Zoo. The sequence was all over, with
a minimum of fuss, inside half an hour. As we left Patra shot
back in with Syl again and as far as I could tell stayed with him
for the next two days as we did the trekking and sea island sequences and were hardly near my cottage at all.

On May 19 I went out early to the wildcats and found I had
forgotten to re-open the gate between the pens—which I usually
set temporarily in place each night so Syl could eat his food before it was stolen. As I approached Patra ran from the gate back
towards her den box, only to be repulsed by Cleo who snarled
and clawed at her from the entrance. Patra ran around the pen,

then as soon as I opened the gate she shot, with a fearful look on her face, straight into Syl's den. It was the first time I'd ever seen any of the cats actually fight, apart from the females' snarls and foot stamps over food, and it was puzzling. Cleo seemed to be actually banishing Patra from their den box and I wondered if that was why Patra was now so often in with Sylvesturr. On the other hand, she could have escaped Cleo by just running into Syl's pen, yet she was, some of the time at least, actively seeking his company inside his den.

Watching them quietly from a distance it certainly seemed Patra was in oestrus because her vagina seemed enlarged and she behaved very kittenishly before him, rolling on her back, sniffing bluebells and playing with loose leaves. Oddly, Sylvesturr seemed merely to be putting up with her behaviour as if not wanting to hurt her feelings by any show of disapproval. When Cleo came out of the den box I noticed she seemed fatter than usual, probably because she had caught a vole or two which she sometimes did in the pens, or because she had eaten some of Patra's share of last night's meal.

The day after the filming was over, glad to be alone again though I'd enjoyed the heady company, I planted all my vegetable seeds, then sat by the cottage corner to watch the cats. Patra, who had been crouching a yard away, made a sudden pounce and caught a short tailed vole that came out of a small hole a mere foot away from Syl's door. I'd noticed the hole a few days earlier but had doubted any vole would have the nerve to make its actual home in a wildcats' pen. Syl, apparently, had not bothered it. But this one had now paid with its life and Patra ran with it like a small parcel in her jaws, and growling, took it through the gate and right up to where Cleo was sitting on top of their den box. There she dropped it and ran straight back into Syl's pen.

In view of Cleo's recent belligerence towards Patra, now that she was keeping her out of their pen most of the day, it was the oddest incident I'd yet witnessed with the wildcats. Cleo dropped down with a growl and ate the vole head first. Was Patra actually trying to placate Cleo in some way? At dusk something just as strange occurred. When I took out their food, Cleo first drove Patra away from it with a sharp spit then came to eat it without her normal hesitation in my presence and actually, for the second time only, let me stroke her through the fencing as she ate. She walked as if her feet hurt and still looked swollen and I wondered if she was ill or even had a tumour in her stomach. Was she perhaps being more friendly towards me now because Patra had clearly made a conquest of Sylvesturr. Maybe she was now driving Patra through into Syl's pen in jealousy that he had finally chosen the plumper cat's company? It was all most odd and I couldn't see any sense in all this strange behaviour.

During the next three days I went on lengthy treks, making up for lost time when filming. Judging by tracks and flattened undergrowth only two of the five badger setts were occupied and only one had young cubs. The first crane flies were flying now, making succulent food for young salmon and trout who sucked them down after swirl strikes when they fell into the loch, and for the few grouse who nested on the hills. When I saw the female was not on it herself, I checked the tawny owl's nest in the hollow tree four miles away and found she had hatched all her three eggs. With their feathers half grown through their thick white fluffy down, the youngsters retreated into a far corner, clopping their beaks noisily at the strange apparition that loomed briefly in their entrance.

On May 25, my forty-seventh birthday, I trekked along the lochside then back up along the high ridges to the north-west of my home. As I walked along there was a sudden flurry as a meadow pipit thumped her wings down on the grass and flew away. She had been on her nest under a heather clump which contained four round pinkish-brown eggs with dark markings. As I left a cuckoo flew from a dwarf rowan growing from a small rockface—she had been watching the pipit, so she could lay her egg in its nest next time it went to feed. On a hill face, over a mile away, three antlerless stags were grazing while a fourth watched us with interest. Deer have a hard task identifying stationary objects even at fairly close distances but their eyesight is extremely keen for anything moving.

When I got back I saw Cleo once again drive Patra from the females' pen with Syl-like ferocity. I decided to put their small den box in Syl's pen for Patra's use—the old tom would not tolerate her in his den *all* the time, I felt—and give Cleo a new den of her own, and to seal the two pens off. Much as I'd have liked to let the females go free, I couldn't until the nesting birds had all reared their young, though I was momentarily tempted to take the newly belligerent Cleo some miles up the loch. Luckily, on my last trip south, my father had given me a superbly made pet box, lovingly fashioned by an old Sussex craftsman, one of his gardeners, which had a hinged front and top. I roofed and insulated it with plastic and rubber sheeting and set it on the logs under the roof that filled one end of the females' pen. I was sure then that Cleo was ill; her stomach was more swollen and white fluid seeped from her rear. She had eaten almost nothing of last night's meal. And yet she didn't look ill—her eyes were bright, her fur in good condition, and she seemed in good shape.

As I put the new box in, Patra, next door in Syl's pen, started to make an awful squawking sound as if she was choking. Then she regurgitated a whole vole skeleton and fur in the shape of a large dropping onto the bracken on top of Syl's den. I wondered if she too were ill, or if it was part of wildcat courtship ritual, a sort of declaring herself on his territory.

In the evening I stole out very quietly at dusk to see if Cleo had eaten her food but to my surprise both she and Patra were in Syl's pen but several yards apart. Putting in the new den box I must have knocked the gate open as I came out again. I stayed there silently and after a few minutes Syl's old head came through his door hole. He looked furtively to left and right, came out very slowly, then walked up to Cleo and sniffed her. She did not retreat but lifted her nose to his. They appeared to be kissing. Their mouths were twisted sideways and they seemed to be biting gently at each other's tongues. After a few seconds of this they stopped, pulled back a few inches then both started licking their chops. Then, although he hadn't seen me, Syl seemed to sense my presence and he went back into his den, moving like a ghost in the twilight. What on earth was going on?

When I came out next morning Cleo was once again in Syl's pen, as was Patra, but as I got nearer Cleo ran back through the gate and into her new den box. I noticed she looked somewhat thinner. As I was running out of meat for both Moobli and the cats, I had now to go on a supply trip. I wrote a few last minute letters, then as I left to go down to the boat I noticed Patra easing herself through the gate. I felt sure Cleo would drive her out again as usual now but Patra walked up to her den box, made an odd noise in her throat, a sort of turtle dove *brrrooo* trill, then reached in slowly with her right paw, claws well in, and made a gentle movement as if she was giving Cleo inside the box a soft playful swat. Oh well, I thought, as I went on down, it's good the two girls seem to be friends again.

On the way up the loch, three gulls from the island colony came beating along in the bright sunshine. They kept just a few yards behind. Lowering and raising the level of their individual flight paths slightly, they followed all the way to the Land Rover parked in the far wood. I felt like the leader of a small naval flotilla with my own personal air escort.

Chapter 9

For four hours after returning from the supply trip, I noticed Cleo just seemed to be lying asleep in her new den box. And when I put her food and water-milk mix in she didn't come out at all, which, although she hadn't eaten so much these past two days, was unusual. At 8 P.M. she had touched neither food nor milk and feeling worried, I bent down for a closer look. Suddenly I saw one of her legs moving but it was an odd light, tawny colour, unlike Cleo's browny grey, and far more finely striped. Then I saw a tiny tail. I thought I was seeing things. It was a kitten! My first thought, although I never normally saw another boat on the loch from mid-September to mid-June, was that a local wag, to play a joke after the TV filming, had come along during my absence and put in a domestic kitten.

Cleo lay on her side with a blissful expression and her teats were pink and swollen, with half an inch of thick pink skin around the protruding centres. I clearly wasn't dreaming and now I had to find out how many kittens she had.

I put on the three pairs of gloves, three sweaters and the old thick jacket, feeling I'd only thus have to protect my face and eyes as I was sure she would attack. Then I crept into her pen on all fours, because of the four-foot roof, expecting a blitzkrieg but Cleo was just too happy to be angry. Motherhood, far from making her fiercer, seemed to have finally tamed her, for she stayed where she was.

There were two kits, both exceptionally large, with big feet and claws. They were fully furred with beautiful chestnut brown and brown-grey stripes and elongated spots on a light buff and tawny background, big broad heads with ears set low down and eyes tightly closed. One was suckling away for all it was worth, making little squeaky noises. When I went a little too close, Cleo only growled warningly but she still didn't move. There was no way I was going to go any closer or try to touch them right then.

I backed out of the pen with thudding heart, let down the hinged door and to relieve my excitement and joy, did a stumbling race round the rough front pasture in my wellingtons, yelling "We've done it! We've done it! We've bred wildcats!"

The whole area round Wildernesse seemed to be smiling now. The sun had shone continuously for thirteen days and the woods were a patchwork quilt of differing greens—the feathery larches covered in the light green fuzz of new needles, the tiny oak leaves now khaki before turning dark green, the beeches thrusting out brilliant green fans on their long horizontal plate-like branches, and flicks of varying hues of jade adorned the twigs of hazel bushes, the birches, rowans and ash trees. Around the cottage the ground was carpeted with creeping buttercups, and the four-petalled yellow flowers of tormentil lay on their weak stems against other vegetation, while the white stars of stitchwort thrust their heads high, and in the marshier places the yellow suns of hawkbit insisted they were no mere dandelions. Almost everywhere bluebells raised a foot-high canopy of blue like a background canvas to the magnificent riot of huge pink, crimson and lilac flowers that filled the rhododendron bushes. As I looked, thinking of the kittens, I thought, what a wonderful world in which to be born!

Later, as with trembling hands I fed Cleo and the other two cats the best meals they'd ever had, I realized the whole long lonely winter experiment, all the difficulties, had been more than worthwhile. To think, she had them on my birthday too, that I had never suspected it, that Cleo was the wildcat I least liked, had even thought of turning free down the loch, or giving to a zoo, because of her wildness, bad temper and yellow eyes. Sylvesturr who I believed had tried to make love with Patra in the workshop when I'd thought he might die after his days of freezing unplanned freedom, and more recently, had clearly preferred the thinner wilder one. That was why she had darted in with him when I was transferring them all to the woodshed for my trip out in March. She had been in oestrus then and although Syl, whiskered dignified old gentleman that he clearly was to female cats, had tolerated Patra's proximity, it was Cleo with whom he was breeding. I recalled, too, how he had defended her that day—March 13. And I also now remembered my impression a few days back that Syl had seemed to be merely tolerating Patra's kittenish behaviour outside his den, as if she were just too young and silly to be angry with or reprimanded.

How foolish and clumsy my attempts to breed them and understand their behaviour had been. Only by chance had they succeeded, it seemed. Even my rare trip out for just over a week had been a blessing for them, for they had been left totally alone and could meet and mate without any human disturbance at all. It was odd, though, that Cleo had been in Syl's enclosure for much of the previous two days, when tom wildcats are reputed to kill kittens. And this morning, when I hadn't looked in her den box at all, I'd noticed she looked thinner when she went through the gate, so she had obviously gone into Syl's pen after having the kits. It was also strange that she should have had the kits on the very night I had given her the new den box. But the oddest thing of all was this morning, just before my supply trip, when Cleo, who had been driving her away for days, allowed Patra to come right up to the den box and give her a playful swat with her right paw—when she had been lying up with her new kits. It all seemed to go against everything I'd read or been told about wildcats.

I went back indoors to open my forgotten mail, and received a shock. A new editor had taken over in New York and my book required extensive and urgent revisions. Hell! That would curtail my spring treks this year but, when next day dawned gloriously sunny again, I left the book right in its drawer. Having wildcat kits in such a wonderful natural place was rare and nothing was going to hamper my studies.

I went carefully into Cleo's pen making the soothing sounds she associated with food and friendliness, spent some time winning her confidence, and after a while she let me stroke the kittens. She didn't mind me actually picking them up—until they cried out, then she growled and I quickly put them back. But they hated being handled and called loudly, not like domestic kittens, but with piercing buzzard-like calls, *meeeoo! meeeoo!* that could have been heard two hundred yards away. Then Cleo stood up, stretched herself up high with arched back and began making an odd breathy clattering sound in her throat which was, as I only heard it once before, probably wildcat for purring. Both kits were 8½ inches long, with 3-inch front legs and 2½-inch tails, and at 1½ days old, unlike adult wildcats who have black feet, their soles were pale pink. Their eyes were closed, little upward slanting Chinese slits and as they groped for their mother's teats with bright red mouths they often fell over on their backs, their feet waving comically in the air. Cleo kept the den spotlessly clean, licking their little vents to induce excretion before they soiled the bedding.

Patra was intensely interested in all that was going on, and as I took several photos, she sat up like an otter, dangling her front paws and peering over into Cleo's den from the top of her own box. Whether she was happy at Cleo giving birth, or going all out to secure Syl's attention now Cleo was busy, I didn't know, but she clowned about in the sun most of the day. She pushed bluebells down and watched them spring up again, hauled them towards her and sniffed them delicately. And when I fixed a small plastic pipe of running water into a bowl in the pens from the kitchen tap, she spent much time trying to catch the falling drops. All this activity Syl watched with what I felt was silent disapproval. But for the thought that Patra might just be pregnant herself—she now also seemed fatter than usual and had spent much time with Syl—and the nesting birds, I would have turned Patra free to allow Cleo and Syl sole use of the pens.

During the next month I managed a few treks, found the tawny owls had fledged two young successfully, the black-throated divers only hatched out one of their two eggs, but all seemed well with the kestrels and sparrowhawks in the west wood. But the bulk of my time was spent slaving away on the book revisions and studying the wildcats.

One morning I heard a slight clonk as I sat at my desk. I went out—to see Syl's long tail floating into his den like a disembodied bush snake. One of the six-foot boards I'd put along the front fencing had been completely turned over and of seven black slugs on its underside, three had been squashed in the centre as if he'd struck them mighty blows with his paws. Apart from this new revelation of his strength, it seemed astonishing that he had actually worked out that slugs shelter by day in dark damp places near their food source and if he turned the board over he would be able to destroy the slimy wretches from which he had to cover his food each night. I had not credited him with such intelligence. The rough curved hole I had cut in his door was now acting as a comb on his back and flanks as he went in and out and was now helping his summer moult as it was covered in long, soft, downy fur.

Patra was still clowning outside his den and once, in a most uncat-like way, actually fell off a rock and landed on her back. She got up again looking really silly as Syl solemnly ignored her. On the whole, he tolerated this virgin buffoon pretty well.

By May 29 the kits were still tottery but were not falling about so much. Two days later their eyes were still closed but they now gave gentle little high-pitched trills when seeking mama. I picked one up, wondering if I ought to handle them more from now on in case I decided to try to tame one later. After a few seconds it opened its crimson mouth wide and squalled with a high piercing *mau* or *maow*, different from the earlier "meeeoo" sound. I noticed its four canid teeth, almost transparent white, were now showing through. Syl showed no reaction whatever to the kitten's loud calls and, recalling at that moment that wildcat toms are supposed to often eat kits, I crawled to the front of the pens to see if he reacted to the actual sight of it. His expression didn't change but Cleo came after me with a low growl and I quickly made the soothing sounds she knew, hastily held the kit near her and crawled back to her den box with it as she walked close by my hand all the way. I had foolishly gone a bit too far, and, as I might have broken the trust I'd now built up with her, I never took a kit out of the pen again. But Syl, I was pleased to see, showed no adverse reaction. Even so, the day wasn't far away when the kits would possibly crawl through the fencing and then I would probably have to put Syl back into the woodshed, Patra into the female run with the gate closed, and give Cleo and her family the run of the big pen and its larger den.

By June 1, as soon as the kits heard any disturbance, although unable to walk and with their eyes still closed, they turned towards it, opened their mouths and tried to hiss and flare. But as they had no lung power yet, no noise at all came out. They wrinkled their little pink noses, opened and closed their mouths in what were meant to be ferocious snarls like those of their father, then usually fell over sideways. But even at the tender age of one week they were prepared to have a go. Cleo now spent a great deal of time grooming them all over with her rough tongue, and often lay down deriving great sensual pleasure from feeling them crawl all over her. She had taken to looking into my eyes now as they were busy with her teats, as if noting my reaction. She was immensely proud of them.

Next day the kits made their first spits. Unable to stand, still blind, they reared up on wobbly front legs and spat at my sounds, but still so weakly I heard nothing. Then they subsided, resting their heads on the hay in exhaustion but with their mouths still open as they breathed quickly, still trying to hiss. As Patra was walking up and down the fencing, I lifted the gate. She immediately walked in and up to the den box, making a brief "turtle dove" trill in her throat. Cleo didn't drive her away but let her sister poke her head right inside and look at the kits. Patra made no attempt to touch them, however, and after a minute went back to the top of her own den box. It seemed she just wanted to check up, and give sisterly approval.

About an hour later as I was having a brief sunbathe, I heard a shrew squealing shrilly and saw Patra dive below Cleo's box. She missed the shrew and drew back. Straightaway Cleo came out, went right under the box, caught the shrew in the thick grass and bracken tangle, bit it to death then instead of taking it to her kits or into her box to eat, she trotted into Syl's pen and dropped it before his scowling face. Then she went back to her den box again—on which Patra was sitting calmly as if agreeing with Cleo's gesture. I knew my two females caught but seldom ate shrews but as the shrew had gone an hour later, it was clear Syl was partial to them. Either that or he needed more furred meat than I was able to trap. But how did Cleo know that, if indeed she did? If this gift of food to Syl surprised me, I was to be even more astonished a few days later.

Not wanting to take any chances, I drove Patra out of Cleo's pen at dusk and put up the gate again. By now the kits were ten-and-a-quarter inches long and their paws measured one-and-a-quarter inches across—a full two-fifths of an inch growth in one week. I noticed after they'd fed to completion at Cleo's milk bar, they often lay sleeping against her warm furry body with their heads upside down.

On June 3, Cleo greeted me with the same kind of rolling *brrrooo* trill that I'd occasionally heard Patra make, and she repeated it again when lying in the den box and one of the kits was flopping about in a far corner, unable to find her. I now knew what the call meant—it was both a greeting and a means of self-identification. It could be used to indicate friendliness when one cat walked towards another or to call young kits. Cleo spent most of the morning with her kittens, biting them playfully and turning herself suddenly on her back as if to make them keep groping and searching for her teats—good exercise! And she was still licking their rear ends clean, a practice she continued until they were weaned. I handled them both for a brief period, feeling that, while I intended to free them later, it might help soften their ferocity, as handling and constant presence had helped half-tame Cleo and Patra. Although Cleo occasionally trod on the kits as they moved around, she was careful not to put her full weight on them with her paws. Nor was she growling any more when I went with her food, though she was back to attacking it fiercely again. Patra had long since ceased to growl at food time, unless she thought I was about to take it back if I moved the bowl slightly.

It was hard keeping her in the same pen as Syl now for she

was as greedy as ever, and after finishing her own food would immediately take after Syl's, and he, not eating till after dark, still never tried to stop her. Today I noticed Patra had a subdued look, as if she felt Cleo was the real star of the show, as it were, and that she herself had failed. Her flirtatious and kittenish behaviour, which Syl largely ignored, had now stopped completely. I thought then that either Syl's mating season was now over or the theory that wildcats are monogamous and true to one mate only was correct. When she passed his door or sat by it now, he seldom even looked up.

In the afternoon, as the kits could still not walk, I put the gate down and despite a sudden cold snap and a freak snowstorm that whitened the tops of the high mountain across the loch, Cleo walked about the two cages, leaving the kits alone for long periods, as if she felt it would be good for them. She was definitely "Queen Cat" now and, when she was in Syl's pen, Patra kept well out of her way, though Cleo again allowed her to inspect the kits in the smaller pen without protest.

Because I wanted to observe their behaviour more closely, I set up a small sacking and hazel hoop hide a few yards from the pens which I could reach from the corner of the cottage without the cats seeing me. Sitting in it next day I was surprised to see Syl come out of his den and go to sit a foot apart from Cleo in the north-east corner of his pen—while Patra stayed in her den box. Apart from a brief whisker and nose contact of greeting, they didn't touch each other and after a minute or so Syl went back to his box.

That night, as she was definitely not pregnant and Cleo's kits would soon be walking, I let Patra go. Although the great tit pair were now feeding young in the bird table nest box, the chicks were safe in it and the adults far too wary to be caught by her, and all the wrens and robins had now flown. At dawn Patra wandered about the house *mauing* loudly as if she was lonely, but she went back naturally to sleeping again on their old sacking bed in the woodshed.

On June 6, as Cleo was prowling up and down the fencing as if bored with being cooped up so long, I let her out for a run but left her door up, and she headed for the west wood. I handled the kits but as if they knew the danger was greater now they couldn't hear mama close by, they struggled, scratched and spat audibly.

By 4:30 P.M., Cleo had not returned and I felt worried she might stay out all night. I set Moobli to work, "Track the pussy coots," and he immediately began dodging, nose down, through the long grass on the edge of the west wood, then into it. Suddenly I heard the *tchee-tchee, chirr . . . irrr . . . irrr* warning notes of great tits and the ticking noises of wrens in the rhododendron bush by the path. It was the noise these birds make when mobbing a cat. Now Moobli burst out of the wood following a scent and headed straight for the bush. In a trice he had cornered Cleo under the tangled brown stems. Ears back, open mouthed, she growled and spat as I clambered through the foliage towards her and Moobli blocked her escape route. She clawed at my gloves but didn't bite and, when I seized her by the scruff, went limp and let me carry her back to her pen. But as soon as I went out with her food and milk, back in the security of the pens, she was once again as tame as she had been since having her kits, and was soon clatter-purring away. After eating she went back into her den, trod, carelessly it seemed, on her kits whose feet groped helplessly for something to turn them back right side up, and within seconds both were squeaking and feeding away lustily from her full teats.

Sylvesturr surprised me when I went out with his food, coming out to get it with a loud *PAAAH!* and a foot stamp—something he hadn't done since late autumn when he'd been at his hungriest, putting on his winter fat. Perhaps he did it now because he had seen me carrying Cleo ignominiously into her pen and didn't like to see his wife treated in such fashion! Or maybe, as I went close with the food, it was to tell me not to try the same thing with him.

Next day the kits' eyes had started to open, from the insides outwards. Instead of being mere slits, they were now triangular with bright china blue in the open part nearest the nose. They spat and flared as they heard me coming, and their little red tongues curved upwards and inwards at the edges, just like Syl's. From then on their progress was rapid.

June 9—one kit's eyes were completely open, the other's almost and the vivid bright blue of their irises made a beautiful contrast to their light tawny and grey-striped bodies and legs. But their eyes couldn't focus at all yet. Their heads were big and square with their ears set low, sticking out sideways with no upward slant, unlike those of domestic kits. Cleo often threw her head back between her kits now as if she liked to feel their big feet and claws struggling over her face as they sought for her teats.

June 10—Cleo licked the whitish film from the lower eyelids of both kits' eyes. The first kit was now beginning to focus, its head trembling as it nodded up and down, the other was only a few hours behind in development. But their tiny teeth were still half transparent. Neither kit could walk properly yet. They put their rear hocks flat on the ground first, then raised the "heel" as they moved forward onto the ball of the foot, swaying precariously from side to side as they did so, before collapsing into Cleo's warm fur.

June 11—both kits' eyes were now fully open, rounded and filled with bright china blue, and they could also make out my looming form for they flared and retreated when I was still outside the pen. Lovely fat little creatures, over a foot long now, and as I picked them up and stroked them, they cried out with even more piercing *wheeows*, more like a whistle than a call. It was an almost exact replica of the calls their mother and aunt had made when I first brought them up the loch. Each time I handled them, Cleo stood up, watching closely but usually giving her *brrrooo* call, which meant she didn't mind too much. She was still cleaning their vents and was being a marvellous mother. Maybe Syl's instincts had told him that as he watched both girls and compared Cleo's slinky wildness with Patra's clumsy clowning, greed and air of irresponsibility.

I noticed that when Cleo was angry with me, the kits too would spit but if she was clatter-purring or making her throat trill, they did not. Wildcat kittens' psyches would be set early in life by their mother's upbringing, like those of other animals or humans. Being taken so young from his mother could well explain Sylvesturr's mistrustful and angry outlook, for he was thrust early into the artificial concrete zoo environment instead

of being brought up like Cleo and Patra, in the natural surround-
ings in which they were born and in which all their inherited instincts were rooted.

At dusk I was watching from the hide and saw Syl leave his
den and walk towards the gate. Instantly Cleo left her box,
danced up to him and with a loud spit, reared herself up as if
about to attack. Syl swiftly pulled his head back an inch, stared
in disbelief, then amicably turned away and trotted back into his
den. It seemed possible wildcat mothers can repel toms if they
wish at such times for Cleo was a fair bit smaller than Syl.
But my impression was that Syl merely wanted to take a look at
the kits; there was certainly no belligerence about his investi-
gation.

June 13—the kits could now see objects up to three yards away
and were taking more of an interest in the world outside their
box, looking out of the door and trying to focus on distant objects with up and down motions of their heads. But as they grew
bigger they disliked being handled even more. When I picked
up the largest kit, it called so loudly that Cleo snarled but with a
bewildered air, as if she wanted to rescue it but not get too nasty
with me. I put it back quickly and as soon as I did so Cleo broke
into her clatter-purr again. Perhaps she was more tame since
having the kits because she realized I was sole food provider and
without me she would have had a much harder time bringing up
the kits. But one must be wary of ascribing human motives to
any wild animal behaviour.

The summer midges were now at their height and to stay still
outside for more than a couple of minutes was to be transformed
into an itching, scratching maniac. Even the gulls on the island
were shaking their heads, blinking, shuffling their wings and digging the irritating insects out of their plumage with beaks and
feet. Syl's and Cleo's heads were constantly twitching, Moobli
scratched them out of his eyes with his paws, and even the kits
had learned to flick their heads. Cleo ate her food and milk in
short shifts, running back into the dark of the den box when they
clouded up around her head too badly.

By now Patra had turned into a furtive sneak, was very subdued in the shed and had left half her food on the previous two

nights. She had a sad, big-eyed look about her, as if she was ashamed at not having had kittens herself. She really looked lonely. Sorry for her, feeling she wouldn't steal Syl's food any more, I put her back in his pen.

Three days later, so I could try to get them at least a little tame before they adopted Syl's recalcitrant habits totally, I brought the kits and Cleo into my study in the den box and set them on the bed. The focussing ability of their exquisite blue eyes still took time to adjust as they transferred their look from one object to another. Every time I went near, they spat and flared, then immediately adopted a bewildered look.

They seemed to feed just as and when the mood took them. But the moment one sleeping kit stirred and touched the other, it too started to struggle to reach a teat. Often they burrowed between Cleo's back legs. When she was bored and needed a stretch, she stood up and arched her back, seemingly unmindful of the guzzling kits, who dropped off one after the other from the teats. Then she lay upside down again, purring as they struggled back over her body to the nearest part of the milk bar.

If one of them crawled too far away or put its head over the hinged front dropboard of the box, Cleo called it back with the *brrrooo* trill, and if that didn't work she called louder with a *mau* which made them turn and crawl back. And when they were feeding I noticed how the kits kneaded, pummelled and trod the area round the teats with their big fat paws, to stimulate milk flow.

After lunch Moobli and I went on a trek to 1,500 feet. The hill slopes were filled with red and green grasshoppers, and, despite the clouds overhead, common blue and small pearl-bordered fritillary butterflies flitted between the orange-yellow spikes of bog asphodel, the blue flowers of milkwort and vetches, and the lilac and white flowers of the heath spotted orchids which looked like little old women in full skirts and poke bonnets. When we returned, an endearing sight greeted us—the entire great tit family were lined up in an ash tree north of the cottage. I felt a bit peeved that, after all the food I'd given them, they'd chosen a moment when I was away in the hills before leaving the nest box, and that now it was dusk the light was too poor for photos.

June 17—the brief stay in the house seemed to have helped for the kits actually let me chuck them gently under the chin after Cleo had responded to my usual calls with a little welcoming trill. The bigger kit took its first faltering steps down the front dropboard in the afternoon but when it tried to turn round on the flat sloping surface and started slipping, Cleo *maued* and biting its neck scruff very carefully, hauled it back in again. Three days later, although still wobbly, the bigger kit scratched an ear with its hind leg for the first time. It also made its first attempt at play—propped up on its right front leg it swatted out gently at Cleo's face with its left paw. Patra, her good spirits restored, began to steal Syl's food again, so out of his pen she had to come. An hour later she had caught a vole and eaten all of it, except the stomach which she usually left, in the woodshed. I felt she could probably look after herself now without much trouble.

June 21 was not only midsummer day but gloriously sunny and the first without clouds or wind for over a week. My main revisions to my book were finished and it was time for a day off, so after a three-hour fishing trip, I sunbathed. As I lay quietly roasting, I had an idea. Having decided I would not now try to domesticate or tame either of the kits, I did want to observe their behaviour in the wild later if I could. So it would help if they became used to my presence outside the house. And now that I was just lying in the sun this seemed a good time to start the process. I went into the pens and brought them all out in the den box and with Moobli indoors, set it down against the cottage wall. As soon as I left the front dropboard down, however, Cleo leaped out and ran back into her pen. I hadn't expected her to leave the kits so I fetched her back. She stayed for about a minute with the sleeping kits, then sneaked out and when I looked up she was once more in the pens. She wasn't acting scared and I thought maybe she was glad of the chance to have some time to herself, as if she was willing for me to take charge of the kits for a while—or maybe she wanted to visit Syl.

For the next hour I tried to make friends with the kits. I placed them on the open grass for photos and soon they were either run-crawling towards the shade beneath me as I crouched on all fours, or into the thick grasses and buttercups by the cottage wall. Their immediate instinct when in the open was to hide. But once in the undergrowth they explored it without fear, calling with little *maus*, sniffing the flowers, swatting out at each other from behind grass clumps, and generally having a fine old time. At noon I put them back in the box and carried it back to the pens but Cleo was now gone. I thought she was probably in the rhododendron bush as usual when she was free, and I decided I'd let her enjoy herself for a while.

But towards the end of the afternoon she had not returned and Moobli was also absent. I called—no response. I went indoors to change into trekking gear to search for them both but when I went out again, Moobli was at the front door—wet. Knowing his habits—he'd probably found something interesting on the loch shore or the burn—I waited until he slipped off again, then followed. He had found Cleo. She had discovered an old natural den in the bank of the burn at the far edge of the east wood, a full 250 yards from the house. Perhaps she was intending to move her kits there, as she was clearly not just hunting. I intended to release them later but it was too early yet, before they were even weaned. Telling Moobli to keep her there, I raced back for the thick gloves. When I returned Cleo was crouching in the hole, growling with ears back, and the earth outside had been deeply scratched. Although he liked the females, Moobli had probably thought I meant get her out and had pawed at the entrance while I was away. Cleo wouldn't know he meant her no harm and as I was not there, his actions had scared her. Her pupils were wide and black and when I reached in she spat loudly and clawed. I took hold of her neck scruff and hauled her out as she started to kick with her strong back feet. Then she got her claws into the gloves and twisting her head round bit down deeply through them. I tried to hold on but her teeth went into my hand and her rear claws were drawing blood from my lower arm so I had to let go. She ran straight back and crouched inside growling. She was really worked up now and I wasn't going to try and catch her by hand again in that mood.

Just before dusk with Moobli indoors I went back again but she was nowhere to be found. I knew from working with cougars in Canada that mothers *will* leave their kits alone for two, even three days at a time but I didn't want to risk it with my wildcats. With Moobli playing bloodhound, we went twice round both woods hoping the noise might drive her back to the pens, as we'd done once before, but without result. About an hour after dark I went out with a torch but although I'd put her food in its normal place, Cleo was still not back. I then had some awful visions—the kits could be killed by Sylvesturr if they staggered to the edge of the pens looking for their mother, or by gulls or ravens, a fox at dawn, or even by a weasel in the den box itself. It was going to be a clear, very cold night and at less than a month old, they'd had no food all day. I panicked and brought them and their box into the bedroom, put on a paraffin heater and tried to feed them.

It was quite a performance trying to get warm milk down them from a baby's bottle and a cut-down rubber lamb's teat. They yowled, swallowed some, dribbled it down their chests and over their feet, yowled again, spat, flared and scratched but never once tried to actually bite. After each feed they started cutely trying to wash themselves clean with their tiny tongues, and biting at the wet milk between their toes with little nibbles. After some two hours I managed to get a mere three table-spoonfuls down each kit. Then I dried them off and covered them with warm cotton wool for the night.

I was just climbing into bed at 2 A.M. when I realized that if Cleo came back at night and found them and the den box gone, she might just leave for good herself. And it would all have been through my own stupid fault. I dressed again and praying it would not be too cold, put the den box back into the run, made a really deep bowl of dry hay for the kits, then fixed the pen door slightly open—big enough for Cleo to squeeze through but not, I hoped, any large fox. I had seen no evidence of weasles in the area but I had no choice.

Uppermost in my mind as I finally turned in was that Cleo had, without being scared away, left the kits in my care this morning. And her own mother had abandoned her and Patra when they were kits.

Chapter 10

Dawn came in a lemon sky, heralding yet another sunny day and after putting on my boots and clothes, ready to track for Cleo with Moobli, I hurried out to check the kits first on my own. As I reached the pens, Cleo calmly ambled up from the rhododendron bush by the path with a murmured *brrrooo*, a complete contrast to the spitting virago of the night before, and walked round the enclosures as if looking for a way in to her kits. She had clearly mistrusted the slightly open door.

As I let Cleo into her pen, the kits looked awfully still lying in the hay nest. I *maued* and up they stood and staggered to the box entrance, peering like little old men without their glasses. As soon as mama came into focus they tried to clamber out to her but she ignored them totally and began tucking into the food I'd left out for her overnight. Clearly no fox had been around for it could have forked the food out with its claws.

Cleo seemed not at all worried about her kits. She had been away on a well-earned break, had no doubt clobbered a vole or two, and after she'd eaten and drunk her fill, she ambled into the den with a light *brrrooo* and sank down among her kits while they went crazily for her teats.

After writing a few letters I saw clouds heading over from the south-east, so to enjoy the last of the sun I went swimming. As I donned black rubber suit, face mask and flippers, Moobli stared at the strange black apparition that had just been me in disbelief, then I set off towards the island some two hundred yards off shore. I didn't make it. Halfway across I felt something thumping me on the back, then whacking me on the head. I looked round. It was Moobli! He had swum out behind me and with his powerful trudgeon dog-stroke, he had caught me up and, as if to assure himself it was still really me, he was scratching at me with his huge thick claws. "Get away you fool!" I gasped. But the more I tried to keep him away the more he tried to clamber on top of me. He would have had me in trouble had I not turned my hand into a scoop and dashed water into his face. And when I got back he began running up and down the rocky shore with loud barks, something he never did unless intruders appeared in a boat. It took a good half hour to accustom him to the fact that it was *me* in the black suit and finally he was content to just swim beside me.

When we got back to the cottage, the kits had climbed out of the den box and were taking their first faltering steps over the pen floor. They wobbled and shook, paused, fell over, but kept trying. Then Cleo decided they'd had enough and carried each one back into the box by the neck scruff.

Next morning I found Sylvesturr had not eaten his last night's meal and in fact had carried one large piece of meat over to the gate between the pens. There was no other way the meat could have got there, for Patra was now living in the woodshed again. It seemed he had intended it as a deliberate gift for Cleo. Perhaps Syl had been worried at her absence all the previous night. I took the gate down and a few minutes later Cleo eased through, picked up the meat despite the few blow flies' eggs that were on it, carried it over to Syl's own food dish and ate it there, right outside his den.

It was really odd behaviour, especially as wildcat mothers are reputed to rear their young well away from the tom because he would otherwise kill and eat the kits. Later, I discussed this with leading wildlife photographer, Geoffrey Kinns, who told me of a reliable keeper, who, while watching a den with mother and kits inside, actually eye-witnessed a wildcat tom bring in a rabbit in his mouth for the family. I twice more found pieces of Syl's meat by the gate in the mornings. It certainly seemed to prove that there is some inter feeding between tom and female, though such behaviour would vary. It now seemed significant that while the females fought to protect food, Syl had never once competed with them, or stopped them taking his.

Wildcats, being nocturnal or crepuscular creatures, are hard to study in the wild, so it is probable the wildcat tom gained his bad reputation from the rare instances where both tom and female had eaten their own kits in zoos—in artificial confines with constant human activity and noise. If it did happen in the wild, it could be an aberration caused by a scarcity of prey, a strange tom chancing upon kits that were not his own, or by a "personality" defect in a particular animal. Eight years of wilderness living had taught me that animals, especially my wildcats, varied as much individually as do humans. The animal world also has its unnatural spoilers and fools.

Even so, as I saw the kits actually run over their pen floor on their toes for the first time that afternoon, I felt I ought soon to separate Syl from them until they were large enough not to get through the fencing squares. Instinctively, I felt Syl would not harm them but I'd take no chances.

Three days later the kits launched their first "attack." Instead of visiting them in the morning and picking each one up briefly as usual, I went in late afternoon. Despite the normal soothing words, which brought the usual *brrrooo* response from Cleo, they retreated behind her when my face loomed and spat and flared. When my hand moved to pick one up, they spat again and both swiped out with their claws. The swats did not seem to be aimed right at the hand but near it and they had no idea yet of pulling the finger onto the bite, a wildcat characteristic. They also growled for the first time, like small high-pitched dynamos, baby versions of their ferocious father. But as soon as I showed I was determined and actually picked them up, they went all soft and childlike again, with an odd bewildered look.

Strangely, the slightly larger kit with the broader face could still not focus its eyes completely but it was the fiercest. As soon as I put it down it ran and hid beneath the small plank on which

I set out the food. Cleo seemed not at all concerned by their tiny attacks on me. She ignored their hissing and spitting, nor was she angry with me in any way. I felt proud at such moments that after her wild suspicious youth she seemed to trust me now she had kits, especially as it was the opposite of what I'd expected. Patra now seemed settled in the woodshed and was catching many mice, voles and a few shrews. The ones she left I dropped in to Syl—he ate them all avidly, even the shrews.

The next two days were spent scything down the bracken in front of the cottage—the third time that year—which was at last showing signs of weakening, weeding my vegetable garden, and transplanting over a hundred young cabbages. Having no hose, I watered them in with four bucketfuls of water and a small si-phon pipe. It's surprising how far a small amount of water will go if directed to each individual plant. Within four hours their flattened sun-wilted leaves lifted up and began soaring nicely. This chore over, I went to feed the wildcats. As Cleo was eating, the larger kit sniffed the air and staggered near to her, to be im-mediately repulsed by Cleo growling. The kit recoiled and looked at its mother with astonishment in its blue eyes. As it sat there, broad face perplexed, ears set so low down it looked like it was wearing a cloth cap, I decided it was surely a male and to call it a real workman's name—Fred or Freddy. Wearing gloves, I managed to take a close look at both kits—boy and girl. The male was now fifteen inches long while the slightly smaller, pret-tier kit who had rounder eyes and a smaller face was just under fourteen and a half inches. I called her Mia—after a young girl pen-friend in America with a back ailment who had been writing to me ever since I'd had two articles about wilderness living in the *Chicago Tribune* magazine two years earlier. The odd thing about the kits now was that they would occasionally come to-wards me when I went to the pens with the "Pussy coots" call, Mia in front and Freddy following. But Mia would turn and run back to mama again whereas Freddy would stand his ground longer.

It was now time to transfer Cleo and the kits into the main pen and catch Syl for his temporary transfer to the woodshed—before I tried the first experimental release of Cleo and the kits into my woods in a few weeks' time. I carried the box-cage trap into his pen and leaving his food dish empty, baited it with some sheep flank.

Next morning Syl had been in the trap but had bitten through the thick nylon line to the bait, and had forced his way out again between the side netting and the roof which I'd foolishly forgotten to bind with wire. He was now back in his den wearing what seemed a most self-satisfied air. There was no chance he'd go into the trap again. Knowing his memory it was surprising he'd gone into it at all. He must have been hungry. I now had no choice but to drive him into it. I opened the trapdoor, held it up with nylon line threaded through the roof fencing with my right hand, while I prodded through into his den with the blunt hazel stick, around which I'd wrapped thick wadding, with my left. He immediately turned on the wadding and attacked it, biting and clawing, and I was glad it wasn't my arm in there. Finally he shot out growling, looking furious, glared about for somewhere to go, ran into the trap then straight out again before I had time to release the trapdoor. Then he ran round the edges of the pen like a small cougar, came right towards me, spat heartily in my face, set off on another circuit, then stopped and looked up at the sky. Suddenly he leaped up at the thick wired roof and held his entire weight on the claws of one paw as he looked round for a gap. He had incredible strength, and looked like a large gibbon hanging there, with his long striped tail dangling. Then he walked across the roof by his front claws like an acrobat. I'd never seen a cat do anything like it before. His shoulder muscles bulged powerfully as he moved. What extraordinary agility for an old cat. I'd noticed before that wildcats can be at peak-form in a split second after days of just lying up without exercise. Finally Syl dropped down and ran into the small den box that had been used by Patra, and I transferred him to the woodshed where he had his former half section, the logpile, a nice big window and lonely Patra for company.

Next day, before renovating Syl's den for Cleo and the kits, I found Patra was to be more than mere company for Syl. She had caught a large vole and had taken it to him—for it was lying on his side of the fencing, along with two shrews. For all her faults,

Patra had developed into a fine hunter, and was now as good as Cleo had been before having the kits. Whether she was trying to reinstate herself into old Sylvesturr's favour was mere human speculation but she was sharing her prey with him. Patra was useful at last.

Over the next few days it became obvious Cleo and the kits were happier in the bigger natural den and the whole area of the two pens. Freddy and Mia began to explore the small hazel bushes, the little shady groves beneath the ferns and bracken, the shelter from the archways of brambles, and they stalked each other through the long grass, leaping out clumsily in most inefficient ambush. They often hissed when there was no danger, just if the wind blew a leafy frond. They dived into the half circular entrance in the den door when they saw me coming but often Freddy would poke his nose out again, blinking at me owlishly, his eyesight still not one hundred per cent.

By now, although I gave her all the milk and food she could take, Cleo had grown quite thin with the demands of feeding the two large kits. Oddly, although Syl would crack open and eat eggs, neither Patra nor Cleo would unless I broke them first. But I had once found a chaffinch's eggshell on the shed floor which Patra had brought in. As wildcats climb trees easily, it seems possible they do occasionally prey on birds' eggs, but perhaps only if rabbit, vole and mouse prey is short.

By early July the young kestrels in the west wood had all flown but the two young sparrowhawk chicks seemed slightly later in developing. On July 12 I came back after watching them learning to fly in the high tree tops, and set Cleo's food out early. As she stood by the dish eating, Mia came out of the den, saw her tail and stalked it, pouncing on its black tip with both paws. Cleo took little notice as she ate but kept flicking it about airily, just out of Mia's reach as she leaped and tumbled after it.

Two days later there was a thunderstorm and a great deal of rain. I came back after baling both boats and hauling them above the higher loch level—to find Mia had disappeared. I searched the pen, dug out some loose rocks in case she'd become wedged in a crevice—nothing. I dashed round the area in the rain, but again drew a blank. I then commanded Moobli to track the cats but he just stared at me and for once, just when I needed him most, didn't seem to understand what I wanted. What a time to be obtuse! I forgot myself, yelled at him, shoved his nose to the ground and simulated sniffing. He stared at me as if I was mad—and for that moment I probably was—for what seemed his deliberate refusal to track Mia made me so angry I clouted him hard. This upset his dignity so much he walked straight into the kitchen and refused to come out. When I cooled down, I apologized and at dusk we went out again, and with patient encouragement he tried hard to track Mia. But apart from a whiff of Patra in the east wood, we again drew a blank.

On our return to the cat pens, I heard a weak plaintive *mau*. Cleo came out of the den and began sniffing the air. Then she walked to the little sandpit I'd put down for the cats' toilet, urinated, squatting on her haunches, then went to the big rocks beside the den. At that moment little Freddy who had watched all this, went over to the sandpit, sniffed, then began to *mau* and scrape at the sand. Whether Cleo had actually taught him this or he was just instinctively copying her, I didn't know, but it was so comical I smiled. Then I heard the faint *mau* again, and saw the grass moving at the back of the pen.

There was Mia. She must have squeezed through the fencing and spent the day among the crevices and huge rocks which I had cut through to make the pen in a natural area. And she had been too scared during the thunder to make a move. Now dusk was falling and the thunder had stopped, she wanted her mama. Cleo saw her, *maued* and moved towards her. And fearing she might just dodge back into the rocks again, I crept behind her and pounced—on a suddenly raging, open-mouthed bundle of claws, red mouth and teeth. She couldn't bite as I had her tight by the scruff but she clawed with surprising strength. Carrying her round to the front I put her through the camera hole in the fencing. Cleo waited, then followed her wobbly gait back to the den with a solicitous maternal air. I was surprised to find my hand bleeding from Mia's claws, and that at less than seven weeks old she could inflict such damage.

Next day Mia vanished again but was back before dusk.

Shortly after I fed Cleo, I was surprised when Freddy ran up to her side as she was chewing in the bowl, sniffed the meat, grabbed a piece in his jaws, growled while holding it still as if ready to flee with it, then decided it was quite safe and began to eat. Cleo not only allowed this but backed off slightly when Freddy made his high-pitched dynamo growl. Cleo would never back down to Patra over food and had never had to with courteous old Sylvesturr, yet she had backed off from her own kit at his first attempt to eat, in that way encouraging him. So at fifty days old, Freddy was weaned but Mia showed no interest in solid food yet. As Freddy ate close to the fencing I noticed the bright blue of his eyes was being banished by a light grey which was working outwards from the pupil in an irregular oval shape.

Cleo, who was now eating almost twice her normal rations, was still hungry after her feed the following evening and walked up and down the fencing with loud *maus*. As I brought her more, both kits came running out but this time as Freddy went near, she clobbered him with a clawless paw, bowling him over. Then she carried a piece away and let him have his pick from the rest. Now both kits were spending part of the day in the rocky crevices behind after squeezing through the fencing, but around 8 P.M. both came running back to Cleo for a suck. *Mau* they called as they came, with a responsive *brrrooo* from her. Freddy lay upside down as she stood over him, while Mia fastened onto a rear teat like a deer fawn, down on her front knees with her backside up in the air as her hind legs were bent while still on their toes. I noticed how they had much bigger jaws and canid teeth, now pure white, than domestic kittens. The soles of the feet, which had been darkening since birth, were now all black and the underside fur of the rear hocks was also turning blackish as Cleo's and Patra's and Syl's was wholly.

The following afternoon the cats had a long play session. Watched by the kits, Cleo made mock stalks and pounces on leaves and pieces of grass moving in the breeze. Then the kits tried to imitate her but most times, as they pounced on objects with their two front paws, they fell over to right or left at the rear! Occasionally Freddy grabbed his mother's moving back legs in abortive Rugby-type tackles—which she bore stoically. Both kits had now taken to chewing grass and broken bracken stubs, biting them off and chewing them inwards against their tightly closed furry lips. But they seemed to reject the juices by excessive workings of the tongue, then started grooming themselves. I wondered if there was something in the juices that helped this activity.

As Patra was now leaving much of her food and seemed to be enjoying her wild-caught prey, I decided to give her a taste of freedom. She fought and growled deeply as I put her into my back pack with the gloves, but her escape attempts were foiled by its loose double lining. I carried her across the burn and a quarter mile away into the thick woods to the east and let her go. Then Moobli and I raced back to the cottage.

On our return both kits had once again been in the rocky crevices behind the pens but were now trying to get back through the fencing. Mia got through but Freddy became stuck. As I'd not held him since he was very small, I hauled him out with both hands but he immediately turned, scratched hard, found purchase enough with his left front claws to pull his head round and promptly sank his canines in so hard they met completely in the underside of my forefinger. I dropped him, chased him round the pens, then grabbed him by the scruff tightly so all he could do was smile a big Chinese smile and give a loud squawk *maaauww,* like the prolonged quack of a large duck, and swipe blindly out with his big claws at thin air. I shoved him back through the camera hole and Cleo immediately seized him by the neck and, staggering, half dragged and carried him into the den.

As I was now worried at the kits' apparent desire to leave Cleo and be alone for a while each day, I shut off the rear rocky mound with doubled netting. I felt they were still too young to be out overnight when a big prowling fox might get them. But next morning Mia had again found a way through—so I gave up, feeling Cleo, a good mother, would stop Mia if she felt there was any danger.

When I went to feed Syl in the woodshed he came out early, stamped his foot and spat. Now most of his side fur and some on his back had moulted, so his flanks looked pink and half naked as he walked. At first I thought he was eating too much Vitamin A in his liver but I saw that in places new short hair was sprouting—a lighter grey-tawny colour than before with paler long grey stripes. It seemed he had both a spring and an autumn moult, and the summer coat was lighter than the winter one. It made sense, for it would camouflage him better among all the new growth and increased light of the warmer season.

I left, then a few minutes later crept back and peeped through the woodshed window. Syl was rending a whole ox heart by standing on it with his front left foot, his long claws deeply embedded and tearing the meat off with long upward heaves of his head and front teeth. As I passed the pens I again saw Freddy go and rake sand over Cleo's toilet, adding to the pile he had already seen her rake over it. He was obviously copying her.

On July 18, Mia ate her first meat and this time Cleo actually moved over to make room for her at the bowl. I now noticed Mia's eyes were also turning grey—she was about three days behind Freddy in physical development, yet she was the wilder of the two kits, still squeezing to the rocks behind for an hour or two each day.

When I went to feed Syl, Patra, who had come back the previous night, shot into the logpile. And Syl who was on the floor of his section, again faced me down with a loud *PAAAH!* As he glared directly into my eyes, growling, fully extended on his front legs, I thought I'd learned one secret of his "attack." Caught out in the open, he was probably afraid to turn his back on potential danger, because it meant he was more vulnerable. Instead, he launched a full frontal display of ferocity without actually attacking, just to set you back on your heels and thus gain enough time to make his escape. At the front he had sight, teeth, claws and an awful aspect. But from the back he had none of these, nor could he see so well. Sure enough, when I retreated a few paces, he slid into his box. His "attack" was therefore based on fear, on defence, and not upon overt aggression—unless he was cornered. I put down his food, and some for Patra, and left.

Next day dawned bright and sunny for the first time in over a week and Cleo and the kits seemed to revel in the morning heat. She now seemed to be positively teaching the kits to hunt with her tail. Wherever she moved, she switched it about so the kits dived, jumped, rolled, and grabbed at it with their claws or teeth, or pinned it to the ground with both paws and bit at it as though they were holding a mouse down. The jet black blunt tip made a fine target and hunting Cleo's tail now seemed a regular feature of their daily play. Perhaps this is why wildcats have black tips to their tails. Cleo, recovering only slowly from the strain of carrying and suckling the kits, could easily flick her tail about when feeding, even when lying down and sunning herself, thus help make her kits faster, stronger and more secure on their feet, yet needing to expend little energy herself. It seemed logical.

By now the kits' eyes were almost all grey but before the bright blue disappeared from the outer edges, the lighter yellow-gold colour of their mature eyes was already starting to oust the interim grey.

Despite the tail-twitch training, Cleo slowly became more fierce with the kits at feeding time and she began to growl if they attempted to thrust their heads into the feed bowl. She now ate her fill then walked away, leaving them to get their own, and now they also began to flare at each other over food. Cleo would not have actually attacked the kits, of course, but seemed to be teaching them food was something to be valued, and once reached, kept strictly to oneself.

By now I was busy with summer time activities and for many days I'd been hay making, cutting back new bracken growth, bottling gooseberries from my four prolific bushes, black and red currants from the canes near the west wood, cutting windfall logs, building the log windbreak in front of the cottage, making a refectory table, tending the garden, fishing, as well as writing wildlife articles and further revisions to my Canada book, and replying to mail. The BBC producer Colin Morris had written that the TV show had doubled the normal *Look, Stranger* audience, a fact I thought due more to the beauty of the scenery than anything else. I'd seen the show with mixed feelings and while understanding the BBC's problems regarding popular content, had been disappointed that the long sequences on badgers, deer, otters, foxes and some birds had been left out. Also that the special ending had been replaced by remarks totally out of context. I felt my attempts at humour had misfired, too, so that more *quirk* than the real *work* had appeared. However, I received mail from 137 interested folk—men, women and youngsters—to some of whom I later gave short free wilderness courses. This flood of letters surprised me as much as those from 509 people when I'd written two articles about the wilderness life on the sea island three years earlier. All these letters had one thing in common—their senders were fascinated with the dream of a life in the wilds among all its wonderful creatures. To hear from nearly 650 folk helped bolster a weakening conviction that I had been right to opt for a life in the wilds, and I now felt it my pleasurable duty to reply to every new writer, as well as many of the earlier ones despite the extra work.

But on this golden day, knowing it was rare for a really fine mistless spell to last for long in late July in the Highlands, I pushed all aside and went for a long trek. After three miles, having seen little of interest, I was thinking of turning back. But as we passed a small lochan at 1,500 feet and were heading west, rounding a large boulder, I saw a hind sitting down chewing the cud with a small calf standing nearby. I dropped behind the boulder, managed two good photos, then she rose and was joined by two more hinds and fawns. Wanting to get closer, with Moobli waiting back as he was now trained to do, I slid on my belly like a ponderous lizard through the grass and heather tufts, glad the knoll to my right was making the south-west wind curl eastwards towards us, when a large hind with two calves came grazing slowly up the hill towards the others.

There wasn't another deer in sight. These had to be twin calves, which in red deer is rare. Everything was perfect. The sun shone down upon them, lighting the lovely white spots on the calves' red coats, the mother's eyes, the green grass and the flowers as if by an expert stage director. They chased each other onto hillocks, had suck, one tried to mount its mother. And as I took what proved to be the best wild deer colour shots I had so far taken, small clouds passed across the sun, mingling soft shades with stark brightness. I finished the whole roll and feeling triumphantly happy as they passed out of sight, went home.

When I went to feed Syl he was again out on the shed floor and as I put his meat down he once more banged down a foot and spat. He was now in superb shape and as he was showing so much activity I really wanted to let him go. But if I did I could not release Cleo and the kits for he *might* just kill his young if he got too hungry and didn't take the food I put down for him.

On a supply trip in heavy rain two days later, I telephoned Dr Michael Brambell and he agreed I should let the mother and kits go while it was still summer. I decided to do so at the end of the month when they would be fully weaned, then move Syl back to the outdoor pens before his release later.

During the next few days, Mia spent much of her time alone in the rear rocks while Freddy had clearly decided he preferred to stay around his mama. This coincided with what I'd learned about cougars in Canada—the young females were far more independent and became skilful hunters quicker than the young males, who often made mistakes when hunting their first big prey like deer, and at that stage in their lives preyed more often on easier farm animals. Naturally, this caused an outcry from farmers to have the marauding cougars shot despite their relative rarity. There is a similar situation in the Highlands where, because of their occasional "offences" of predating on loose poultry and upon game birds and their young, the wildcat was brought to near extinction before World War One, and in its pure form is still rare today. We tend to forget that we have taken over most of these animals' hunting grounds, reducing their natural prey, and thus forcing some animals to prey on stock in order to survive.

Towards the end of July, I formed my final plan for releasing all the wildcats except Sylvesturr. Cruising the west wood I found a completely dry spot in tangled undergrowth between four large, criss-crossed windfall trunks a few yards south of the cairn of boulders on the east edge of the granite escarpment. Two of the trunks ended in a five-foot-high, upended root cluster which also had sheltered tunnels and a natural chamber beneath it. To make sure it all stayed dry I erected a sloping sheet of corrugated iron between the trunks, so the undergrowth fell back and almost obscured it, and large fronds of dark green bracken hid the open area below. I would put Cleo's box there and they could choose between it, the area under the roots or the rocky cairn as their future home. Just to the left was a large square rock whose flat top was covered in lush green moss. On this I would regularly put out their food and drink each evening so whenever hunting proved poor, they would always regard the mossy rock as the place for food.

But what was I to do with Patra? She was now idling away her days in the woodshed, leaving most of her meat, so was clearly earning most of her living from the two woods. On recent supply excursions I had noticed a pair of kestrels had moved onto the small green island that was a Highland burial ground six miles up the loch. Wondering what had attracted them, I wandered over it and was astonished to find a plague of voles. Wherever I looked in the open areas between the azalea, whin and rhododendron bushes, voles were scudding to and fro like little animated cigar butts in their day-time tunnels in the grass. At first I thought my eyes were playing tricks—zip, zip, zip, the little furry bodies shot here and there through the tangles between the old gravestones. There must have been thousands on the island and they would certainly be causing damage to the young trees and bushes which helped make it such a picturesque place. The kestrel pair would barely dent such an overcrowded population. Here seemed the ideal place to release Patra, at least for a few weeks. Not only would she keep herself healthy, learn full independence, but also perform a useful community service.

By now the kits were more than two months old, and even Mia was finding it difficult to get through the fencing into the rocks behind. They spent much time stalking moths and flies in front of the den, some of which they ate, and in grooming each other. Freddy could now repel Moobli easily when he came sniffing at the pens, with a show of ferocity like a mini version of his father. And all Moobli did was whine and look up at me with hurt eyes. He was, thank heaven, because he was still growing up with them himself, remaining goofy and gentle as far as the females and the kits were concerned.

One morning as he sat on the grass outside my study while I typed the last words of my book revisions, I saw him suddenly look up into the sky. I went outside—two ravens, looking almost as big as buzzards but with longer necks, were circling over the wildcat pens and croaking loudly. Cleo and the kits looked up too but seemed not at all perturbed. Indeed, Freddy, who, like his father, often sat with his red tongue sticking slightly out between his white lips, didn't even bother to pull it in as the black ravens made a deep dive then flapped away to the high ridges to the north. Clearly, wildcats had no instinctive fear of ravens.

As I pulled the last sheet from the typewriter, I recalled I'd arranged to meet some friends next day, a local estate foreman and his young daughter, and bring them back by boat to have a look at Wildernesse and the wildcats. Well, tomorrow would be the big day, I decided. My friends could not only see my home but also usefully witness Patra's release on the green island and the freeing of Cleo and the kits in the west wood. As I made final adjustments to their future home site, I congratulated myself on how well things seemed to be dove-tailing together. Cleo and the youngsters would have plenty of time to become used to the area, to find the best hunting places before winter, and the kits could grow strong and fast before I finally released old Sylvesturr.

Chapter 11

Freedom day did not run according to plan. After the post and supply trip, I brought my friends back in a following west wind but, when we arrived, Mia had escaped again into the rocky mound. I would just have to catch her later. Wearing gloves, I managed to coax Cleo and Freddy into their old den box, then we carried them growling slightly to the sheltered spot between the windfalls. I set food and milk out on the large mossy rock which was now to be their regular feeding place, and let down their front door. As we stood twenty yards away, Cleo looked carefully round the new view, sniffed the air, then lay down casually while Freddy nuzzled into her furry belly for a teat.

After lunch, I tried to put Patra into a deep-sided thick cardboard box so I could drop her off on the green island when running my friends back to their car. But she *maued*, bit the gloves, scratched and fought like a fiend, and despite my efforts to hold the lid down forced her way out again and ran like a huge hare towards the burn in the east wood. My friends laughed at my futile attempt to contain Patra. I was glad they had seen Syl's ferocious spits, matched by Freddy's juvenile imitation and witnessed Patra's fierce herculean struggles. For apart from Allan MacColl when Cleo and Patra were kits, and the TV crew, no-one else had ever seen my wildcats.

Before taking my friends back, I instructed Moobli to stay and guard the place, which he had obediently done on two previous occasions. But we had only gone half a mile when we saw him running along the shore after us. He ran the three miles to Sandy Point, well behind as I had turned up the throttle, but when we saw him plunge back into the undergrowth, I felt sure he'd turn back for home again.

But on the return journey, although I slowed down from the point and called and whistled as I crept along, there was no sign of him. And he wasn't at the cottage either. I fed Syl in the woodshed and waited for Moobli to show up. But as he wasn't back by dusk I decided to go and look for him. As I went out, Cleo walked up to the pens from the rhododendron bush by the path, *maued*, then out from the rocks behind came Mia. As I stood well back she came to the front of the pens *mauing* anxiously, and as Cleo greeted her with a little *brrrooo* trill, rubbed nose and whiskers with her mama then followed her through the undergrowth to the west wood.

I hauled down the boat again and set off to find Moobli. I didn't want him wandering the hills alone, maybe picking up some old poison, or falling victim to trigger-happy poachers. Indeed, a local farmer had found one of his cows shot dead a week or two earlier. I went all the way back to the Land Rover and home again, a total of nearly forty miles in the boat that day, but in the near dark could not see him anywhere. As I mechanically prepared a small supper for which I had little appetite, I looked at his bed and empty bowls on the kitchen floor, and felt suddenly lonely. He had never stayed away overnight before and already I was missing him. I left the front door open as I went to bed but I could hardly sleep.

As he was still not back when I rose at dawn next day, it seemed that not only had I lost my only companion but my wildcat release experiment was now doomed to failure. For I had hoped to use Moobli to track the kittens occasionally so I could check their condition.

Once again I hauled the boat down, now in mist and drenching drizzle. As I putted along the shore, hand screening the rain from the binoculars, two buzzards shot up suddenly from near some bracken in a clearing in the far woods. Fearing the worst, I beached the boat and hurried over but found nothing. I could now only continue on to report his loss to the police and offer a reward in the local paper.

The grinning fool was standing by my Land Rover in the woods! And as I clambered over the tangle of naked pine roots on the shore, he came running down wagging his huge bushy tail, whining with pleasure and leaping up to lick my face. He had obviously run on from Sandy Point and must have missed seeing my boat's return while he was in the thick forest, so had decided to wait by the vehicle until I showed up. At any rate, all was well again.

Shortly before dusk, Cleo came back to the pens again and just behind her were both the kits too. There was no fencing between us now to make the kits feel secure, and as I walked slowly towards them Cleo showed little fear but Freddy and Mia scattered, shot away a few yards then hid by crouching down very low, totally immobile, in the long grass and bracken. Which was precisely what Cleo and Patra had done when Allan MacColl had first shown them to me.

Although I'd seen exactly where they stopped, they were difficult to see, for their thin dark stripes blended perfectly with the stems of the surrounding foliage.

It was hard to do but they now had to regard the west wood as home, not the pens, so I clapped my hands at Cleo, shooing her back to the south edge of the wood. This also started up the kits who, seeing mama ahead, bounded after her with their tails high. When I went to feed Syl, I found Patra was back in the woodshed but she was now very wary after yesterday's attempt to take her to the green isle.

An hour later I gave the usual calls and put the food down for mother and kits on the mossy rock. Cleo came out of the undergrowth after a minute as I called but the kits kept their distance, though I could hear their little *maus*. The calls must have started off one of the young sparrowhawks who were still roosting in the pine tree nest above the rock escarpment, for, as I left, its thin breathy little *pee-a-ous* blended in with the kittens' calls, so the darkening wood seemed full of little fairy voices.

When I went out next day there was a large wildcat dropping in the centre of the doorstep. Perhaps it was a mark of rejection by Cleo, or anger by Patra. At dusk, Cleo came to the feeding rock when I went to take a look but again the kits kept in the undergrowth *mauing* faintly. As I walked back to the house to get their food, Cleo followed a few yards behind, not along the open path but in the undergrowth by its side, then stopped at the rhododendron bush. It was good that she was still associating me with food. When I came back with it, she again followed but would not let me touch her now she was out of the pens. She jumped onto the rock when I was a few yards away and began to eat, while the kits still called but again kept out of sight.

Towards midnight in almost complete darkness, I crept down the edge of the wood from the north and waited. Before long the wildcats began calling to each other. But now it was an oddly thin call that a human could easily have mistaken for a wind sound, a high-pitched, drawn out *awrooori*. It was a sound that carried far but as if coming from a ventriloquist, it was hard to tell exactly where it came from. I heard this strange call many times later and realized it was a special wildcat sound, made so a family can keep in touch yet confuse any would-be predators on the as yet fairly feeble kittens. It was an interesting discovery.

For the whole of August and early September I kept close watch on the movements of the wildcats, while still allowing them complete freedom. Now Moobli proved absolutely invaluable, for he really looked forward to the days when we went out to track them by scent. As soon as he located any of the cats in the undergrowth, they immediately shot up the nearest tree where I could more easily check their condition. And by noting exactly where he found them, and when, I could work out the rough pattern of their movements and their hunting areas, which became wider with each passing week. Without Moobli the wildcat release project would have foundered at this point for, in such woods and dense undergrowth, plus the six-foot-high bracken forests on the north hill, contact with the kits, for a mere human, would have easily been lost. This was the way I'd worked with cougar hunter Percy Dewar on Vancouver Island the previous summer when we had followed on foot behind his trained Blue Tick hounds to track, tree and radio-collar the big, wild mountain lions.

Along the rocky shore on August 3, Moobli got a good scent and shot off seventy yards over the big rocks that were obscured by bracken and started whining. It was Patra and she had treed near where the secondary burn came out on the shore line. We left her, tracked all through the east wood, back along the foot of north hill and all though the north end of the west wood without finding any scent. Cleo and the kits were not in the den box but Moobli found Cleo and Freddy in a tangle of thick bracken and fallen tree branches that I had piled up during the winter on the wood's eastern edge. And while his mother shot up to a small branch of a larch at fifteen feet, Freddy scrambled to the top of a seven-foot cluster of fallen tree roots where he perched spitting loudly. Of Mia there was no sign, but Freddy seemed in fine shape.

At dusk, with Moobli in the house, Cleo came to my calls at feeding time. And as I left, Freddy came skulking along under the two fallen larches and for the first time in my sight, sprang up to join his mother to feed on the rock. Later that evening, back at the cottage, Moobli whined at the front door. We darted out—to find Mia under some spare hay I had piled in the open porch to keep dry, and Patra fleeing into the dark. As Moobli sniffed closer, Mia spat and swiped out and he narrowly missed losing his nose. Wilder now, her tail as wide and bushy as a flue brush, she was fat and healthy looking. She was easy to hold at bay with the hissing paraffin lamp because she could not see past it into the dark. But we left her, happy to know that she too was still all right.

Next day, sultry and hot, I cut a quarter acre of second crop hay before the irritating hordes of midges stopped work, then I put armfuls of loose green bracken over Syl's main den, preparatory to putting him back in the pens. The winter frosts and snows, the spring and summer winds and rains, and sexton beetles working away at Syl's old dung had reduced the original ten armfuls to a few mere handfuls of dust.

Tracking round after the cats before lunch, Moobli put Patra up an old ash tree on the far side of the burn, well beyond the east wood. It was the first time we had found any of the cats *across* the burn and, as she was seldom in the woodshed now, it seemed she was going wild easily. Maybe I wouldn't need to put her on the green island after all. She recognized me but growled loudly as she glared at Moobli below, probably because she didn't know the newer terrain and its best escape spots so well.

In late afternoon we were walking along the shore directly below the cottage when Moobli began an anguished whining up ahead. He had Cleo at bay in a natural blind burrow that went deep into the bank under the front fence. She knew well enough he could not get in so just lay there, ears back and growling. I called him away. Near the south-east land spit, 200 yards further on, at the mouth of the burn, Moobli got another strong scent. He ran through the bracken, and up a tiny fir tree shot— Mia. The odd thing was that *Patra* was with her, but she bounded away westwards, towards the temporary refuge spot Cleo seemed to have found under the fallen tree branches. Mia was only up a small tree, her front and rear feet straddled about eighteen inches apart on its top twig-like branches—a perfect picture. I ran back to the cottage for the camera. There I had to change lenses and put in new film but when I got back, Mia was still there, and I got a good shot.

She stayed in the tree for half an hour after we had left. It was clear now that, while adult wildcats deliberately try to go up big trees, the young, inexperienced kits go up the first tree, stump or root cluster they can find, even if it is small and unsuitable. And, just as the cougars had in Canada, wildcats would stay up trees for a long time, making sure the danger had gone before venturing down again.

That evening Cleo came alone to my call at feed time in the west wood and there was no sight or sound of the two kits. She was very hungry, springing onto the rock as I put out the food. I saw she was still very thin, though her milk glands were full, so she was obviously still feeding the kits.

A possibility then dawned on me for the first time. As we had found both kits nearer Patra than Cleo in the past few days, it seemed Patra had assumed some maternal duties and was in fact helping train the kits to hunt and forage—at least during the daytime. In this way Cleo would be left to get the best of my free food and rebuild her energy and strength. This was certainly in line with Percy Dewar's discoveries regarding cougars in Canada —he'd found that sister cats would run together for up to two years, and that the unmated sister would sometimes help on hunting expeditions with the kits. That wildcats might also follow this behaviour was interesting.

On August 5, after hearing both kits *awrooring* in the west wood in the morning, I re-lined Syl's old den with new hay and after boarding him up in his box, transferred him back to the pens. Once again, after the usual growls, he dropped to the ground and with perfect memory, head down, he padded off straight into the den like a furry tank.

The thick bracken jungle behind the house had become the favourite pre-dawn hunting area for the kits and, two days later, the most eerie experience I ever had with them occurred there. Moobli ran through the bracken on a strong scent line, then abruptly shot a few feet backwards. He had cornered Freddy far from any tree, and what a packet of ferocity the kitten now was —back on his haunches, eyes glaring, ears flat, tail as thick as a bottle, he spat and swiped out with claws so far extended his paws looked like round black metal plates filled with sharp scimitars. As the looming threat of Moobli kept him there, I decided to try and measure him and get a good close-up photograph.

I took off my jacket, knelt on its edges, my elbows holding down the sides, and threw it tightly over the hissing bundle. There was no sound, nor any struggle, so he was clearly just crouching underneath. Bit by bit, ready to grab his neck scruff with my gloved hand, I peeled back the coat. There was nothing there. The wildcat kitten had vanished. It was as if a magician had performed a disappearing trick. I dug into the soft ground with my fingers—nothing. Even Moobli was still staring at the spot. The comical expression on his face must have been nothing to the one on mine.

We had heard nothing, felt nothing, seen no movement nor one stem of bracken quiver. That young wildcat, a tangle of tendons and lithe sinew, with reflexes Muhammad Ali would be proud to own, had shot away faster than my or even the dog's eyes had been able to follow. It was one of the most astonishing and uncanny experiences of my life. Even now, years later, I still find what happened that day to be hard, if not impossible, to accept.

A quarter of an hour later, as we worked our way through the bracken to the north-east corner of the west wood, we treed not Freddy but Mia. She ran up a small willow tree. I photographed her several times and, as we turned to leave, I saw both Freddy and Patra sneaking along the level trunk of the huge fallen silver fir that lay along the top of the rock escarpment in the wood. I was now certain that Patra had taken over training the kits to hunt, at least some of the time. But where was Cleo?

We found out when we returned home—she was in the workshop at the back, whose door I had left open, and was helping herself to Moobli's sterilized meat sausages. Her first time since her own kittenhood. She had two sheep ticks behind her right ear and again I felt she looked run down.

But what an odd reversal of roles. When young, Cleo had always been the wild one, the explorative expert hunter. And surely this was one reason why Syl had chosen her. Now Patra, strong from not having kits to feed, had become the mighty hunter and Cleo was allowing her to run with and help teach the kits to hunt. To think, I had intended to release Patra on the green isle a week or two ago. She was certainly earning her keep now.

In the heat of the afternoon, not calling out as I wanted to see what the cats were up to, I sneaked down to the bottom of west wood with binoculars. Cleo was lying in the den box and both kits, now almost as large as their mother, were suckling away from her teats. But there was no sign of Patra. What an odd lot they were, I thought, scratching my head as I walked back. At dusk feed time, only Cleo came to the rock while I was there but I saw Patra run through the wood with one of the kits behind her.

As I cooked supper later, Moobli whined at the front door. Instead of letting him out, I went into the dark study and peered through the window. Mia was sniffing a small dark object on the ground beside the log porch. As I watched, the object jumped forward a few inches—*flub*. She poked out a tentative paw. Again it jumped, weakly, heavily—*flub*. It was one of the two toads that had moved in to hunt insects in the hay most evenings now. She sniffed it again and this time it jumped towards her. Immediately she shot backwards, looked at it again fearfully, then ran away towards the west wood. Mia was interested in frogs but this old fat toad, with its dry, warty, poisonous skin, who had no fear, was clearly something to be left alone.

Next morning I turned my hay crop in blazing sunshine, laid out some edible toadstools to dry, and went to post some urgent mail. As I boated home later under gathering clouds, a loud thunderstorm broke out overhead and small spikes of lightning struck the rock faces of the higher mountain ridges. I hurried to gather my crops before the deluge but luckily it missed Wildernesse, while three miles to the west the clouds dragged dark grey skirts of rain across the loch. At dusk feed time both kits followed Cleo when she came to my calls and stopped six yards away as she leaped up to feed. As I backed away Freddy also jumped up and was followed by Mia who sneaked round to the rear of the rock. All the cats growled as they ate and Freddy swatted Mia for coming too close to his piece of meat, but as it was the first time I'd seen all three on the rock together, it was a small moment of triumph.

When I returned, Patra was stealing Syl's milk right in front of his eyes. She poked her head through the fencing, couldn't quite reach the bowl, so stuck her tongue out a good two inches, gathering enough on the tip to slowly lap up as much as she wanted. I clapped hands and she shot behind the pens and back to her own supply in the woodshed.

After leaving them alone for three days, we tracked the wildcats again on August 10 and Moobli treed Freddy near the den box in the west wood. At feed time Cleo came to the rock followed closely by only Freddy. After feeding she went into the den box while her son hid in the natural root tangle chamber below. By now Cleo had thrown all the hay and sacking out of the box, perhaps because of the hot, close weather.

My practice each morning the sun shone was to pull Syl's door up for an hour, to warm up his den. Each time I did this he built a barricade from his hay bed and hid behind it, his glowering golden eyes just peeping over the top. Whereas we often found the kits and young females out hunting by day, Syl seldom came out until evening and certainly never ate until it was almost dark. It seemed to me possible that young kits learn to hunt first by daylight, and that nocturnal hunting is something they have to learn as they grow older, taking advantage of the evolutionary adaptation of their eyes to see in near total darkness.

Two days later we treed Mia from the rocks and bracken on shore below the east wood. She ran nearly 200 yards through the undergrowth and scooted up a small fir from which she could have been shaken by hand. But Patra, who was with her, shot along the banks of the burn and disappeared. Moobli, who was slow at actually sighting the cats because he was low in the bracken himself, could now run nose high on a fresh scent.

Later we treed Cleo from the fallen-branches refuge near the west wood and saw Freddy running into the root tangle den near their box. On August 14, after a long search round the woods, we treed Freddy up a small willow on the north-east edge of the west wood, and saw Cleo running away. But Mia was still running with Patra in the east wood. The theory of sister cat helping out was clearly established. I recalled how Cleo had kept driving Patra from her pen before the kits' birth but afterwards she had allowed her to visit and sniff the babies without protest. Perhaps it only occurred with inexperienced cats, or when the two sisters happened to remain together.

Next day, as if to blow the theory apart, we had just returned from a long high trek, when we found Patra in the workshop raiding the box of dog sausages. Fat and heavy, her tail really bushy now, she spat and shot out as we entered. And at dusk both kits came to feed with Cleo on the rock.

Next evening after feeding, I made myself a stew into which I poured some old oats without checking them first. It tasted awful so I tipped it onto the grass outside and kept watch, as I made a fresh stew, thinking Patra would scent it. To my surprise, Cleo arrived, closely followed by Freddy and Mia. They ate a little but weren't hungry, then took off again for the west wood, Cleo leading.

Two mornings later, before leaving on a post trip, we checked the west wood but Moobli found no scent at all—and the previous night's food and milk hadn't been touched. I wondered if Cleo had taken the kits to forage further down the loch. Flies and sexton beetles crawled over the meat and some of the beetles had drowned in the milk. There had been a small plague of these black and red striped beetles around Wildernesse for the past few days. Like little insect vultures they hovered in the air, trying to locate the meat I set out for the cats.

After returning in the boat, I went down to the feed rock. Nearly all the meat and milk had now gone, and I startled Freddy who had been calmly scraping moss and leaves over both bowls, standing high on three legs while scraping away with his right front paw. This real wildcat trait was a perfect example of inherited instinct from Sylvesturr, who was now scraping even larger mounds of debris over his nightly left-overs against the slugs and the new onslaught of the sexton beetles.

As I drew near with fresh food, Freddy vanished into the herbage but Cleo emerged, jumped up onto the rock and started to clatter-purr. Maybe she had taken the kits down the loch last night but had decided the pickings were better at home. The milk bowl, I now noticed, had been licked clean and there wasn't a beetle in sight. In the twilight near distance I heard Mia *awrooring*. As the shyest of the three, I supposed she had eaten a good share of last night's food during our afternoon absence.

As I read my mail that night there was a note from Dr Michael Brambell of London Zoo whom I'd asked to visit me on his next holiday in the area. He and his wife Patricia and their two young sons, hoping I'd get the message in time, would be at a small pier at noon in four days. I was delighted to have the chance of showing them not only that old Sylvesturr was thriving, but that he was indeed the father of two lovely kittens—*if* we could tree them on the day. I could possibly live-trap them both but it would be better to show him they were alive, healthy and above all, free.

Two days later in dull drizzle, we tracked all round the north hill and the west wood and along the shore without any sign of the cats. I felt a little worried. For the cats to leave the area just before Dr Brambell came would have been very disappointing. I took Moobli to the north edge of the east wood. He picked up some scent near the waterfall, then we scrambled south along the banks of the burn. Twice he lost the scent, stumbled through the rushing burn as I crossed on a creaking dead larch, then he went back across the burn lower down as I negotiated the treacherously slippery trunk of a fallen beech to follow him. Suddenly a buzzard, perched low on a stunted beech near the shore, shot away through the wood, flying with curved back wings like a huge hawk. My heart jumped. A buzzard's eyesight is eight times better than a man's and what was it doing perched so low in a wood? Maybe it had spied something dead—like a wildcat kitten. And the dense bracken had prevented the scent of the corpse reaching Moobli.

We ran over, found nothing, then Moobli picked up a strong scent, dived under the shore fence and as I caught up, both kits shot up two alder trees. I hadn't photographed the kits for over a week now so I climbed up close to Freddy. He looked really mad and evil, ears back and down, and snarling with flat lizard-like head. I took two shots and was about to get down and to go to the alder five yards away up which Mia crouched, when Freddy walked down the branch towards me, then leaped—all four limbs extended, claws out, like a sky diver trying to control his fall—and almost glided the sixteen feet down to the ground. He landed with an audible plop on a flat rock as if all the air had been forced out of his lungs. I felt sure he was badly winded, if not worse, but he bounced up immediately and high-tailed it into the east wood, heading for the beech tree which bridged the burn.

It seemed an astonishing escape device for he hadn't dropped straight down. His slanting air flight must have been a good twenty feet and reminded me of the flying squirrels I'd often seen in Canada. He really had half glided. I was so surprised, I forgot to try and photograph his flight.

The moment Freddy landed, Mia scrambled backwards down her tree and scampered north-west through the bracken. As she reached the top of the rocky bank, Patra sprang out of hiding and went with her. I had a task restraining Moobli as the two went lickety-split for the north hill.

Freddy and Mia on their first outing, June 21, a day short of their four-week birthday. They explore the sunny world of grass, buttercups and brambles, playing and *mauing* to each other. (Freddy at top.)

At exactly eight weeks, Freddy *(left)* and Mia have been enjoying the freedom of Sylvesturr's larger den and pen, while their crusty old father is temporarily banished to the woodshed.

Cleo, thinner during weaning, plays with her eight-week-old kits for several hours each day in the sun, allowing them to have mock fights but watching closely so that they don't stray too far.

August 12. The kits, Cleo and Patra had been running free for nearly two weeks. I tracked them every few days by aid of Moobli's fine nose, otherwise all contact would have been lost. This way I checked their condition and movements. On August 12 Moobli put Mia up a tiny dead fir, which no mature wildcat would have chosen as a refuge.

"A sad look of defeat came over his long-whiskered face." Sylvesturr, live-trapped after fifty-two days of freedom, had eaten the raw venison bait and was in fine condition, despite overnight rain. Having proved he could survive alone, he was freed minutes later. (Early September or end of August.)

Freddy in February 1976, at about nine months.

In her third season with me, on June 5, Cleo gave birth to four kits, smaller than her first two, after mating with Sylvesturr in the wild woods. Here she carries the smallest and weakest of the sixteen-day-old kits, Liane, back to the den.

Playful Liane at four months. She often performed a wild ears-back, toes-outwards, sideways dance as she made mock attacks on blowing leaves or small moving objects, stopping suddenly to look about her for danger.

As I now wanted to determine whether both kits, or just Mia, were really running with Patra, we went out again in late afternoon. We quickly put Patra up by the rhododendron bush southeast of the cottage. I held Moobli back and watched her run. She headed south-west to the gate and shore, then turned left and was lost to sight. I let Moobli go after a minute and he sped away, tracking nose-high, following her route exactly. She had doubled back from the gate a full 250 yards along the bracken-filled shore and when I reached him, Moobli was showing great interest in the root tangle of an old stump on the edge of the secondary burn mouth. From the snarls and spits that erupted when Moobli put his nose down, Patra and at least one kit were in there. This, at last then, was Patra's den. And it explained why we had so often found her and Mia in the vicinity, and today, Freddy too. Cleo's den was still the den box and the nearby root chamber in the west wood.

It now seemed finally and definitely established that the kits, but more often Mia than Freddy, ran with Patra during the day, yet returned to their mother at night for the dusk feed and for her milk feed during darkness. Patra, if not a surrogate mother, had become a real working aunt. And Cleo, once the wilder of the two but who'd had less chance to develop fully as a summer hunter while rearing and being penned up with her kits earlier, had been happy to allow Patra to take over daytime training duties. This also explained her recent tameness for, as she recovered full bodily strength, she had become more dependent on me for food.

Next day, after torrential rain and south-west gales for some twenty hours, there was no sign of any of the wildcats in the wood at feed time. No wonder—I found they were all in the woodshed. Again here was proof that while they didn't mind light rain, they didn't like strong winds, with, possibly, the noise and danger of falling branches. Neither kit had been in the shed before so the two adults had obviously brought them there. Although I had wanted them to stay in the wild area of the west wood, I took pity on them that night. As I went in with a second supply of food Freddy flared from his new bed in the hay box that the females had spurned as kits. Cleo was high on the rear logpile, Mia had squirmed among the log crevices until she was out of sight, while Patra sat on their old bed with half-closed eyes.

In the morning the gales had abated but a steady drizzle was falling and all the cats were still in the shed. I spent the afternoon leeward of an occupied badger's sett two miles away but none came out to have their portraits taken. When I went to feed the cats at night, Patra and the kits had gone, leaving Cleo behind on the bed. I walked down to the feed rock, calling out, and she must have followed me down, sneaking through the herbage, because as I set the meat and milk out, she suddenly emerged from beneath the windfall trunks.

On August 22 I met Michael and Patricia Brambell and their two boys at the little old pier and brought them back by boat. Sylvesturr should have won an Oscar for his performance that day. As I raised his door, confronted by this new mass of humanity, he flung a whole pile of hay outwards, *PAAHED* louder than ever as he braced up on his powerful front legs and easily stared us all down. The Brambells were delighted to see him alive and in such good shape but Michael commented: "He hasn't got any nicer, has he? I thought you'd have had him eating out of your hand by now."

After a fine lunch which Patricia provided, we put Moobli to work. I was anxious to tree the kits—to prove their health and their actual existence. But as we tracked round both woods without scent and I felt so many people walking and talking plus the drizzle had probably made all the cats seek deep cover, Moobli suddenly put his huge black nose low and took off along the shore from the south-east land spit. Twenty yards from Patra's den, he bounded into thick bracken, and up a hazel tree shot Freddy. He growled, then spat, superbly on cue, a perfect replica of his crusty old father. At this fine moment of proof for Dr Brambell that the whole experiment had been a success, I resolved to track the cats for only two more weeks. Then, although I would still set out food for them, I would leave them to revert naturally to the wild.

Two hours after boating the Brambells back to the pier, I took the night's meat and milk down to the west wood. Cleo came running through the undergrowth—and ten yards behind her Freddy sneaked along. As I left, Mia also headed towards the rock to join the others. But Patra was nowhere to be seen.

When I reached the cottage I knew why. She was in the kitchen with Moobli, eating at his huge bowl. It was another example of the duplicity of the wildcat mind. All the cats were afraid of Moobli in the open but Patra knew from kittenhood he was harmless in the house. As she ate his left-overs, Moobli sat smiling but kept his distance, looking proud as if he had herded her indoors just for me, and his tail was wagging like a great hairy flag as I walked through the kitchen door.

Chapter 12

Over the next week our trackings established that both kits had now gone back to Cleo in the west wood, they were using the dry chamber beneath the root tangle as their main den, and that Patra's duties as a hard working aunt for three weeks were over. Cleo was now restored to her former lithe sleekness and this was probably why Patra had relinquished her temporary daytime care of the kits back to her sister. Towards the end of August Patra began coming to the rock for the dusk feed and to compete with the kits and Cleo for the free food.

On August 28, Cleo and Patra spent most of the day in the undergrowth near Sylvesturr's pen, leaving both kits alone in the west wood. On a brief cruise round it, Moobli and I started Mia up an old larch snag from a small clearing in the bracken. She had been feeding from a wood pigeon, a small flock of which had colonized the wooded loch shores that summer. Only the wings, tail and green gizzard with gravel teeth in it, had been left, and one of the wings and some breast meat had been carried a few yards away, probably by Freddy.

At the dusk feeding time, Cleo and Patra followed me through the side undergrowth down to the rock. Then, as I kept calling, both kits also came from beneath the fallen trunks and leaped onto the mossy surface and squabbled over food. Freddy aimed a paw swipe at Cleo, who backed off from her son and took another piece of meat two feet away. Then Patra growled and swatted out at Freddy.

When I saw that, I decided it was time for Patra to go free. I didn't want her upsetting the new fine balance between mother and kits, for Cleo was still giving them milk. It would be better to let Patra go while it was still summer. A visit to the green isle recently had shown that it was still seething with voles. The kestrels were still there but had barely affected the little rodent populations.

Oddly, next morning Patra was asleep in the porch hay. I enticed her into the kitchen with meat but as soon as she'd eaten it, she sensed something odd was occurring, began *mauing* and sneaking round the floor for some way out. I drove her into the dark of the small den box, then took her to the island.

She hated the boat journey, growling and thrusting her big claws through the ventilation holes in the box. As I saw them I appreciated what a big, tough cat she really was, and how lucky I had been to handle her occasionally without gloves, but not in this mood. As soon as I put the box down on the lush green grass below the thick azalea and whin bushes, she ran out, paused to look back, then vanished into the shrubbery. As I watched her go, I decided I would try and pick her up again before winter.

On my way back from fetching mail, I stopped at the same spot on the island and called with my usual imitation *maus*. Within two minutes she emerged from the bushes. She looked lonesome on the shore but I put down a whole fifteen-ounce sausage for her. She came down cautiously, grabbed it and carried it off dangling, like a plastic covered rabbit, from each side of her jaws.

At dawn next day I saw Cleo and both kits troop past below my window. Freddy and Mia looked like two beautiful little cheetahs with their lithe long striped legs, such an accentuated wildcat feature in kittenhood. Every so often Cleo peered up over the grass like a weasel, and the kits paused too, looking nervously about them. They went down into the pasture, skirted the spruce glade and on through the east wood towards the burn.

In the afternoon as I was photographing a red squirrel on a larch trunk, Moobli started yiping. He had treed Mia on the far side of the burn, which was quite swollen so Cleo and the kits had clearly crossed over one of the two fallen trunks. I made the usual soothing sounds which showed we meant no harm when treeing them and let her go again. This was the family's first crossing of the burn and it was obvious they were now wandering farther afield.

Now the big problem was how and when to release Sylvesturr. That night as I picked the first blackberries from the brambles I'd trained to grow among bamboo canes in front of the cottage, I heard Moobli bark. I stole up to the cottage corner. For sheer devilment he had stamped playfully in front of Syl's pen and Syl had come out of his den to attack. Moobli growled but the old cat not only held his ground but resting on his left front foot, PAAHED and swiped out at Moobli's nose with the flashing hooks of his right. Moobli's barks deterred him not at all and he only shot back into his den when I came round the corner. It was the first time Moobli had barked at Syl since the day of his arrival, and he received a hand whack across the rump for his pains.

Clearly, I could not let Syl go free in the area without possible trouble for both cat and dog, yet I didn't want to release him miles away where I couldn't set out regular food for him and at least try and keep a check on his movements. It seemed a big problem. Harsh old recidivist Syl had not grown up with Moobli as had the girls. I also felt he might go for the kits when all were ranging the same area. But I did have several reasons for optimism too. They were just about big enough to look after themselves and could certainly scoot up trees faster than his big bulk would allow. He had never shown any belligerence to them or either of the two girls. Also, two days earlier, I had found the first fox scats in the west wood since last winter. There wasn't a fox in the wide world that would face up to Syl's devastating ferocity. If they did happen to meet, one encounter with Syl would probably convince the fox that safer hunting grounds lay over the hills and far away. Syl's fierceness with Moobli probably partly stemmed from the fact that he had now recovered his full appetite, which increased greatly in the autumn when growing his darker thicker coat and as his body prepared for winter.

By early September both kits were ranging away from Cleo during the day and seemed to have set up their own daytime headquarters amid the thick foliage and bracken beneath the large silver fir that lay across the rocky escarpment. But each night they came to my feed calls, a few yards behind Cleo, then seemed to spend time with her in the roots chamber near the rock, still suckling milk. One afternoon after checking the boats were still above the loch level after two days of drizzle, I came up the path and saw them leap from the bird table and hare off into the east wood. When I went to feed them I heard their faint *awroori* calls coming nearer and nearer but though I tried I could not see them until they were mere yards away. They had somehow covered the whole distance between east and west wood under cover. And, again, the ventriloquial quality of their calls made their exact positions impossible to determine.

In these few days I noticed Mia was once more becoming warier, and would not jump onto the feed rock until I was many yards away. And she would swiftly seize a piece of meat and jump below the fallen trunks to eat it. By contrast, Syl was now advancing out of his den for food each evening. He was in magnificent shape and I decided the time had come to let him go.

I had long been overdue for a short research and working trip to discuss writing projects, so here was the ideal opportunity—I would set Syl free while Moobli and I were away, so he could acclimatize to freedom and the whole area in peace.

On September 5 I boated up the loch to buy the cats' meat and by sheer coincidence my Highland butcher asked me if I had any use for ten pounds of hearts that had become unfrozen. On the way back, I pulled the boat in to the eastern shore of the green island and made the usual feed calls. To my surprise I heard Patra *mau* in return, the calls coming nearer until she emerged from some thick brambles. She looked carefully all about, half ran until a few yards away, then became scared and skulked in the thick grass. I kept *mauing*, broke two eggs for her, and she overcame her fears and came down to eat them. She was fat and in fine shape.

A great problem when releasing animals to the wild is that one can so easily upset the balance for other wildlife in the area, especially when predators are involved. Hence I intended to check the isle at regular intervals, to make sure that Patra and the kestrels could co-exist without either destroying all the wild prey or take so much as to affect each other's survival. As I left again, I threw one of the hearts into the deep grass as a treat for Patra.

Next day I cruised the woods for a good place to release Sylvesturr. The only suitable places in the east wood, which was far too open, were the dens in the burn banks but these would be flooded in winter spates. But at the top of the west wood, near its north-east edge, I found a huge inward-curving stump and roots cluster that was heavily screened with long bracken and had thick heather sprouting from the top. It faced south and the area below was dry with powdered dust. It was nearly 150 yards above the area where Cleo and the kits had their den, with a marsh, many tangled windfalls and the rocky escarpment between them. It was the ideal place. That evening I set the box-cage trap in his pen.

But next morning although he had eaten most of the meat, he had once more forced his way out where some staples had come loose, and was back in his den, growling at the indignity. Leaving him to calm down, I hauled the big boat up under the alder tree, picked all the blackberries that might rot while I was away, boiled and bottled them, and painted a fifth of the cottage roof. After lunch, I hung cooked and half-cooked beef ribs, liver and flank in strategic positions—Syl would have to go a yard to get three hearts tied to a fallen log and three yards to reach four more and some ribs nailed to a tree. I distributed other fresh meats and sausages in the thick bracken. Nearby where the den box was going to be I set a large plastic bowl with seven pints of long-life milk and water. Then I did the same around Cleo's den.

The moment for the freeing of Sylvesturr had come. I set the den box in his run and after driving him out with a broom, when he once again performed his one-handed gibbon act on the pen roof, he dashed into it. I wedged a pine sheet over the entrance and after several pauses, managed to carry box, broom and a now strangely silent Syl through the tangled undergrowth and over fallen logs to his new home site in the wood. It seemed strange he wasn't growling as he usually did when being carried, just as Patra had behaved oddly before I took her to the green island. Wildcats are possibly psychic, seeming to sense when something momentous in their lives is about to occur.

I had never had a confrontation with Sylvesturr in the open and I don't mind admitting my heart thumped when the last moment came. To forestall any possible attack, and the resulting fracas which might be a poor start to his freedom, I lay over the heather on the stump, well above his box, and prised the pine sheet free with the broom handle.

I saw his great head emerge slowly, take one glaring look this way, one glare that, both slow and terrifying, his golden eyes like great black-centred orbs, then he shrank back again into the box. He always took a careful look at anywhere strange before making any move. I knew then he wouldn't leave before dark.

As I said goodbye to him and walked back to the cottage, I felt slightly bereft. He had never shown any love or even liking— it was just not in his make-up. Plucked from his wild heritage as a kitten and jailed by man for all his long life, his motivation sprang from his inherited fear and distrust of man. He had learned only to hate the human species with all the inviolate unchanging character of his heart, with instincts inherited from centuries of persecution against his kind. I loved Sylvesturr. I respected his pride, his courage, his refusal to compromise. I would not sentence him to another winter of imprisonment. Although he was nearing his old age, I was happy to have given him a natural home, to have shown him the long-forgotten wilds of his childhood, and provided him with a choice of wives from one of which he had produced two magnificent kittens. And, if I could achieve it safely, it certainly behoved me to give him his freedom.

Before pulling out on our trip next day, I checked Syl's box, approaching with caution in case he attacked. Syl had gone, so had two hearts, but the milk seemed untouched. I decided not to track him. His life was now his own. Knowing his memory, I would put food out for him in the same place on my return. As I boated up the loch in mist and rain with Moobli, I felt I had done my best for all the wildcats.

Chapter 13

Eight days later we returned to my old small boat upturned in the woods to find the larch trees bending to the fury of Force 9 south-west gales, and heavy showers of rain hissing into the foaming crests of the deep-troughed waves that were marching up the loch. At the village shop I had been told an outdoor sports and survival centre were using the loch, and as I reached the small bay I saw four men in black rubber diving suits were fixing a forty-horsepower outboard onto a large rubber boat which they had in the water, which although turbulent was out of the main onslaught of the waves.

As I laid a pathway of broken branches over the gravelly shore, overturned my boat and hauled it down and set it to ride just off the rocks on a small anchor, I noticed they were standing around and looking at the sky.

It was to be a really rough trip but if they were going out, I, used to the loch in the storms of icy winter, ought to be able to make it all right. My twenty-horsepower outboard should be equal to the task. Besides, I had lost time visiting friends on the way up and had slept the night in a pine forest south of Edinburgh. I was anxious to get home to check the wildcats. But as I carried the final load down and covered the gear with a rough plastic sheet held down by rocks, I saw the men had removed their engine and were now carrying their boat back to its trailer. As I set off they stared with open mouths.

As I hit the main run of the waves and the hissing rain made vision difficult, I felt they were the ones who had made the right decision. It was a really hard trip home and any question of stopping at the green island to check on Patra was out. As I sat in the back with Moobli crouched down in the bow with round fear-filled eyes, I had to make continual adjustments to the throttle, accelerate just sufficiently up the broad slope of the rolling waves to avoid being swamped by the following ones, then throttle right down when slide-racing down the far sides to avoid ploughing the bow into the bottom of the next wave, thus turning boat, dog, gear and self into an unwilling submarine. Yet all the time the boat had to be kept under power, slightly faster than the waves, for to have veered sideways would have meant being instantly swamped. While Moobli and I could probably have made it to shore, I doubted I could do so with my only valuable possession—the heavy brief case of photos and notes I had amassed during my Highland years. But we reached home safely.

Later, Cleo came to my feed calls in the west wood, with huge Freddy following with stealthy lion-like walk behind her. Eight days mean little to wildcats, or even domestic cats, who are far better left with food on their own familiar territory than being transported around in cages or left with strangers during the temporary absence of their owners. I then checked Sylvesturr's den box. There was no sign of the old boy but while all the hearts, liver, mutton and most of the milk had gone, a cooked beef flank still hung untouched on the curved stump. And some of the sterilized sausages were still intact. There were no fox scats anywhere.

Next day, with the bracken on the shore and in the hills already turning yellow before the final brown, we went tracking. We found no scents until Moobli reached the roots chamber near the feed rock. He sniffed and whined but though I couldn't hear any growls, I presumed one of the cats was down there, probably Mia, for when we returned we found Cleo and Freddy had spent the night in the woodshed!

At dusk Cleo came to the feed calls again, walking near my

feet like a dog, and Freddy came down, sliding along furtively like a small wolf through the herbage. I didn't see Mia but could hear what I thought were faint *maus* from some fallen trunks about thirty yards away.

Tracking the woods again next day still produced no sign of Syl and I wondered if he had left the area entirely. I was fairly sure he was not dead because Moobli would have scented his carcass easily, even down a hole. Moobli could scent sitting woodcocks and even tiny mouse carcasses, so it seemed human-hating Syl might now have made his home elsewhere.

Apart from the two woods around the cottage, there was the long hilly oak, birch, rowan and hazel wood running eastwards after a 300-yard gap on the far side of the burn. And there was a similar wood, over two miles long, with plenty of open grassy patches, rocky cairns, small burns, and old hollow stumps that began a mile to the west. I felt he could well be in this wood. He was powerful and fast and in fine shape when I had released him but, as the days went by, I had a nagging wish to see him again, to know he was all right. I was in fact missing his harsh, proud old face.

Over the next three days Cleo and Freddy alternated between the west wood and the shed, both coming to the dusk feeds, and Freddy began jumping on the rock at the same time as his mother, so both were feeding while I was near. He was still try-ing to suck milk from Cleo and once as he nuzzled beneath her in the shed, he lifted her back feet right off the ground, and she looked quite embarrassed! He was now longer and more burly than his mother. As far as I could tell he got no suck at all but Cleo seemed to enjoy her huge kit's caresses, and turned over on her back twice as he pushed and probed. But I was now worried about Mia, whom I had not seen at all. Maybe she had left, per-haps with Sylvesturr? It made sense that she could be the first to leave—she had always been the wildest one, escaping from the pens long before Freddy showed any desire to go. And yet she was weaned several days later. The odd thing was that the new meat I left near Syl's den box and release point remained un-touched. So it didn't seem much use setting the trap for her.

By September 23, after four days of incessant gales and the

first hailstorm of the coming winter, it seemed certain Cleo and Freddy were going to make the woodshed their main quarters. Much as I wanted them to go wild, I just hadn't the heart to drive them away. As this meant putting out sand and gravel as litter, I took advantage of a calm sunny spell in late afternoon to row to a beach one and a half miles away to the west with a shovel and some heavy duty plastic sacks. Moobli ran all the way beside the boat but as I was filling the sacks and lugging them down, he disappeared. I whistled—no response. Darn him, had he gone after some deer? I walked to the end of the beach and climbed up the high bank covered with bracken and scrubby birch and alder trees, when he came running back with an odd look, whined, and took off again into the bracken, but he was not on a trail.

He had found Mia—dead.

She lay in a puddle below the tangled roots of a fallen birch. Blow fly maggots writhed under the skin of the carcass which gave off a putrid stench, and the half-open eyes were sunken and opaque. I couldn't pick it up for it would have fallen to pieces. I felt awful as I stood by the shattered birch in that bleak inhospitable place, feeling I had failed. Yet in the wild they would all have been together in the open from birth. Perhaps neither Cleo nor Freddy had let her feed from all the meats I had left, and yet there had been enough for ten cats for a fortnight, and there was much left on our return. Had she run foul of a fox, a big otter or even Syl himself? I poked the remains about but there was no sign of external injury. The fur looked darker than hers and the carcass seemed smaller too.

I went home in a black mood, perplexed too for the carcass seemed too decomposed for not even two weeks' exposure. Then I remembered Patra on the green island. Trying to reach her old home, she could have swum the 250 yards to the mainland. Then weakened by the swim, losing heat from being wet on the long rough foot journey along the shore, perhaps hungry, she could then have fallen prey to something. That thought increased my misery. Maybe all three cats were dead somewhere, and I had only found Mia's, or Patra's, remains because of Moobli's wonderful nose. I would now have to quickly check Patra's presence on the green island—she had come twice to my calls before and if she *was* there the remains just had to be Mia's.

After hauling up the boat I went to check the meat I had left for Syl in the west wood—it had all gone, seven days after I had put it down. Perhaps he at least was still alive.

That evening as I prepared the cats' meal in my workshop, I saw Freddy emerge from the bracken with a vole in his jaws and take it into the shed. When I went in he was curled up in the old hay box and Cleo was eating it. He had clearly brought the vole for her. It seemed odd that a kit should hunt for its mother, yet he was a tom and the incident lent more credence to the possibility that toms do occasionally feed females. I fed them in the shed, weakening from my earlier resolve because I didn't want to lose Freddy as it seemed I had Mia. He was now a superb, very pretty, long-legged wildcat indeed, and for the first time I thought what a fine source of inspiration he could be—for youngsters who might grow up with a desire to help conserve these rare creatures. But when they came out to get their food, Cleo growled and swiped at Freddy when he came too close to her first piece. He just backed off good-naturedly. At least they were hungry so it seemed neither of them had taken the meat from the west wood. It had to be Syl.

Next day the south-west gales were blowing again and whole twigs of leaves were being torn from the ash trees and the first-to-fall alder leaves were whirling about the beach. We had run out of meat, I needed to go to the post, but I had a hard task launching the boat in the big waves. Two strong kicks launched us clear of the rocks, the engine started first pull, and we banged our way up through the troughs until I could pull into the lee shore of the green island. I *maued* and called Patra but there was too much wind, my voice didn't carry and we didn't see her. But I left a meat sausage in the usual place. The New York publishers had sent back my edited book, for me to explain some passages more fully, tidy up chapter endings, and they wanted it all returned urgently so they could go ahead with publication. I had a hard week's writing ahead.

Over the next few days between work spells, I saw Freddy bring three more voles to the woodshed. He was now hunting totally alone as Cleo lazed in the shed most of the day. On September 29, the book that had filled most of my writing life in the past five and a half years now complete, I boated up the loch to get it off my hands. I could now get all my outdoor work completed and set out in earnest to find the truth about the missing wildcats.

I pulled into the green island on the return journey, once more without result. And my heart sank when I saw the sausage was still lying intact on the shore. But next morning the meat in the west wood had again gone from where I had left it. And there was a large four-toed wildcat footprint in a small patch of mud nearby. It was too big for Freddy. My hopes rose. That night, after hauling firewood from the east wood all day, I set the box-cage trap on the spot with a sheep's heart.

I spent October 1 collecting the tasty honey fungus that grew on several ash tree boles, cutting firewood, and picking over five pounds of blackberries from my "trained" brambles—there were still three times as many unripe ones left. At dusk I checked the trap—the door was down. But when I sneaked hopefully round to the front it contained Cleo. She had smelled the meat on the west breeze from 250 yards, yet more proof of wildcats' scenting ability.

I would have to pen up Cleo and Freddy again while I tried to trap Sylvesturr. I carried her to the pens, set in food and milk, and because Freddy was waiting for his food in the shed, laid a small trail of meat pieces from it to the pens. From the workshop window, I saw him leap onto the half door, sniffing the air, then drop to the ground and run towards the pens. Then I ran out and slammed down the swing door behind him. Now they were safely out of the way I could set the trap with impunity.

Next morning the trap was unsprung but the meat bait had gone. And the thick nylon trigger line had been neatly chewed through. No fox would enter such a trap, at least not unless it was desperate from starvation in the harsh depths of winter. It could only be Syl—his perfect memory enabling him to chew the bait free and make off with it without setting off the trap. With great excitement, wearing plastic gloves which I dipped in boiled spruce needle juice to reduce the man scent, I set the trap again with all the cunning I could muster. And this time I tied the bait on with plastic-wrapped wire fishing trace. He wouldn't chew through *that* in a hurry.

Next day the trap was unsprung but a large dumb-bell wildcat dropping with the usual twisty ends lay near the untouched bait just outside the trap. It seemed a mark of contempt. Spreading butter to lubricate the moving parts, I set the trapdoor on a knife edge, hoping the windfall trunks would screen the westerly wind enough not to blow it down.

The south-west gales sprang up again overnight and when I saw the trapdoor was down after breakfast, I felt sure it had been blown loose but as I crept hopefully round in my usual half circle I saw the mousetrap spring had gone off. As I came round the big larch and pine trunks with Moobli, I saw a cat crouching in the box part. I ran up. It was Mia! She was bigger than before and as we came near she became a raging monster. With her tail almost three inches thick, she flared and spat like a huge firework, and closed and opened her eyes slowly as she glared round with head still for a way of escape. Then she dashed at the thick wire netting at the left, right, then straight at us, hitting the netting as if she was blind or thought a mad rush would force her through it. Moobli whined, then barked, and I had to order him away and sit which he reluctantly did, whining and staring at the mad cat in the trap.

Beside myself with delight, I raced back to the cottage for my camera to record the victory, fell over in the small burn after catching my boot in the rusty traces of some old fencing, grazed my palms on its stony bed, but feeling no pain, shot indoors and feverishly changed the lens and ran back. I took three shots as she crouched, her face full of hate and ferocity, in the box. It was certainly Mia, the same light golden tawny fur that Freddy still had, and the yellow-gold eyes with jet-black pupils. Her spit was not as strong as Syl's but this was his daughter all right. I went back to the house and sat down. What was I to do with her? Put her in the pens with Cleo and Freddy? Would they still get along? They had been apart a long time now. Well, I'd try it for a few days anyway, using the gate if necessary.

I went out again and chased Freddy, who suddenly became

blockheaded and started spitting, out of the small pen and into the main one, and shut the gate. I cleaned out their old den box, filled it with dry hay and set it back on its old logs in the small pen corner. Then with Moobli in the house, I went back to the wood with thick gloves to carry Mia and the trap up to the pens.

She had gone. The wire netting on the roof at the point where I had sewed the edges up with wire had been chewed through in three places and through that hole, barely four inches in diameter, she had forced her way, leaving some fur. Although Moobli tracked her for a while, her scent petered out on a wet rock face north-west of the wood, and he lost interest and started playing with sticks.

I felt sad I would probably never see her again for with her shy spirit she was not likely to come back again after that experience. Yet I felt an enormous relief. She was alive and in superb condition and as she had always been the wilder one, it was right she should stay free. My disappointment was really based on pure possessiveness. Oddly, however, it seemed right to keep Freddy about for he at least seemed to *choose* some contact with our isolated little civilization, and to be still around his mother.

But I felt sad as I thought of the cat carcass down the loch again. It seemed it just had to be the remains of poor Patra. Yet it hadn't seemed large enough, though of course a live angry cat looks much bigger than the same animal dead. Could it have been the carcass of another cat altogether? This was, after all, the country of the wildcat.

I had never found any evidence of wildcats in the long wood to the west but I decided to go there and make a long search. On the way I checked the droppings in the west wood again. They seemed too large to have been made by Mia. Reaching the long wood a mile to the west, we searched in ever increasing spirals outwards from the carcass. Within an hour we had found wild-cat droppings on a grassy patch between the browning bracken. They were as large as those in the west wood.

Surely, they were Sylvesturr's. It seemed likely, hating man as he did, that he had now made his home in this long wood, yet was returning occasionally to his old home for the meat I put out. When I checked my diaries I found that meat, plus the last meat in the trap when the bait line had been chewed through—before it caught Mia—had been taken every seven days. It was possible he was traversing over a mile of loch shore territory each week, the largest section of it open, boggy, tussocky ground. If only I could now trap him, know for sure he was really still alive. But there were plenty of voles about, and mice too, judging by the many woodmouse "dining" areas filled with holed hazel nuts below sheltering roots in the woods.

Seeing the hazel nuts eaten by the mice reminded me that I had not yet gathered my own winter supply, but next morning as I collected them from under the east wood bushes, Moobli suddenly began to bark and ran off.

Some men with guns had landed in a boat below the west wood and were now walking through it to stalk the stags on the hills. Red deer need to be culled, especially after mild winters and as more and more land is fenced off against them for man's purposes, they overgraze their dwindling ranges. My feelings, and findings, about this and about those who only come to the Highlands for a brief period once a year for the sole purpose of killing, and related matters, don't belong here. But my main fear was for my experiments with the cats if the stalkers were to make this a regular occurrence. Wildcats are not protected in law; many folk still regard them as vermin, and I didn't want Syl, Mia, Freddy or Cleo to be the recipient of a rifle bullet should they, by some mischance, show themselves. But the stag stalkers proved to be courteous men, listened to my explanations, assured me they would not shoot any wildcat and indeed were kind enough not to bother us again.

Autumn now came to Wildernesse. The leaves of the ashes, following the earlier alders, were turning yellow and falling, the bat colony in my roof were flying every dusk, feeding on the last flying insects to put on fat for their winter hibernation, and on October 11 the first heavy winds came, scattering the nuts, rowan berries and tree seeds. A large flock of redwings who had worked their way across country after landing on the east coast during their winter migration from the continent, moved in. Fast, powerful fliers for such small birds, the woods were full of their little *quip quips* as they thronged the rowans. In three days they had taken every single berry, then off they flew westwards for the farmland pickings. The big green, blue and black Aeshna dragonflies that had hawked their beats for insects all summer were now weakening, their wings clattering audibly as they flew, and they roosted lower than usual on the trunks of trees, leeward from the stronger winds. At night now the woods were filled with eerie hootings as the tawny owls re-established their territories and the year's young looked for their own areas. And as the air grew colder red deer hinds came down from the hills to shelter in the warmer glades.

Cleo and Freddy were both happy in the pens and if I let them go for a day or two, they always returned to them at dusk to be fed. Freddy now greeted me with *maus* and odd spits and flares when I came with the meat, reaching through the fencing to swat out at the bowl. Competing with Cleo, he soon learned that the springy sterilized meat sausage would bounce when it hit the ground after I poked it down through the roof. He watched the operation carefully, timed his run to catch the sausage in the air after the first bounce, seized it with a growl and dashed a yard or two away to eat it in the herbage. If Cleo came near he shot a paw out onto her forehead, just as she did against him when she had meat and he approached too close. But none of their claws were ever extended. And when I scattered meat in the grass, Freddy located it first by scent, then after his sight confirmed its presence, he pounced on it with a little growl.

On October 20, after a hard circuitous fifteen-mile mountain trek with Moobli in perfect sunshine and south-east gales which we used to best advantage, I took photos of no less than six stags with their hind harems. We returned tired but triumphant, just in time to see Cleo swat Freddy for trying to suckle her empty teats. She swatted him so hard he stumbled. But it was more a displacement activity on his part than a serious attempt to get milk, as if he was seeking re-assurance. And I noticed when he tried to stalk her twitching black tail tip now, she shot a paw out at him. Once she even did it when he was only staring at her tail as if about to pounce.

That week the winds switched south then south-west, bringing heavy rain, and the hills began to look wintry, not green or even green and brown any more with the dying bracken, but an increasingly uniform grey. The rain pelted on the roof, along with leaves and small twigs, the gales moaned about the eaves and with lighting-up time now before 6 p.m., the hissing of my paraffin lamp vied with the foaming and crashing of the waves on the loch. Winter was coming and it was time to plant new trees.

On October 24 we fought our way up the loch and drove 320 miles to a forestry nursery at Fochabers near the east coast to fetch 150 young spruce, sweet chestnut, Canadian hemlock, Douglas fir and oak. These, with the trees already there, would help make my woods as balanced and varied a wildlife habitat as possible, for it is the well-balanced woods, with a variety of many broadleaf trees among the conifers, that are the best for birds and animals. On the way I called Patra at the green island but in the winds there was again no response.

When I cruised the west wood next day for the best sites for my new trees, I found two huge wildcat scats and one large footprint I was sure could only be Syl's. I hauled the trap from where I had been setting it without success by his release point, determined to try once more before winter. And I set it near the print which was on a tiny patch of mud in what seemed to be a new animal trail, using bloody, strong-smelling raw venison from a dead deer calf we had found near the burn in the east wood. Around the trap I scattered a few pieces of meat sausage.

On our next trip up the loch, when I received still more queries on my book that needed swift answers, I called again for Patra but the wind was strong and although I fancied I heard a faint *mau* she did not emerge. It was probably my wishful imagination. On the way back I checked the cat remains—just a skeleton now. I decided to let it rot even further then pick it up and try to re-assemble it so Patra's demise would at least allow me to examine wildcat bone structure.

Checking the trap that evening, I found it unsprung but all the sausage pieces outside it had gone. Well, mice or shrews perhaps could have eaten them, possibly Mia, though I doubted she would return. I threw more loose meat inside the trap, feeling I was probably wasting my time, and went indoors.

All next day, most of the night and the following morning despite sunny weather, I chained myself to my desk determined to finally beat the book. I went out at noon, walked moodily round the garden with Moobli, then remembered I hadn't checked the trap. I climbed onto some rocks on the edge of the west wood and looked over. The trapdoor was down, but that didn't mean much as gusty winds overnight could have blown it loose from the trip nail. I crossed the small burn, the two fallen pine trunks and over the marshy land, treading on the criss-crossed logs that were embedded in the moss-covered ooze, and over two more windfalls.

As I peered round the side of the box part, there was a loud *PAAAH!* It was like a small bomb going off, with debris flying in all directions. *Sylvesturr was there!* The sudden unexpected blast of his spit and the noise of his big foot thumping on the wood seemed enough to nearly throw me backwards. I felt as if I were in a dream. Driving the whining Moobli back and away, I turned round again, heart beating like a trip hammer. The ferocious old devil was caged there at last, braced up on his two powerful front legs, his head touching the top of the two foot, four-inch-high netting.

PAAAH! again and a sideways whack this time, his huge horn-coloured claws sticking through the mesh as he held his foot there. He held his ground, not retreating into the wooden box part but glaring up at me, and as it was when I had first seen him in the Zoo, I seemed to see flames springing behind his eyes, matching the tears of joy that had sprung into mine. Hell, was I glad to see the lovely proud old fool, the big tough old warrior whose unchanging character and cussed independence had made him resist for over ten years the attempts of a succession of human experts to tame him, to have him show just one moment of gratitude, or even compromise which characterizes most of our human lives. But no, it wasn't in him. He was now, even now, after fifty-two days of freedom in this harsh wild landscape as wild, tough and resolute as the day he had been found and taken from this land.

He was a truly terrifying sight, but I knew his way now, knew his memory. "Sylvesturr," I said slowly and softly, bending down to take a closer look. To my surprise he didn't spit again but flared and hissed, looked sideways with that terrible, slow series of glares, his eyes switching from object to object, then walked slowly, growling, into the wooden box. Had he been there all night? In the late setting sun's light he looked vast, his tail wet and wrapped just under his white lipped face. He did not rage about as I expected him to, like Mia had, but now crouched low, and the box was splashed with the raw meat as he must have turned to run after grabbing, only to meet the fallen trapdoor. He crouched down shifting slightly from foot to foot as if he would make one powerful leap if he saw the glimmer of a chance. Then, for a few moments, he cast his eyes down at the ground as if I was no longer there, and a sad look of defeat, of self-disgust at having been caught again, at the realization this was again the end of his late-earned freedom, came over his long-whiskered old face. Written there again was all the gloom, the despair that ten years of solitary confinement, of endless prison days, that had been the principal cast of his countenance when I had first had him and seen in him during unobserved moments of repose. It was heart-rending.

I checked the netting was secure, ripped the trip nail from its nylon line and shoved it through the staples so the trapdoor could not be opened from inside, and I went back to the cottage to think.

He was in first-class condition, his fur thicker than I had ever seen it, fat and solidly healthy. To imprison him again would not be a victory but total defeat. This cat had proved he could make it on his own and though he was now old, if he only lived one more year in the wild it was better than five in jail. He had well earned the right to be in his natural element, to take whatever this Scottish wilderness, his heritage, could now give him. I put on the sweaters, double trousers and thick gloves in case he attacked, then with a square of heavy fish netting held before me, went back and removed the nail and lifted the door right out of its runners.

There was a pause as he looked, then Syl came straight out,

leaped to the top of a rocky mossy ridge in three bounds, stopped, turned back briefly as if for one last glance, then disappeared into a thicket. There was no attack, no need for the netting. I whispered a soft "Goodbye, old fellow," then sat down on the box for a minute or two to collect myself. Then I carried the trap back to the house. There would be no need to use it again. Sylvesturr and Mia, after I had long thought them both dead, were alive and free. The rest was up to them. Only Patra, it seemed, had lost out, and it was no-one's fault but mine.

Chapter 14

In early November as the first skeins of white-front geese began to fly in from the Arctic to winter among the small flocks of greylags on the rare four miles of mossy marsh and meadow land at the far end of the loch, I planted my new trees in the more open spaces of both woods. Although I had fenced the front and rear of my land and had intended to fence the woods too so deer could not destroy tree seedlings, I now realized to do this would make me guilty of what I am against in land use. Deer were originally woodland animals but with more and more land fenced off for intensive forestry, farm stock and agriculture, they have been driven out onto the bare hills—still oddly referred to as "deer forests."

There is often high winter mortality on these rough open grazings. Few estates feed their red deer in winter, the view being, apart from cost, that artificial feeding creates artificial herds who could not survive on the actual land. But there must be a difference between a little beneficial supplementary feeding in the worst periods and the creation of artificial herds. Even fewer estates plant forests for the deer, being more interested in merely culling populations for the revenue from the venison, hides, tusks and antlers. Many deer used my woods for refuge in winter, as they had for centuries, and I felt it wrong to deny them this shelter. Instead I built protective wire netting cages round my trees and some of the natural seedlings, so they could grow yet the deer could still use the woods.

As I worked each day until near dark, I heard the tawny owls calling *k-whick* while from further away others answered with their mournful *hoo-oo-oo-oos* and I wondered if they were seeing old Syl or even Mia prowling below. Some meat I'd put down had disappeared overnight six days after I let him go.

Once the tree work was finished, I picked the last of the blackberries which ripened during a four-day sunny spell, brined vegetables, cut the last winter firewood, went on two more stag treks, then on November 14 decided to have one last try to find Patra.

It was a dull, misty but totally windless day and I landed the boat gently, stern first, on the grassy shore, then walked up the hill between the gravestones giving the usual feed calls. Hearing nothing, I had just turned to come back when I heard an answering *mau*, very faint. I stood still, kept calling and slowly the sounds came nearer. Suddenly, out from the thick azalea bushes stepped—Patra. She looked the same as she had before, not bigger but plump and well fed. She began walking to and fro but not actually coming to me. I went to the boat, ripped open a meat sausage and gently threw her a small piece. Very gingerly, looking all about her, she came down, took it and ran into the undergrowth. Again I stayed still and as she watched, dropped a piece near my feet. Out she came again, *mauing* and walking up and down looking at the meat, then as she finally came close I picked her up with the gloves, expecting an explosion. But she neither spat nor struggled, as if she was glad to see us both, for Moobli was staring with intense interest from the boat where I had told him to stay.

I put her loose into the boat but as soon as the engine started up and we were eight yards off shore, she ran round the boat, leaped over the stern with all four feet splayed out, swam the last six yards to the beach, shook herself and ran into the bushes. Whether she jumped off because she was scared of the boat or now really liked the island, I wasn't sure, but it was wonderful to know she was still alive after all. The carcass, then, was that of another cat entirely but I suspected not a domestic one, for my nearest neighbours, six and a half miles away, had told me they had not lost a cat.

I picked up the skeleton on the way home and though I have it to this day, I never did solve its mystery.

Five days later I went up the loch again and one of the local tradesmen told me he had been on a grave party on the island when they'd heard odd mewing noises, and one of them had glimpsed a large grey-brown cat in the bushes. To me Patra, apart from earning her own keep, had been performing a useful community service, and it would not have bothered me to know a wildcat was hunting a living round my own or a relative's grave space, but I realized others might not share this view. I'd intended to fetch Patra back before winter, so on the way home I stopped at the island and called loudly again in a light drizzle. It was almost as if she had heard the familiar engine coming and had waited for me, for she materialized out of the bushes almost immediately, *mauing* away, and came down for the meat in my hand.

I caught her easily with the gloves but now I held her on the seat next to me until the boat was well off shore and this time she stayed. She walked all round *mauing* noisily, the semi-cabin acting like an echo chamber, then stood on the centre seat next to me as I controlled the wheel, put her front paws on the little roof, and peered all about her like an otter. She was still playing the clown. I caught her before the boat landed and leaving it to bump up and down in the light waves, ran up the path and put her in the pens with the others. After hauling up the boat and carrying up the supplies, I went to feed them.

Cleo and Patra were having a fine reunion, walking round each other and banging their heads together like a pair of rams. Freddy seemed quite left out of things but as I pushed meat through the roof, I found he'd learned a new trick. Hungry, he stood on his hind legs as Patra often did, then when the meat got momentarily stuck in the mesh, he leaped up from that position, without putting his front feet down first, just like a kangaroo, clung to the wire, grabbed the meat in his jaws, then dropped down with it. A full five-foot leap from the standing position, just from his back feet alone, seemed nothing at all to him.

Next day when Freddy walked towards Patra, his old hunting teacher, to bang his head against her in friendship, Patra growled and clouted him with both paws. He went to Cleo, who did the same. At feed time, though, Freddy was the quickest and most powerful and he even drove Patra off food, more by his heedless rush at the meat than an actual attack. Cleo was usually the first at the milk but after the first few laps she would allow Freddy to thrust his head in beside hers—but Patra stayed well away until both had finished.

On fine days now I let them all run free as they came back to the pens at dusk for food. I also set meat out in the old trap spot in the west wood, noting it still vanished every six or seven days. As this regular date came up, I shut the three in the pens until the meat had gone, and occasional large droppings showed Syl was almost certainly the taker.

But on their free days the other cats ranged widely. As usual, they were far more wary in the open than behind the pen fencing, and even Patra no longer allowed herself to be picked up as she had on the green island. Cleo and Freddy had long ago learned not to raid the bird table, having fled after being greeted by a violently thrust open window, clapped hands and a spit louder than Syl's! But Patra, more persistent, was soon back to this old trick. Luckily the birds came to the food I set out mainly in the worst weather—when the cats were in the pens.

There were moments of comedy. Once Patra and Cleo were drinking from the milk bowl when Freddy, who had already had his turn, heard their lapping noises and decided he'd swig a bit more. He marched in, gave Patra a swift sideways butt with his big head, knocking her right off balance, and started drinking. But when he tried this with Cleo, she still gave him a thump, just to let him know who was the real boss.

On their free days, Patra started raiding the house for extra food, whenever I was closeted writing in my study, for unless gales were blowing I usually left a door open for Moobli to go in and out. I'd go into the kitchen, find her on the sink where I kept their nightly sausage which I mixed with other meat, and she'd snarl defiantly until clapped hands and human growls drove her out again. Patra, it was now obvious, lived only for her stomach, would eat twice as much as the other cats until her gut was like a balloon.

By the end of November the first snow blizzards arrived and suddenly the mountains took on the look of vast icy cakes topped with white sugar, an impression that was soon dispelled on photo treks when at 1,600 feet one had to shelter from solid walls of snow that swept in from the north-west. The Highland mountains can be savage in winter, soon reducing a man to size, but Moobli loved snow, gulping down great mouthfuls when he was thirsty, and as we neared home again, with no more need for caution, he'd charge around like a runaway horse, his great half-webbed feet going plap, plap, plap as he made his terrifying mock charges, leaving massive footprints that were five inches across. Many was the time I was glad Moobli was so placid by nature for in a confrontation it would have been like fighting off a tiger. I noticed when he was climbing up rocks, small chimneys and gullies his huge claws were partly extendable and he could hook them into crevices like a cat. And his molars were more than an inch across the base. When we found newly dead deer, I would often take their haunches and shoulders to help his and the wildcats' diet, and Moobli cracked the big thigh bones with just one bite to get at the marrows, with a sound as loud as pistol shots in the kitchen.

It was on December 4 that violence first occurred among the cats. At feeding time, Freddy suddenly seized Patra by the side of the throat and dragged her away screeching after both had gone for the same piece of meat. He left her a yard away and went back for it. I thought I'd separate them but it seemed a one-time occurrence with no harm done to Patra, for she soon went to another piece. But it was not a nice way to treat one's aunt. Next day all were amicable again but both Cleo and Patra began to give their burly six-months-old son and nephew a wide berth in the scramble at feed time. Just in case Freddy was turning nasty, or it was the natural time he should leave his mother, I now let the cats run free some nights too.

But when Freddy stayed away for two nights and three days I

became worried. I was sure Cleo and Patra were safe from Syl, but it was likely the two toms would fight and I wanted neither of them hurt. At dusk on the third day, after feeding the girls in the pens, I set a steaming pan of meat right on the bird table, after all the birds had gone to roost, so its smell would waft round the estate. Within a quarter hour as I watched from the study, I saw Freddy emerge like a grey ghost from the direction of the west wood. He had scented the meat from over 250 yards away. He crept up to the bird table, head raised, sniffing away, stood on his hind legs, and was about to perform his kangaroo leap but was forestalled when I went out to put the meat into the pens. He was very hungry and for once stood his ground like Sylvesturr and flared and made passing swipes at my shooing hands as I walked along. But when I put the meat into the small pen he shot inside and I didn't open the door again until he had eaten his fill.

Generally, the new system of alternate freedom and being in the pens seemed to be working splendidly. Some nights, however, I was woken up by the cats *awrooring* around the cottage in the dark early hours, and once by greedy Patra delving into my waste sack in the porch and hauling out the tins.

One afternoon I was greeted on my return from a supply trip by all three wildcats running down close to the path but while Freddy approached with the others, he flared, ran away a few steps, ran back, spat with ferocious expression, then ran off again. He clearly wanted food but not the company! He began to spend more time alone in the woods while on wet days Cleo and Patra holed up in the woodshed, back on their old logpile bed. One morning I watched Patra sneak along past dozing Moobli. He scented her, got up, but she made a quick feint to the left, put him off balance and swerved around the porch. When I went into the kitchen she had the open butterpack on the floor. She was becoming a nuisance, and she knew now she was not welcome in the house as she always stole things.

By late December a pair of eagles were cruising regularly in the area, after the grallochs (gut contents) left on the hills by the hind stalkers. They often flew tantalizingly close before heading off to the big mountain across the loch again—exciting but only good for silhouette photos. I had little fear for my wildcats, for eagles won't fly in woods where they would get their huge long wings damaged.

Christmas Day that year was spent as usual, half-hearted and short-lived whisky sipping while pounding out philosophical reflections. I shared a small turkey with Moobli, and Cleo and Patra seemed hardly able to believe the goodies that came their way that day but at first Freddy spurned turkey—until he tasted it.

On the afternoon of New Year's Eve, I left food for the wildcats in the woodshed and went off into the woods to spend two nights out in the open—cooking suppers on campfires and sleeping in the fresh air—a yearly habit of spiritual renewal close to nature among the trees that I had acquired and adapted from an old Indian in Canada.

When I returned on the afternoon of January 2, the other two cats were still around the woodshed but there was no sign of Patra, nor did she appear over the next few days. This was odd as she had always been the most fearless of the wildcats. I wondered if Freddy had driven her away.

Snow began falling in a cold north wind on January 23 and a small herd of hinds with a young six-pointer stag, which was unusual, were grazing in the front pasture in the early morning. After stalking and photographing them in a brief sunny spell as they moved to the lower ridges to the north-west, Moobli and I came back through the west wood. He immediately picked up a strong cat scent and within minutes led me to a sheltered mud patch where there were two large four-toed prints and nearby a huge double wildcat dropping—almost certainly Sylvesturr's. Excited that he was still about, I put some meat down that evening and fed Cleo and Freddy a large meal, hoping that would stop them venturing into the west wood, though missing Patra could find it if she was in the area.

More snow fell overnight, covering the ground with a four-inch white blanket. Determined to try and find out more about the cats' nightly movements, we went tracking again. Cleo and Freddy, whose prints were slightly the larger, had foraged all round the house, along the north hill almost to the west wood,

doubled back to the rhododendron bush by the path, down to
the loch shore, then along the front fence and its bracken tangles
to the east wood. There, with the snow only lying in brief
patches, it was impossible to track further on the wet ground,
but we found Cleo's prints going in an almost straight line, like a
fox, across the fallen larch that bridged the main burn. Before
that Freddy had clearly diverged to hunt alone. By morning
though, both cats were back in the woodshed where they stayed
all day.

When we went to the west wood all the meat had disappeared
but the two cats had not taken it for there were no prints in the
snow-filled open area near the south-east corner of the wood.
Nor could Moobli find any scent. We zig-zagged up and down
westwards and there in an open patch amid the big tussocks on
the wood's far edge were Syl's tracks in the snow. But they were
heading out of the wood and try as we could, we could not find
any tracks leading in. He had probably come in higher up where
the trees were thicker and he had found it easy to avoid the
snow patches. My theory that he was now quartered in the long
wood a mile to the west was probably right.

We went out again in the afternoon and walked a good half a
mile into the long wood, and found Syl's fresh tracks in snow
that covered the tops of some large fallen trunks. They were firm
and his strides were well apart so I felt sure he was still in good
health. But the snow was again too patchy and the ground too
wet to track him either by sight or Moobli's scent to any den.

During the next few weeks, by timing the disappearance of
meat, finding his tracks and scats, I established that Syl was indeed patrolling a distance of at least one-and-a-half miles and he
was reaching the west wood roughly once in every seven nights.
It was interesting that he would cover the boggy terrain which,
apart from a few rocks, heather patches, tussocks, small rowan,
birch and holly trees, plus leafless bog myrtle bushes, was almost
totally open. He clearly didn't live in just one den and operate
from there but lived, on his wanderings about his territory, in
various day dens from which he hunted by night. We found one
a few days later. Walking along the shore, Moobli put his nose to
a trail of flattened yellow tussock grasses and stopped behind

some rocks about two hundred yards south-west of the west wood. Three slabs formed a small natural chamber from the edge of which grew a stout dwarf birch tree. And beneath was a perfect dry oval bowl of mosses and grasses, just like Syl had often made from the hay in his den in the pens.

By now Freddy had become shyer and refused to come at dusk to my food calls at the woodshed. But he certainly heard them, for after I'd gone into the workshop to watch, he would emerge from the corridor between the cottage and shed walls, then go in to join Cleo and feed. One late afternoon, I banged the dishes together and called as usual, then waited in the trees east of the shed. I saw him emerge from the west wood, sneak along a low natural ditch despite small pools of water in it, then leap into the rocks of an old ruined wall where he waited until he could see I had gone, his eyes peeping through a hole between the rocks. Obviously, this is what he did every day. Once he was in the shed I took Moobli over to exactly where I had seen him running along. But Moobli could find no scent and I remembered how the cougars in Canada, when tracked by the hounds, often ran over wet swampy ground because the water de-scented their feet. The hounds wasted minutes on the other side trying to pick up the scent from the dried feet again—by which time the cougar was much further away. This was probably why Moobli could so rarely track Sylvesturr and it was an interesting comparison that wildcats could obscure their scent in the same way.

When Patra had not returned after two weeks, I became worried. I wanted her to go free but I also wanted to know she had not met with a tragic accident. After finding smaller tracks in the snow near her old east wood den, I set the trap for her there. Next morning, however, Freddy was in it, raging about and hurling himself at the netting just as Mia had done. He was covering a lot of ground at night now. To keep them out of the way while I tried to catch Patra, I carried Freddy into the pens and later enticed Cleo in with food too. But for two days the trap remained unsprung.

In late January, we were coming back from a supply trip in the boat when Moobli suddenly became agitated, sniffing, looking at the shore. I thought he just wanted to go for his normal run which because it was raining heavily I had decided to make shorter that day. As soon as I let him onto the shore, he was greeted by a wildcat coming out of the dead bracken. It was Patra—a full two-and-a-half miles from home. Moobli stood there, as huge as a small donkey, big soppy smiling ha'porth, while she walked all round him, but she immediately fled when I stepped ashore. I managed to entice her back with meat and the usual calls and put her into the boat. She was certainly glad to see us and what a noise she put up, walking round and round inside the semi-cabin which rang with her loud cries of *mau* as we took her home again. When I put her into the pens the other two appeared to accept her but there was no friendly head-banging reunion between her and Cleo this time. And on the following nights Cleo and Freddy slept together in the main den while Patra seemed banished to the small den box in the smaller pen. Now he was back in the pens, Freddy, who had become furtive and extremely shy in the open and fierce if cornered, was quite tame again and walked about quite happily with the other cats.

One gloriously sunny day in early February, I let them all free again for a run in the wilds. At dusk Cleo came home with a vole and took it into the pens to eat—crunching its head first, biting with her side carnassial teeth to crack its skull, then rending the softer parts with her front teeth. As she ate, as usual scraping the green part of the gut aside, Patra came into the pens but Cleo growled, not letting her near until she had finished the vole. I fed them both but just as they finished, Freddy turned up in the near dark. I put in some more meat and shut down the pen door behind him as he chewed hungrily. His voluntary return to the pens while I was still there, in the open, was exceptional. Then I had a sudden thought—had he been scared away from the wood by Sylvesturr? I quickly went down and put some meat in the usual spot.

Next morning, not only had the meat gone but the fresh remains of a woodpigeon had been moved eight yards where strewn feathers showed it had been killed, to below a tangle of bracken and honeysuckle. And a few yards further away was one of Syl's huge, tapered, twisted scats, bigger than anything

Freddy ever released in the pens. I looked at my diaries—it was eight days since he had taken the last meat. I supposed a day or two either way was not important, for his visits would depend on the success of his other hunting. I felt sure a fox had not taken the meat for there was a high deer mortality that year and on treks we were finding plenty of natural carrion in the woods and hills. So much so that several eagles, who usually migrate eastwards to the mountain hare moors, were wintering in the area, and I had hauled several carcasses out of the woods into the open hills for them.

Through much of February as I studied the birds now able to eat without risk on the table, Cleo and Freddy shared both pens at will yet Patra stayed mostly in the small pen. Freddy pleased himself about dens, sometimes sleeping with Cleo or alone in the small den box. Occasionally I saw Patra about to enter the latter, pause outside and peer into it as if to make sure he wasn't inside. But at feeding time all three cats milled around together, with only Patra intelligent enough to reach into the meat bowl as I was washing out their dishes, hook out a handful and transfer her full bent claws to her mouth. On two occasions I saw Patra bang her paw down against Cleo over food, only to be promptly clouted with hard clawless swats by Freddy. And once, when she started into the den box while he was having a quiet siesta, he spat at her in a way his courteous old father would never have done.

February 16 was dull and windless so I again let the wildcats out for a day off. The west wood meat had not gone at the usual seven day interval and I felt Syl might have graduated to eating fresh wild deer carrion, which would mean not only was he almost completely weaned naturally to the wild in winter, the hardest time, but the chances of a confrontation with Freddy were now far less. On each of the next three nights both Cleo and Patra returned to the pens at dusk to my feed calls and ate and drank their fill, but not Freddy. Worried by this new absence, I set the trap for him on the second night and also put a dish full of food on *top* of the pens. Next morning the trap meat was untouched but the food in the dish had all gone—only a cat could have taken it and I felt sure it was neither Syl nor Mia who, I felt certain, had long since left the area.

Next day the trap was sprung but the meat was still there. Had Freddy worked out that he wouldn't get caught if he sprung the mouse trap trigger device on top first? If so he still hadn't reached the meat because the door had fallen. At about 2 P.M. Moobli disappeared. I whistled. Out he came from the west wood and ran back whining. He had cornered Freddy in the rocky cairn below the escarpment. As his growls and spits came from between the rocks, Freddy sounded almost as fierce as his father. One hour after feed time, when only Patra had turned up to the pens, I went out with more food, when up came Cleo and some way behind her—Freddy! I kept very still then in went Cleo and Freddy followed. I shut down the swing door. They were all back inside again and Freddy seemed in fine condition.

On February 26 I noticed the cats had begun to behave oddly. Patra and Freddy had a brief fight, making loud *rowwl* noises at each other, then Patra flew into the small den box. Later Cleo also attacked Patra and now the claws were out and some fur flew. I felt the wildcat oestrus period was due and the sisterly bond was drawing to a close. It appeared rather inappropriate that they should start fighting on the day the first daffodils came out, heralding the approach of spring. But at the dusk feed they seemed all amicable again.

It did not last. On the next two mornings I came out to find Freddy had kicked the heavy main den door outwards, just as Syl had done last spring, and on March 2 I saw Cleo launch a fierce attack on Patra, driving her into the den box where she crouched growling. Moments later after Cleo had returned to the main pen, Patra poked her head out of the box, then Freddy went in to attack her, whirling claws from his burly body in a fighting style reminiscent of the late Rocky Marciano. Patra fought back, grabbed his head with both sets of claws at one point and tried to bite but he was too strong and drove her back into the box.

A few hours later I saw both Cleo and Patra apparently sitting amicably a yard apart in the small pen, where Patra was now *piling* her droppings, not burying them like Cleo and Freddy were theirs. Suddenly Cleo glared at Patra, set her ears down, crouched, then pounced—poor Patra fled again into the box. In late afternoon when I went out for another look, all three came milling to the front fencing and I thought all was well again. But as soon as Freddy realized I was carrying no food, he looked at Patra's expectant face and again assaulted her, driving her once more into the den box.

Were they attacking her because she was dirty with her droppings, fouling up the pens? Or because Cleo was in oestrus? Apart from the two attacks on Patra, she was certainly very playful all day, attacking emerging daffodils, and she seemed skittish with her son who was looking more and more like Syl with every passing day. Once I saw him lying down supine and allowing Cleo to bite closer and closer into his throat, while his eyes remained sleepily half-closed, as if in ecstasy. Was it possible Cleo would mate with her own son? I didn't want that. I wanted her to mate with Syl again and for any chance of that I would have to release her and hope the two would find each other again. But that would mean keeping Freddy safely in the pens for a while longer.

The immediate problem however was Patra. Clearly, amicable sisterhood was now completely at an end, though it had lasted twenty-one months. After the attacks, Patra again assumed the frowsty, spinsterish look she had worn after the birth of Cleo's kits, as if she knew she no longer fitted in. It seemed likely that the reason we had found her two-and-a-half miles down the loch five weeks earlier was because the other two had driven her away.

Now the days were lengthening and small animals were emerging more and more as the occasional sunny spells stirred plants into new life. It would soon be time to release all the cats. I felt Patra should go first.

I carried her den box from the pens and took her in the boat to some thick woodland three miles away where there were many mice and voles. On the way we picked up a fresh deer calf carcass and before releasing her I axed it open on the shoulders and haunches so she could get the meat easily. I felt sad as she went up the beach in short trotting bursts from bush to bush, *mauing* loudly, but she had long since proved herself able to earn her own living.

She was back in thirty hours, on the sacking bed in the woodshed. I softened when I saw her crouching there and fed her. Wondering if the earlier attacks had perhaps been a temporary aberration, I put her back in the pens. Within an hour Cleo attacked her. She fought back but only half-heartedly, as if she knew Cleo was right. A few minutes later Freddy chased her into the den box. It was no good and I was sure they would probably kill her between them, so out she came.

Patra now began behaving atrociously, like a spirited child that feels itself unwanted. She leaped onto the bird table every afternoon, intent upon avian annihilation, despite eating and drinking as much as the other two cats put together. She had become a compulsive eater, her stomach constantly distended, as if psychologically trying to make up for being the odd cat out. She raided the kitchen at every opportunity, once knocking over some bottles and smashing one on the concrete floor, and on March 10 she left her scats right on Moobli's bed.

Finally, after hearing from a local gamekeeper that a female wildcat had been accidentally caught in a fox snare in a riverside wood nine miles away, I took her there by boat and Land Rover. Foolish though it may sound, I found myself talking to her before the moment of final release, trying to explain that the time had come to let her go, that she would fill a niche left by another wildcat, that a young tom was known to be in the area!

She ran a few steps, looked back, gave a last *mau* and disappeared into the green curtains of foliage. There were many rabbits in the riverside fields and I felt sure she would make out all right. But as we drove away again, Moobli whined and stood looking sadly out of the rear window. I knew how he was feeling for I felt the same but it was in her best interests. She would not meet a mate in my area, for Syl would not breed with her. And to have five wildcats running loose in my territory would certainly have meant the ultimate death of the least efficient. It would also have caused a major upset to the overall balance of nature that I was trying to enhance.

Chapter 15

Now Patra had gone, Cleo and Freddy seemed far more relaxed and happy in the pens. On March 13 I noticed Cleo had undergone a spectacular colour change. The inside of the rear parts of her thighs had taken on a new brighter orangey hue mixed in with the normal rufous and the thicker hair made the backs of her legs seem smoothly rounded. The under side of her tail, which she now held upwards more often, was also much ruddier. I was sure it was a seasonal phenomenon to make her more attractive to the male. She was extremely active, rubbing herself over the daffodils, rocks and undergrowth. I checked the diaries —it was today, exactly one year ago, that Cleo had taken refuge in his den with Sylvesturr, when I had been trying to put all the wildcats into the woodshed.

It seemed certain she was now in or rapidly approaching oestrus, so I checked my diaries. If the sixty-three days gestation (the most quoted figure) for wildcats was correct, Cleo would have mated with Syl on March 23. If the sixty-three to sixty-nine days gestation theory, confirmed by Berne Zoo, Switzerland, where copulation had been observed, was correct, Cleo could have mated with Syl as early as March 17. All these dates fell into the week when all the wildcats were housed in the woodshed, with the females having access to Syl, during the days Moobli and I were safely away on the research trip.

If there was any chance of Cleo mating with Syl again I had to let her free right now. After a gap of three weeks, the meat had now begun to disappear from the west wood again, so in the hope she and Syl would have a romantic rendezvous there, I let her and Freddy out of the pens.

My only real guide to managing the wildcats had been my experience in Canada with cougars—apart from the conflicting references to the animals in nature books. I often smiled when I recalled how at the end of those cougar chasing days on Vancouver Island I had sworn never again to have anything to do with wild felines. I knew that the mountain lions often run with their cubs until the following year but when the mother comes into oestrus in the spring (cougars can reach oestrus almost any time of year but usually mate in spring so they can hunt, feed and rear their cubs more easily in the summer months) the incoming male often drives the cubs away. They are then totally on their own for the first time. I felt this would not be a bad thing to happen to Freddy. And Cleo, feeling the urge to mate, would then feel it was right to let Freddy go. Although I had been introducing Freddy slowly to the wild, with brief periods of freedom alone, he would never starve for he had proved he would come back for food when hungry. He, unlike Mia, had chosen to stay around the cottage area.

Next day, after a trek in which first my hat, then my pack and thirdly nearly myself had been blown off a high ridge by sudden easterly gusts, we returned to find Freddy denned up alone in the rocky cairn in the west wood. But Cleo came back to the pens for food at dusk. I shut her in and put food on the roof mesh in the hope Freddy would come for it there as he had before. One hour after darkness it had gone, and I let Cleo go again.

Next evening the roof meat vanished within ten minutes and I just caught a glimpse of Freddy trotting back to the north end of the west wood. He was using the ditch and various damp gullies on a circuitous route, and when I set Moobli to track him he could only do so for a few yards. I was now certain that wildcats, like cougars, could deliberately obscure their scent in this way. It could also explain why wildcats are almost never tracked to their lairs by dogs. Cleo spent the day in the woodshed but was away all night.

On March 16, Freddy again took the meat from the top of the pens shortly after dusk. But in the early hours I was woken up by an awful yowling noise, a sound that gave a real meaning to the word "caterwaul." Then I heard Moobli scratching at the kitchen door. I shot out of bed but could see nothing in the darkness. I had read that male wildcats will call noisily during the breeding season, also that females will screech when wanting to mate. This was certainly no fox bark. Thrilled by the thought that Sylvesturr had perhaps come back or that Cleo was looking for him, I refrained from investigating the noise. Half an hour later, as I dropped off to sleep, I heard the thin metallic *awroori* sounds wildcats make to contact each other yet not give away their positions. I wondered which of them it was.

But next day Cleo was resting up in the woodshed—she had not left. Moobli and I searched the west wood but apart from Freddy in the rocky cairn den there were no signs of Syl's scats or prints at all. Then I had some new thoughts—if Freddy and Cleo were together at night and Syl now associated them totally with humanity, he might just not come back for Cleo. And if he had come back and gone to the rocky cairn den, which he had used several times, he would possibly have encountered Freddy. The young tom was now strong and fierce and although not yet Syl's size, he would have found it easy to repel Syl if the old cat had poked his head into the narrow entrance between the rocks, and the den being occupied might send Syl away again.

I decided to take Cleo *to* Syl. It was a calm sunny day, the first of real spring, and it was also the day the common gulls first came back to my small island. Primroses had started to spring up in sheltered places. Soon there would be plenty of natural prey about and as Cleo was in oestrus—I was sure she had made that awful screech, and probably from a desire to mate—she would be needing Syl and, no doubt, he her. She deserved a real chance for freedom too, while she was young. As I needed to go out for mail and supplies anyway, I put her into the large den box in which she had given birth to her kits, and on the boat trip up released her on the edge of the woods at what I judged to be the far end of Syl's territory. She immediately ran up the shore into the trees, not pausing or walking about as had Patra, and didn't even wait to see where I was putting down a meat supply. I had a slight lump in my throat as she trotted away, wending through the pines and firs without once looking back.

That evening I left a fish head with the meat on top of the pens. Both had gone within an hour and in the early hours the *awrooring* sounded round the house. Now I felt sure it was Freddy who made that noise. He was probably looking for his mother, but as he never showed himself by day any more and now made no attempt to join her in the woodshed but had chosen to make his own den in the west wood, I hoped he'd work out in his feline way that he had to lose her some time.

Cleo was back at 11 A.M. the following day! She had covered a good three miles of extremely rough country in less than twenty-four hours—a faster traveller than Patra had been. She went straight into the open pens and fell asleep in the main den. Later we found Freddy had taken last night's fish head right inside the trap which I had left propped open in the west wood in case I wanted to catch him to check his condition. He had carried it some 250 yards. This seemed odd behaviour. Had he felt safer inside the box-cage because Sylvesturr was about? Had Syl in fact followed Cleo home? I threw more sausage meat in the trap but didn't set it.

Next day Force 10 gales came hurtling over from the south, blasting heavy rain across the loch, and Freddy's nightly food had been left untouched on the pen roof. When I checked the wood after dark the meat was still in the trap but eerie *maus* followed me part of the way home. I became worried when the roof meat was again untouched next evening, and let Cleo out again in the hope she would find Freddy and bring him back.

On March 22 I returned in the dark after meeting some friends and was rowing home quietly in the calm moonlight when I noticed what looked like a new rock on a high knoll below the west wood. It was rounded and a lighter colour than the surrounding heather but suddenly it changed shape, the top

part of it moved, I saw two distinct ears, then it suddenly became smaller and melted away into the landscape. I was sure it
was Syl, for it was too large for either Cleo or Freddy, and he
had disappeared at a spot just above the den we had once found
below the stout dwarf birch, which I had thought might be one
of Syl's temporary hunting refuges. If Syl had indeed followed
Cleo and she was now out in the wood with Freddy, it seemed
certain the kit would be in the way. And if Syl caught him in the
open, not when he was merely defending the narrow rocky
cairn den mouth, he might just kill him. But if I set the trap I
might catch either Cleo or Syl instead and the resulting psycho-
logical upset would ruin any mating attempt. It was a problem.
When I reached the pens I saw the meat had gone but the sausage had been chewed where it was and pieces of both had
fallen into the pens below. I was sure Cleo, not Freddy, had
been eating them.

That night in my mail was an unexpected letter from Nobby
Clarke, who had been head keeper of small mammals at London
Zoo when I had first taken Sylvesturr away. He was now head of
the Animal Department at Edinburgh Zoo Park. He referred to
Sylvesturr, the "marvellous specimen of wildcat," and asked if I
could help provide a male wildcat, female pine marten or otters
as it seemed a shame that they, a national zoo, were short of
these particular animals.

Coming when it did, the letter seemed an unusual coincidence. I replied that I might let them have Freddy, provided I
felt he was not likely to make out here in the wilds on his own,
their accommodation was good and they had a fine natural run.
But before I made any final decision I would telephone them
first and discuss everything fully.

Next morning the pen roof meat had again been chewed
where it was, undoubtedly by Cleo who had already eaten a full
meal. She spent the day in the open pens and was as fat as a
balloon but because I wasn't sure if she was meeting Syl at
night, I didn't set the trap for Freddy.

South-west gales blew all that day but in the early hours of
March 24 I was woken by loud *maus* and *awroorings* around the
cottage and in the morning all the new pen roof meat had totally

gone. It seemed Freddy had been driven to return by sheer hunger but hating the gales, had waited for the first lull before making his move. Again Cleo chose to spend the day in the open pens, while, far above her errant son, on the topmost twigs of the larch trees, a thrush sang loudly above the wind. When we cruised the wood later, I found tawny owls had moved back into their cleft in the big silver fir and a kestrel pair, perhaps the same as last year, were prospecting among the old nests in the top end. Spring, as far as wildlife was concerned, was well under way.

Three days later, really worried about Freddy, I locked Cleo in the pens to make sure it really was him taking the roof-top meat now. It had gone within an hour of darkness. Next morning something had been in the open trap eating the remains of meat and the old fish that must have been nearly rotten. Freddy clearly had no more fear of the trap, so I hauled it to beside the pens where he was coming some nights and set it carefully.

I was out early next morning and there he was, nicely caught, but he had lost some weight after his fifteen days of freedom. He yowled with anger when he saw me approach, flared but didn't spit until I picked the trap up. Then he did, loudly, and right in my ear. He landed in the pens, then with perfect memory, just like Syl in another age it seemed now, headed straight into the den, his head snaking up and down with each stride, like a small lion. Despite the slight loss of weight, his body was broad, his legs and paws more powerful than his mother's, and his head was big and square. His eyes were huge and golden with great black centres, just like Syl's.

It was wonderful to see Cleo, who had watched the entire operation from the small pen, hurry into the main area to seek Freddy. She passed by the den door, he saw her from inside and immediately came out although I was still standing there, and began to follow Cleo among the grass and new primroses.

The sudden change in Freddy's personality was astonishing. Throughout his fifteen days of liberty he wouldn't let us even see, never mind get near him. But within an hour or two of being back in the pens with Cleo, knowing as before the wire fencing between us meant total security, he walked about a mere two yards away, glancing up at me occasionally with casual unconcern. He plodded doggedly after her, twisted his head against her body, lifted his tail, lowered it again, arched his back, flicked his tail again. Once when she was on the den box in the small pen and he was looking up at her from the log below, he made a deep trilling noise in his throat. Suddenly Cleo darted a paw onto his right ear, pushing his head down. He took it, easy-going oaf, twisted his head from under after a few seconds, then plodded after her round the pens again. My fears they might fight after the long separation were not founded. That night I put meat down in the wood in case Syl was around.

Running out of meat next day, I cut a haunch from a newly dead hind east of the burn and gave some to the cats. Both stared at the first piece, then at each other, and started growling. Then Cleo pounced on it as Freddy stayed immobile. I threw a bigger piece to him but he sniffed it carefully before just taking a few licks. It seemed odd that Freddy was keener on sausage meat and tinned cat foods than on raw venison when all the other cats loved it.

That afternoon Freddy again followed Cleo about, crashing his head against her and raising his tail, but I noticed after that first initial greeting Cleo never did this back to him. Several times he sniffed her rear parts. Cleo took this at first but the third time, when both were standing on the den box, she uttered a brief yowl and swatted him. He just lowered his head, took it without any reaction, then followed her again, his head going up and down, an oddly ponderous walk for a wildcat. But if he was trying to mate with his mother, he wasn't having much luck.

I had noticed last year, when Cleo and Patra had been with Syl during his convalescence, and later when Cleo had taken refuge in his den, there had seemed a definite overlord and underling relationship between the old tom and the young females. I felt wildcats would not mate with any but a dominant mature male. As I now thought of Syl again I went to check the new meat I'd put out in the west wood.

It had all gone. And in the mud nearby was one of his unmistakable large prints, far too big to be Mia's. That convinced me. At dusk I herded Cleo into the den box, carried her to the wood, fed her near the unset trap, left more meat nearby, and returned to feed Freddy. When Cleo came back to the pens later, as I'd thought she would, I chased her back to the wood, hard though it was to do. And I blocked off the woodshed. If she was still in oestrus, I wanted her to have every chance with Syl. I felt sure he wasn't now in the area for nothing.

At the end of March I woke to see three whooper swans cruising down the loch and a pair of buzzards circling over the cottage. A pair of great tits, as last year, again investigated the nest box on the bird table on their first search for a nest site, filling the air with their loud see-sawing song. Chaffinches were chipping away in the bushes and, on the table itself, which was right on the edge of their territories, two male robins constantly fought and chased into the woods. A greater spotted woodpecker began a loud rat-tat-tat-tat on a dry snag tree to its mate and the bluebells were now sending up their first rich leaves, like green starfish upon the earth.

Cleo stayed away for four days, not even showing herself at dusk feed times when I returned from long treks, and I began to fear we had driven her away for good. But I refrained from letting Moobli try to track her.

In the early hours of April 3 there were loud *maus* around the house and when I went out later, I found Cleo walking round and round the pens seeking a way in, while the *mauing* Freddy was trying to poke his head through the fencing. I hoped this meant she had been running with and had mated with Syl and I let her in again.

Next morning I found a large dying slow-worm outside in the open grass with a deep bite across its back to under its jaw. I wondered if Syl had attacked it and decided it was not edible. When it was dead I gave it to Cleo who, to my surprise, chewed it up with her side carnassials and ate all but the last four inches. Slow-worms, which are harmless legless lizards, could well be a wildcat food item in the wild.

For the first few days Cleo and Freddy were friendly as before, he going after his mother with low *brrrooo* trills in his throat. Once I saw both cats on the den box again and Freddy bit Cleo's cheek gently, as if in play. I felt it was probably instinctive early courting behaviour on Freddy's part but not a part of mating between mother and son, a feeling reinforced by the fact that Cleo now resented and repelled any attempt by Freddy to sniff around her rear. Then Freddy noticed me quietly sitting there. He suddenly stalked towards me growling, keeping low, ears down, looking all thin and evil about the head like his father. I felt he was about to launch an attack but he stopped two yards away and dropped his glance, then started to sniff the air. It was quite a frightening sight.

On April 10 Freddy jumped and hauled down a slightly rotting beef rib bone I had left on the iron sheet of the pen roof, and chewed it. I'd noticed a hind carcass in the west wood had been neatly chewed on several days last winter, not raked and ripped by a fox who also leaves saliva on the flesh. Now here seemed further proof that wildcats will occasionally eat carrion. It must be a food supply in harsh weather.

As the days passed now and high woolly white clouds occasionally replaced the dull lowering rain-filled layers, revealing the high blue vaults of spring, the sun beamed with greater force and the golden seven-petalled celandines vied with the nodding white wood anemones to cover the woodland floors before finally surrendering to the carpets of bluebells. The larches were sprouting their bright red female flowers, and as the light green leaves of the beeches thrust out from their buds, thousands of the light brown covering scales began falling to the ground with a noise like summer rain. Cleo and Freddy spent hours gazing at the distant woods, the trees along the loch shore, at the new hunting grounds among the emerald forests of bracken, and I noticed they were now often sitting separately.

The time had come for the last decision—to keep or free them, or let Freddy go to the Zoo.

On my next two supply trips I had telephone talks with Nobby Clarke and Roger Wheater, the Zoo's enthusiastic modern thinking director. They both wanted Freddy very much indeed, not only as an exhibit but because they had a lonely young female wildcat there, and wanted to try to breed from her. This put a whole new aspect on things, to which I had already tried to give much conscientious thought.

The wildcat project had all begun by accident, after my return from the grizzly and cougar treks in Canada, when Allan Mac-Coll had found the baby kits Cleo and Patra spitting in that lonely ditch. Even acquiring old Sylvesturr had been sheer chance—for I had initially intended to let London Zoo have Cleo and Patra. But in spite of all the problems, the lack of wildcat experience on the part of their keeper, we had all had many fine adventures, much had been learned, and Cleo and Syl had produced two superb youngsters. Now Syl was free, Mia was free, Patra was free and before long Cleo would also be at liberty. Freddy had constantly shown he was partially dependent on man by coming to the pens for food during his fifteen days at large—which Syl had never done. He was also too large and fierce when in the open to have prowling around the house and risking possible conflict with Moobli who, although well behaved towards the two females with whom he had grown up, showed little liking for the toms. To have four free wildcats in the immediate area with the nesting birds would be too many for a natural balance, and one day Freddy would undoubtedly come up against Sylvesturr. Win or lose, I wanted neither to perish or be injured. And in the Edinburgh Zoo Park, which I knew to be one of the finest in Europe, he would have a far better chance of mating than he would have in the wild.

I had often looked at Freddy and thought what a fine specimen he was, and unlike Syl, he was not so wary and shy of man when he knew there was fencing between. And to that Zoo many thousands of youngsters went every year, some of whom might become tomorrow's active conservationists. If Freddy did sire kittens, they too would be a source of inspiration to young folk, to help them in later years to work towards preserving the last of Britain's wilds. Inspired perhaps, as indeed I had been as a child, by my first sight of real live animals in a zoo.

I told Nobby Clarke I would bring Freddy down—on one condition. If he didn't settle down happily in three weeks, or the two cats didn't like each other and fought, I would take him back and, with care, release him to the wild in a good prey area.

So it was arranged. I would have reared and rehabilitated four more of these rare creatures to live in the wild, and put one into a zoo where, if happy, he would also be useful. It was not, I felt, too bad a thing to have done. As I had to go to London for business talks, research and to visit relatives, and spring was the best time to leave—thus allowing my nesting birds to settle without disturbance—I decided to head out in a few days.

On April 17 I freed Cleo from the pens and she immediately ran off to the west wood, watched by Freddy who reared up on his hind legs as he saw her go. At dusk she returned for food, *maued* briefly to her son, then ran back to the wood again.

Next evening Cleo came up from the rhododendron bush, exchanged *maus* with Freddy but did not try to go in to him. Instead she went into the woodshed where I fed her but she left again soon afterwards. I put in the usual cooked and half-cooked meats, sterilized sausages and long-life milk and water mix in a huge bowl, and making sure the exit hole was unlocked, shut the doors. Then I put meat in the west wood for Syl. Cleo now had her freedom—her future was up to her.

In the morning I managed to herd Freddy into the large den box in which he had been born, and with him and Moobli in the small boat, went up the loch and drove on down to Edinburgh to deliver him to his new home.

Nobby Clarke met me on the high back path of the Zoo, explaining that Freddy would have to go into quarantine for a few days while blood and urine tests were made, before putting him in with the young female. We turned Freddy into a large cage, between a young leopard and a cougar cub, which seemed an oddly fitting coincidence. He immediately climbed up the bars, his eyes huge and black and his big horn-coloured claws thrusting him upwards.

"He's a really magnificent specimen, a junior edition of his old dad," remarked Clarke admiringly. Then as we stared at his tawny underside, we both had the same thought. "There's nothing wrong with his wedding equipment either!"

Clarke showed me the enclosure where Freddy would live. It was superb, three times the size of my own pens, with grass, hollow logs, bushes, flowers, a long rocky den at the back, upon which a fine female wildcat, a trifle larger than Cleo or Patra, was chewing a piece of meat. It was situated in a quiet terrace which Roger Wheater and Clarke use for purely British mammals. As I had felt before, Clarke had a wonderful way with and understanding of animals. When I asked if he could actually touch the young leopard, he immediately opened its cage and cuddled it. The big half-grown cub sank its large claws into his jacket and nibbled his arm, but only in play, and let me stroke it too. If Freddy settled down well, he clearly could not have been in finer hands.

I took no money for Freddy as I didn't want to feel I was turning wildlife into a business, asked only for a small plaque with mine and his new name—Sylvesturr 2—to be put on the run. This somehow gave a touch of reality to all the isolated work with the wildcats, which now seemed already to be assuming a dreamlike quality. As I drove on down towards London, I felt rather like a father who had taken a favourite son to his first boarding school. I felt sad, too, that the exciting months with the wildcats were now over.

Chapter 16

Before leaving London for Scotland again, I telephoned Clarke at Edinburgh Zoo Park. "The cats have settled down perfectly together. Young Sylvesturr 2 is still growing, eating like a horse, and when he thinks there's no-one about is often quite playful." Relieved and happy, I made the 570-mile journey back in the laden Land Rover in one long drive.

As I hauled the boat down from its pine roots bed, the lightly falling rain, the first I had encountered since leaving, suddenly ceased, the sun shone warmly through a large blue hole in the clouds, and as a fresh south-westerly blew us home, one of the local golden eagles flew low over our heads.

In the middle of the grassy path up to the cottage, as if to show us our life with the wildcats was not yet completely over, Sylvesturr had left one of his vast tapering visiting cards. The gull colony on the small island was in full clamour—the first olive green and brown blotched eggs had been laid, while other birds disputed nest sites, and a large pale sparrowhawk, gliding cavalier of the woodland glades, floated past us, looped up into the larch branches and was lost to sight among their fuzz of light green needles.

The nesting birds were all settling down well in the woods, and although the spring foliage was not yet fully grown, the differing array of new greens was a delight to the eye. The oak leaves were as yet khaki-yellow, the rowans silver-green, the birch twigs sprayed with light green tips, while the golden clearings from last year's fall below the smooth grey trunks of the beeches were bathed in brilliant green light. Miniature emerald rain forests of bracken sprang everywhere but below the cottage —three years of sustained cutting had weakened its growth, so it could only throw up a few sparse fronds here and there. The front pasture was now lushly verdant with new grasses, soft rush and the bottle green leaves of thousands of bluebells, some of which were hanging out their first flowers, as if heralding the colour of the summer skies to come. Blue and green should never be seen, goes the old saying, but to anyone who loves the wild they are God's colours.

Early next morning as the leaf patterns danced in the sunlight upon my white walls, I looked out of the window—Cleo was stalking along just above the loch, her long striped tail hung in a low curve. She was perfectly silhouetted against the bright water, hunting through the grass as she walked below the budding crimson rhododendron flowers.

I went out quietly and *maued* to her. She stopped, looked upwards as if she could not believe her eyes, then she *maued* in return. I kept very still and she walked a few steps up the pasture towards me but then turned and walked to the west wood again. It was good to know she was all right.

Having much to do indoors, I refrained from going out with Moobli but decided to try to trap her overnight to check her condition. It was not necessary, for later we found her in the woodshed. As I went in, some two weeks' absence had not apparently made her heart grow fonder, for she hissed and flared and dived into one of the den boxes. Covering its entrance, I carried her into the pens to let her stay there for a few days of really good feeding. But within a few hours, she was her semi-tame self again, and as she·fed I noticed she was plump and heavy round the gut.

With delight I realized not only was she probably pregnant again but with over twenty square miles of roadless forested mountain wilderness behind the cottage, she had chosen to stay.

It is a lovely May day. As Cleo eats at my feet, I look out over the murmuring woods to which Sylvesturr returned to mate with his true but late-found love, and maybe now is not too far away, and I feel a great happiness. My wildcat days began by chance but I feel I have at least done a little to help stem the tide of destruction that by the early part of the century had brought these rare and beautiful creatures to the brink of extinction.

My wilderness wildcats have more than repaid their debt for whatever care I have been able to give, for I have learned far more than mere biological facts from them. In their beauty, independence and natural courage they symbolize what it takes for any living being to be truly free. Shy, proud, faithful in love, their care for their young, for which they will fight fearlessly, is extraordinary. Although relatively small in the feline world, they are not equipped for compromise like the fox. Yet their wild, free natures epitomise qualities which so much of mankind has lost. At last, thankfully, a new wind blows and we realize, through continued study, that, even to man, wildcats are more useful than otherwise. Surely now it behoves us, as the most intelligent, foreseeing species on earth, as responsible custodians of the world about us, to give complete protection to these last pure spirits of our dwindling wild places.

Epilogue

Cleo gave birth to four new kittens on June 5, the last of which, a female, I saw being born. Smaller and weaker than the others, she had to be helped to the teats in early weaning or she would have died in the competition for milk. She has been tamed, but not house-trained, and is with us still. Patra came back into our lives, pregnant, when Moobli tracked her, not far from where she was released and, after two attempts I managed to live-trap her. She too gave birth to kits, three, on June 11. Later in the summer both Cleo and Patra, and their kits, were released in suitable areas. In spring 1977 I heard from Roger Wheater that Freddy, alias Sylvesturr 2, had been adopted by the Cub Scouts of the 64th Edinburgh (Waverley) Group, who are paying for his keep. And that they had re-named him yet again—"Tammy Haggis!" It seemed a fitting end to the saga of my wilderness wildcats.

Appendix

In the Scottish wildcat, *Felis silvestris grampia*, Britain has an indigenous mammal as truly wild, independent and magnificent as any animal in the world. While lynxes, tigers, lions and leopards can become amenable to man's discipline in captivity, the wildcat does not. A sub-species of the European wildcat, *Felis silvestris silvestris*, it is usually larger and darker coloured than its European and Asian relatives. More controversy surrounds the wildcat than any other member of our fauna but in the notes below I have tried to pay due respect to the findings of other naturalists. My choice, if somewhat arbitrary, is based upon studying my own animals and observations in the wild.

I am indebted to the mammal section, British Museum of Natural History, London, for permission to examine their wildcat pelts; to John B. Murray for the Royal Scottish Museum pelt measurements; to Mrs S. Bevis of the London Zoological Society Library; and to Geoffrey Kinns for his photo, two anecdotes and helpful suggestions.

DESCRIPTION, WEIGHT AND LENGTH

Although usually described as a light tawny grey beast with thin grey-black stripes and a bushy black-ringed tail, the adult wildcat has many colourful features. The pelage is overall longer and softer than in the domestic cat. The guard hairs, some over two inches long, are generally whitish grey or dark brown with the grey flank stripes formed by concentrations of dark hairs. Beneath the guard hairs there is a thick-growing fine wool-like fur, varying from yellow-grey to orangey buff, the latter especially marked on the insides of the thighs and the lower inside of the front legs. The belly fur, often frosty white between the front legs, is short and greyish but lined below the flanks with ochraceous buff and there are dark grey spots, stripes or patches on the under belly which vary with individuals. The toe pads, pink at birth, are almost completely black in the adult, and are surrounded by thick short black hairs. These black hair patches extend an inch or two up the rear of the front feet, and sometimes right up to the heel bone on the rear feet. The claws are light horn coloured and like the feet are larger in proportion than the domestic cat's. The short hair covering the top of the feet is a light buff and in the sun has a gleaming velvet look. Two or three broad browny-black bands often partly encircle the forelegs in front of the "elbows." The wildcat skull compared to the domestic cat's is stronger, broader and more robust. Hamilton measured wildcat skulls and found they varied between 78.5 to 89 millimetres in basal length, domestic cats' between 73 and 85 millimetres. In mature wildcats, particularly in males, there is a high nasal arch, giving the wildcat a slightly convex "Roman" profile. The teeth are also bigger and stronger, particularly the canines; the upper two can be over half an inch long and in mature toms protrude even when the mouth is closed.

The wildcat nose is bright salmon pink in a prime animal, the colour fading with age. The nose and inner nostrils are edged with a fine black line which extends down to the mouth. The fur of the front upper lips and the whole chin is white but the amount to which this white extends into a throat patch varies greatly. The chin is thicker and more "determined" looking than in the domestic cat. I believe wildcats signal to each other with their white lips and chins because I often saw my animals opening and closing their mouths when in sight of each other at dusk without emitting a sound— looking *as if* they were *mauing*. The whiskers are stiff and white, grow in greater profusion, and often extend far beyond the head width. They are certainly used as "feelers" when the animal is in narrow places in pitch dark. The lip membranes are black but the inside of the mouth and the long heavily rasped tongue are a far brighter red than in the domestic cat. The eyes are distinctively large, with yellow-gold irises which seem to grow paler with age, and no British animal's eyes are so expressive of mood—from rage and ferocity to peaceful relaxation and pleasure when basking in the sun. I noticed wildcats' pupils stay rounder longer than those of domestic cats in similar light conditions. They also expand to full roundness in bright daylight when they sense danger, are afraid or are hunting. This tendency to greater roundness may link wildcats more closely than domestics with the big "cats" like lions and tigers whose pupils do not contract to vertical slits.

On the wildcat's forehead there is usually a distinct but unjoined "M," the inner ends not meeting in the centre, and a pair of dark lines extend from the eyes to below the ears. The widely spaced ears, held down rather than back when angry, are light tawny, front-edged with dark brown, rimmed with yellow-buff, and sometimes end with longer dark hairs at the tip, though this could not be called a tuft. From the crown of the head and down the nape are four, rarely five, dark lines which peter out before the shoulders. Between the shoulder blades are usually two, rarely three, strong dark parallel dashes and from them, an inch or two away, a dark wavy line runs along the spine to the tail. Occasionally this line breaks into three though the lower lines are usually not joined and consist of paler dashes and indistinct spots. The wildcat undergoes a fairly heavy early spring moult to a lighter summer pelage, sometimes but rarely to sandy or silvery shades, then another slight moult in late summer, before the darker pelage of winter which grows from the end of October, through November and early December.

The tail is nearly always described as "short," but my research (see later notes) proved that in the finest specimens it usually well exceeds half head and body length. It is thick, bushy, ends with a blunt black tip and has broad black rings which vary in number from three to as many as nine, though in multi-ringed animals the last rings nearest the root are usually indistinct. But the tail usually contrasts greatly with the thin, tapering, un-evenly striped or blotched tail of the domestic tabby. It is one of the wild-cat's most distinctive features. (Sylvesturr's tail at one foot, three inches, and my females' tails, plus those of several wildcats I've seen in the wild, were "long" in this sense.)

Southern quotes Kirk and Wagstaffe's 1943 measurements of 107 wild-cats, of which only five were females. The average head and body length of the males was 589 millimetres (23¼ inches), smallest 365 millimetres (14⅜ inches), largest 653 millimetres (25½ inches), the average tail length being 315 millimetres (12¼ inches), shortest 210 millimetres (8¼ inches), longest 342 millimetres (13⅓ inches). The figures for the five fe-males—average head and body length 571 millimetres (22⅓ inches), average tail length 311 millimetres (12¼ inches)—reveal a similar picture, and also confirm they are generally considerably smaller animals than the toms. (See later notes.)

The wildcat is longer and usually stronger limbed than the domestic, its rear legs some half to an inch longer than its front but when at bay it doesn't usually arch itself, fluff out all its fur with upraised tail, presenting as large as possible *side* view to bluff its opponent as to its size. It fluffs its fur certainly, but usually backs into a corner, tail down and rears as high as it can to present a ferocious *frontal* aspect. With ears down, fangs bared, low growl punctuated by violent spits at every movement of the approacher, it is here its extraordinarily long ulnae (top foreleg bones) come into play, for it seems to raise its front to twice normal height, its claws ready to rake and slash any attacker.

Wildcat weights vary greatly. Southern cites 102 males ranging from 6½ to 15¼ pounds. My own well-fed Sylvesturr weighed sixteen pounds. But much larger wildcats have been recorded, including one weighing over thirty-two pounds from the East Carpathians, and Berwick recorded a wild-cat "upwards of five feet" from Cumberland long before they were extinct in England. Wright's edition of Buffon describes the Wild or Wood Cat as measuring "two feet round the body, and, including the tail which is about half a yard long, is about four feet in length." There are several specimens approaching, and over, forty inches in the British Museum (see later notes). Millais records one measuring three feet, ten inches in October 1899 at Kinlochmoidart.

FOOD

Although reputedly able to kill lambs and red deer fawns, I feel such predation would be rare. Red deer calves are strong, heavy and able to run fast within a day of birth. I have never seen remains of either near wildcat dens, nor known of such a kill authenticated. Smaller new-born roe deer fawns, which the wildcat might come upon by chance in the woods, are possibly an uncommon item. The bulk of the wildcat's food consists of rabbits (for which it will wait patiently near burrows), mountain hares, mice, occasional shrews and many voles which can be hosts for the early stages of a tick that transmits the "louping ill" disease to hill sheep. Also taken are birds up to the size of woodpigeon or occasional game birds (8 per cent in the East Carpathians), infrequently eggs and nestlings of ground nesters too. Wildcats will hunt edges of lochs and burns where ground birds take their young to drink in summer, and for ducks and other water and marsh birds too. I once found the remains of a barn owl, far from its natural habitat and probably weakened by its winter search for a home in sparse woodland, that had been killed and eaten by a wildcat. Squirrels, frogs, slow-worms, lizards, rats, moles, water voles, and even occasional weasels are also taken. Eels are probably caught when travelling overland in dewy grass from burns to lochs and ponds or negotiating waterfalls. Fish travelling over shallow rocky riffles can be caught by foxes and wildcats. Beetles, grasshoppers and insects are not despised, nor are larger moths which are chased and swiped down with the paws, particularly by youngsters. Many naturalists believe wildcats disdain carrion, unlike foxes and badgers. But while they will not feed from "high" carcasses as will fox, crow or raven, my wildcats often proved they could scent meat and venison from at least fifty yards, occasionally, depending on wind, up to 250 yards, and would feed avidly, chewing far more neatly than a fox. It is claimed wildcats' teeth are not equipped for chewing through thick fur, but on one occasion the inexperienced, zoo-confined Sylvesturr, knowing that meat lay under the fur, stood on venison chunks with both feet and rended them with front teeth alone by great tearing upward strokes of his powerful neck. His small front teeth were quite strong enough. In winter, carrion is probably an important wildcat food item, especially as the suspicious fox tends to leave a new carcass alone for several days. MacNally once saw a wildcat skinning the head of a ewe carcass in winter. Occasionally an old or hungry wildcat, especially in the cold months, will leave its home grounds and haunt outlying farmhouses and crofts if it finds loose poultry the owner does not shut up at night in a predator-proof hut. Usually it removes just one to eat but will return for the easy prey until the irate owner traps or shoots it, or looks after his birds. In the winter of 1976, a wildcat killed a large goose at Kinlochmoidart but unable to carry it away, ate part of it on a nearby path. But such losses are as nothing compared with those inflicted by feral domestic cats. The intestinal canals of wildcats are up to a third shorter in proportion than those of domestics, which is believed to be due to their more strictly carnivorous diet. Yet, if they don't get enough fur or roughage in their food, they will eat grass, dry hay or bracken stalks to give the clearing roughage they need. I have found wildcat scats in the wild containing vegetation.

HUNTING TECHNIQUES

The wildcat is usually described as a nocturnal hunter, but I feel crepuscular would be more exact as all my wildcats were most active for an hour or two after sunset and an hour before dawn—coinciding with the main movements of their small mammal prey. It locates victims mainly by sight, approaches carefully until within a yard or so of vole or mouse, then with a lightning bound, pounces, clutches the prey with its claws and holds it down or hauls back for the death bite, usually in the skull or neck area. It does not play with its victims. With larger prey, hares or rabbits or the bigger birds, it stalks behind cover as much as possible, keeping low until, because of the prey's longer sight and wariness, it is several yards away. Then it gathers its legs together and with a burst of devastating speed, bounds forward making its attack as terrifying as possible. As Millais wrote "So swift is this final attack that four footed game find it impossible to escape, even if its terror paralysed nerves did not benumb its muscles." Several times I observed that if my wildcats missed with their first pounce at a bird, they would leap high into the air after it, making lightning strokes with both sets of claws, often knocking the bird down from mid air. Certainly the powerful smash of the clawed paw also helps stun victims and the cat will make deep raking slashes with its claws as it is delivering the death bites. It will also occasionally kick powerfully with its hind claws against the victim's body, probably to disembowel, and this activity constitutes a large part of kitten play though they don't exert full force.

In dense undergrowth, in woodland or hill heather and tussock grass, where sight is restricted, the wildcat relies more on scent and also hearing— a rustle instantly alerts it to prey presence and after sighting, the cat pounces with both paws. Millais said wildcats occasionally make a loud scream when hunting which causes prey to squat down. I have seen foxes use a technique where the pocket of warm air expelled by the suddenly squatting bird or mammal helps the fox locate it by scent, but I have not seen this myself with the wildcat, though it's possible. MacNally once saw a wildcat stalking a rabbit entirely by scent.

Several times I saw my cats dash into thick herbage then smite down moths, grasshoppers and other large insects so disturbed. Wildcats can catch water voles, usually when coming to shore, but they will swim readily themselves if there is a good reason—to cross a river, a small sea inlet, or to reach an island where they think or know there is prey. One early summer dawn in a sea loch near my home I saw some terns screaming and diving constantly upon the rocky islet where they had their young. As my boat drew near, I was astonished to see a wildcat leap into the water and swim rapidly, its head and shoulders well above the surface, ears flat as if ensuring water wouldn't get in them, fifteen yards to the main island and bounce off into the woods without even pausing to shake itself. It had probably been after the young birds. Occasionally the wildcat will wait in ambush for prey, behind grass or heather tufts near small trails or burrows.

It is solitary by nature and hunts alone. There is some published evidence that they will occasionally hunt together but I suggest this springs from occasional sightings of male and female being together in the breeding period, and my experience indicates it is unlikely they would hunt as a *team*.

Nearly all prey is taken on the ground though my females twice brought chaffinches' eggs back to the woodshed and in summer, during one of Sylvesturr's visits to the west wood, the nest of a collared dove had been robbed of one egg and the bark on the slim oak tree, up which no fox could have climbed, had been deeply scratched. This is not enough evidence to determine that wildcats will raid tree nests, but they have been known (Millais) to make their homes in large deserted birds' nests and being excellent climbers, it is possible.

GENERAL HABITS, BEHAVIOUR AND TERRITORY

Although mostly active during twilight and dark, wildcats will also hunt by day, especially in the autumn when growing their thick winter coat and laying up fat for the harsh winter. My first wild sightings were of two hunting in open patches between heather sprigs a good two hours after dawn, though it is rare to see them hunting by day in summer after 8:30 A.M. and before 7 P.M. for they spend most of the day resting up. They occasionally bask in the sun on mossy boulders or on broad tree branches. They hunt, depending on individual terrain, in woodland, among rocky cairns and mountain slides and on open moors with great adaptability. And they also hunt in light rain or on crisp dry snow but not during heavy storms or winds unless driven out by hunger, as they distrust waving foliage and fear noise and falling twigs and branches; also most of their prey is in shelter anyway.

They cover uneaten remains of kills, often hauling them under long heather clumps or small bushes, and arranging debris cover to look like the surrounding terrain. This not only hides carcasses from other predators such as fox, crow, raven or buzzard, but also reduces the scent, helps keep it fresher and protects it too from spoiling slugs and insect scavengers. Females with kits old enough to accompany them take great pains to cover up uneaten food, to return to it next evening from a temporary den.

Wildcats make their dens in hollow standing or fallen trees, under dry root clusters of stumps or windfalls, in old fox earths, larger rabbit burrows or natural chambers and crevices in or below ancient rockfalls. Usually they choose dense deciduous or mixed woodland or the steep treed sides of ravines above burns and rivers. They may den rarely in large tree birds' nests but would not rear young in them. In the extreme north and west where tree cover is scant, they den amid the rocky cairns of the open hill, living and hunting beyond the height to which feral cats will range. Wildcat tracks have been recorded at over 2,000 feet and I've found them myself at nearly 1,800 feet. The dens are hard to find for they leave few signs of occupation, no well trodden paths like the badger. They are usually not lined though the female appears to occasionally make some effort to rake in heather or dry grass before having her kits. Syl raked in dry deer hair, made deep bowls of hay in the pens and in the wild, and Cleo also raked hay into a bowl. But Millais recorded one litter born in an open bed of bracken at Drumnadrochit.

Droppings, normally dark grey, grey-green or brown, are usually covered on snow, sand, gravel or shingle but seldom on grass or beds of broken down bracken. But sometimes they are found, fox-like, on a prominent place, a mossy rock or old stump, as if left deliberately. Bang and Dahlstrom suggest this is done, together with urine (also Southern, quoting Lindemann, 1955) to mark the outskirts of territory; that it is *inside* territory that both are buried. This seems feasible. It is also possible such signs are used to warn off other males, inform females of a male's presence, or by females in heat to inform males of the fact and their presence. I do not believe wildcats stay in pairs through the year for both sexes are solitary by nature, but their coming together when the female is in oestrus surely cannot be left to chance meeting by sight and body scent alone. Cougars in North America make special "scratch piles" of their faeces and urine for these purposes.

The figure of 150 acres (sixty to seventy hectares) is often quoted as being a normal wildcat's territory but this seems too simple a generalization for much would depend on the type of territory (woodland, open moor, treed burn and gorges, sea coast etc.), the availability of prey, plus age and ability of individual cat to hunt efficiently. My observations suggest that territoriality in the wildcat is over-rated, but until a research team works full-time on individual cats and families with light radio tracking equipment over several years, information upon territory will be largely guesswork. Males are known to wander widely in spring, as did Syl, during the normal breeding period, but females with young are naturally compelled to stay in smaller areas.

Claw "sharpening" marks are occasionally found on small tree trunks, usually hard birch. But as cats' front claws are retractile, which prevents them being blunted from constant rubbing on rocks, earth and the wood of trees, this digging them into hard surfaces serves only to clean away excess horny outer sheath from the claws, which grow sharp naturally, not to actually "sharpen" them. Having watched my wildcats perform this action many times, I'm convinced that the exercise, where they haul down heavily on the dug-in claws and scratch deeply, is to strengthen the sinew and muscle that control the claws, and also the arms and shoulders, so the entire forelimb weapons stay strong for hunting.

The renowned ferocity of the wildcat is purely defensive. Far from being "utterly fearless" or likely to "spring at your throat like a tiger" as one naturalist wrote in a national paper in early 1977, the wildcat is afraid of man and dogs and will do its utmost to escape either. Only if cornered or surprised at close quarters where it feels it cannot escape, or caught in a trap, will it set up its devastating frontal display but even then its main aim is to make a lightning spring past and escape, still avoiding contact. Only if bodily contact is made, or dog or man tries to prevent its escape or kill it, will it fight. Then, indeed, it will fight like a tiger. St. John, who described how he once stumbled upon one and killed it with a staff and the aid of three Skye terriers, wrote "I never saw an animal fight so desperately, or one which was so difficult to kill. If a tame cat has nine lives, a wildcat must have a dozen." He gave no reason, however, for his foolish act. The wildcat's thicker skull, short jaws and larger teeth enable it to give a harder bite than any domestic cat but no worse than that from a cornered otter or fox, and nothing like the terrible bite that the much-loved badger can inflict, powerful enough to crack a terrier's skull.

The wildcat mother, however, is aggressive and fearless in defence of her young. When Cleo had her second litter of kits, I saw her once face down a fox that had come prowling nearby. She advanced straight out of her den, fur and tail bristling, and with loud growls advanced slowly towards it then stopped, glaring straight at it. And the fox retreated. A wildcat mother was once seen to spring on to an eagle that had just snatched up one of her young. (See *Enemies* below.) It appears male wildcats tend to avoid each other for I have seldom known of a wildcat fight in the wild, which would be a noisy affair, though they have occurred in captivity, even between male and female.

VOICE

More varied and complicated than realized. The kits make a loud piercing note *meeoo* when alarmed and handled at only two days old, which changes to an even louder *maow* at four or five days old. At five to six weeks they can emit the latter sound and also a still more piercing whistling note *wheeoo* when really frightened. This sound is probably given in the wild if straggling kits are picked up by a fox, or eagle. From four days they give a high trilling note when seeking their mother's teats and her warm body. At less than a week old they try to hiss and spit at outside disturbance but neither are audible until the eighth or ninth day. Later they make a special suckling noise by smacking their lips when already at their mother's body but, waking up suddenly, want some milk. This lip smacking noise can continue until five months old and it is often made near the mother's head. When the kits get caught up in a thicket of brambles or in fencing they warn their mother with a loud squawking *mauuw* which is louder but similar to that of a duck grabbed by fox, dog or man. The "turtle dove"-like *brrrooo* trill is not made until about eight months. It is used for greeting, affection, and to call the kits back when they are not far, but from further away the normal loud *mau* is used. When the kits are running wild with the mother a high metallic ventriloquistic *awroori* is used, to help all keep in touch yet not give away exact position to possible predators on the kits. Wildcats can and do purr, just as do cougars and lynxes, a sudden breathy, clattering sound, which often ends suddenly. This purr is slower and louder than that of the domestic cat, but is rarely used. The ability to growl, like whirring high pitched dynamos, develops at about a month. As the cats grow older this growl deepens in volume until in an old tom it sounds like the prelude to a minor earthquake. It is used to display anger and as a warning before the ferocious spits and stamps. The female can emit loud tormented screeches during her oestrus, possibly to help find the male. It is an unearthly chilling sound. I never heard Sylvesturr make such sounds but males are reputed to call noisily in the spring, again probably to help contact a female.

MATING OR "COURTSHIP"

A special rutting or oestrus period for the male has not yet been established, which is true of other cats, and Matthews opines the male's noisiness could be caused by the onset of oestrus in the female. In the wild, I feel, it could also be caused by the scent discovery of a female being in oestrus, a period which lasts up to ten days. Courtship appears to consist of occasional plaintive mewing, the male following the female around and frequently nuzzling her, rubbing his head against her flanks, and I once observed Syl and Cleo "kissing," heads sideways as they bit each other's open mouths, as if exchanging saliva. In zoos, male sexual activity has been known to last from late January, and copulation may continue until after pregnancy has begun. My own experience supports the theory that wildcat males are monogamous. And Pitt recorded that her own wildcat male Satan was so devoted to his mate he "rent the air with hideous cries of lamentation whenever she left his quarters. He would not accept any substitute. I several times introduced other females, but he attacked them at sight . . . He never cast an attentive eye on any female save his mate." My own Patra failed dismally to arouse Syl's interest after he'd mated with Cleo.

BREEDING

Here we enter controversy. Despite assertions by a few authorities that wildcats can have two, or even three, annual litters, my own observations lead me to side with Millais, Pitt, Morris and Cocks, that the true Scottish wildcat, as has been proven for its German counterpart, normally breeds only once a year, mating in late February or early March. Alfred Heneage Cocks first bred wildcat kits in Britain and raised them almost every year from 1875 to 1904. He was first to set the gestation period at sixty-five to sixty-eight days (since confirmed at sixty-three to sixty-nine days) as opposed to a usual fifty to fifty-eight days for the domestic cat. Cocks informed Millais he had never observed a female come into season during the summer. "Many years when, owing to the death of the young or the fact that the pair have not bred together in the spring, I've kept a female and male together all summer, they have shown no inclination to breed."

Matthews examined several female wildcats and found two in an-oestrus for February 16 and 28, two in pro-oestrus for March 1 and 29, and five actually pregnant animals for that month, March. And he rightly concludes oestrus must normally occur during the first half of March. But there was one lactating animal for May 25 which was also in oestrus, and another in lactation an-oestrus for August 29. This valuable evidence shows it is biologically possible for wildcats to have more than one litter a year, though it does not prove that they do. Although Millais records perplexity at seeing young Scottish wildcats in October which had clearly been born in late August or early September, the later scientific supposition that these kits "must have been members of *second* litters born late in the summer," is perhaps not correct. They could just as easily, and far more likely in my opinion, have been *first* litter kits born late. For many reasons, their mother may not have mated at all in the spring. Patra showed great interest in Syl in May, perhaps coming into oestrus again because her early spring oestrus was not, as it were, consummated, though this is surmise.

My own experience showed wildcat kits may not be fully weaned until two-and-a-half to three-and-a-half months old, and certainly even the earliest leavers (like Mia) need to run and learn with their mother for at least three-and-a-half months, but more usually four or even five months, before they are strong enough, their claws sufficiently hardened and developed, to hunt on their own and scoot up trees from danger. I also believe efficient night hunting takes some time to learn. Zoo mothers have been known to drive their kits off at three months but this could be partly due to the confined conditions. Toms appear to need their mothers more—my young Freddy stayed close to his mother through the winter and early spring too when, during periods of freedom, he could easily have left. Millais also felt kits run with their mother until September. So the assertion that Scottish wildcats bear kits in May and a second litter about August seems extraordinarily optimistic and has not yet been proved.

As Pitt first pointed out, in the wild mountains of Scotland where life is strenuous, conditions are not as compatible with the rearing of offspring as in the free and easy life of well-fed domestic cats who can have three litters a year. My own female, despite good feeding, was considerably exhausted during weaning of her kits and while I only once saw her drive off an approach by the tom during this period, it may have happened oftener at night. It seems likely if a mother in the wild came into late-lactation oestrus, with her kits about her, she too would drive off an interested tom.

Trying to clarify this controversy, I examined two papers on the zoo breeding of wildcats—from Berne Zoo, Switzerland, between 1960 and 1967; and from Prague Zoo, Czechoslovakia, in 1963 to 1967. It is fascinating to note that out of the thirty-two litters (sixteen at each zoo) there were only *three* cases of two litters a year. (This substantiates Matthews' findings on late-lactation oestrus.) But the one Berne female who had kits in April and also in August 1961 died at the age of four. The fecund female at Prague destroyed her first litter in the spring of 1963 but reared a second litter in August that year. In 1964 the same female cared for her spring litter until the kits were taken away from her in early June, then in August gave birth to a second litter of only one kit. But this kit died the day after its birth. Prague's Curator of Mammals Jiri Volf comments: "From this it can be deduced that, physiologically, she was unprepared to rear a second litter that year; but other factors may well have been involved."

Monika Meyer-Holzapfel, Berne Zoo director, makes some pertinent comments. She records they did not separate males from females when they had young "for the female is sufficiently aggressive during this period to chase the male away from the nest box." She also writes "The birth season lasts from March to August. This means if a birth occurs in August, it may not necessarily be the second litter of the year: it may equally be the first litter of the year."

From breeding and releasing my own animals, it does not seem possible for a wildcat to rear a family successfully in some two months, then have another and rear that too—not so that both, especially the late litter, survive. For the survival success of the species, it would be against the usual biological "common sense" wild animals show in their breeding cycles. Having late summer or autumn kits cannot be the norm for they would hardly be developed enough in time to cope with winter conditions. But in May or June far more natural prey abounds—young birds, rabbits, hares, voles, mice, frogs and insects. Thus not only does the mother have less trouble hunting, feeding, rearing and teaching her kits but they also have more time to learn the techniques they need before the onset of winter. Spring kits receive a far better and more successful start in life.

All this evidence makes me conclude that in the harsh conditions of the wild, having a second litter in any one year, though possible, is most unlikely, but to rear both successfully is almost impossible.

Another point—why should the Scottish wildcat be different from its continental cousins in having multiple broods? The possibility has been put forward by several authorities that it has interbred for many years, particularly in the southern parts of its range, with feral domestic tabbies who are capable of multiple annual broods. This controversy is dealt with fully in the *Status* section below.

DEVELOPMENT OF YOUNG

Wildcat litters vary considerably. At Berne the number of kits varied between one and eight, though still-birth was probable in larger litters. The average litter size there was four. At Prague it was three. In the wild consensus, and my own experience, indicates two to four young as average. Generally, slightly fewer males are born than females (Cocks recorded thirty-two male to thirty-seven female kits) both weighing about the same—between 120 and 150 grams—though there are uncommon exceptions. Males usually gain weight slightly faster. At birth they are fully furred, mouths and tongues are bright crimson, pads of paws pink, darkening to near black by three months old. The kits, who can crawl at two days, instinctively try to spit and hiss at a week old, before their eyes are open, at any strange disturbance. Between the tenth and thirteenth day the eyes start to open, varying with individuals, the whole process taking four days, with the mother helping by licking away the sticky secretions from the lids. The bright china-blue irises last until about the seventh week, when a greeny-grey tinge begins at the pupils spreading outwards, banishing the blue in some eight to ten days. This colour lightens to the final yellow-gold by about five months old. Weight increase is less than a weekly 100 grams at first but averages between 100 and 270 grams a week once the kits start eating solid foods. Sexual maturity is attained at ten months of age but breeding at Berne showed females gave birth more usually at two years of age—by which time all wildcats are fully grown.

REARING

Apart from her brave defence of the kits, the wildcat is a fine mother. She keeps the den clean and does not take food inside the bed section. She rough-tongues the young kits' rear parts, stimulating excretions which she swallows. As with most carnivores, aggression and competitiveness are encouraged in the sense that the mother will make no effort to ensure a weak or runty kit gets its share of the teats. Yet when they first start to walk, she keeps an alert eye on them, calling or carrying them back into the den with a firm jaw grip on the neck if they stray too far. When her kits were about a month old, Cleo would leave them in the den for long periods, which must happen in the wild when the mother has to hunt. When the kits are weaning off on to meat from about six to seven weeks old, they follow the mother when she defecates and she appears to encourage them to cover droppings on soft surfaces, for they often copy her actions. When the young kits are mobile there is certainly much "tail twitch" training—when for hours the kits chase the black tip of the mother's tail—which she flicks about when sitting, lying or even while eating. As they watch, she "catches" waving flowers, blowing leaves, crane flies and moths and fast walking beetles, which seems the preliminary training for the kits to learn to hunt. Several times, with both litters, I saw Cleo catch voles, shrews and occasional birds that raided left-over food but instead of crippling them so they were half-alive, she killed them, dropped them among her kits, then batted them about, deliberately encouraging the young to chase after them. The first kit to catch this "prey" then defended it with high whirring growls from the others, as if copying the growls its mother made if the weaned kits approached her too closely when she was eating. The kits can walk, unsteadily, at about a month. After two more weeks they are surer on their feet and can climb a little at seven weeks. From two months they accompany their mother on short forays, then stay with her on longer expeditions, lying up then in temporary dens near covered kills.

The belief that females tend to rear young away from the tom who is liable to kill and/or eat them has often been expressed in print. My tom showed no belligerence at all to the kits but *my* fears made me keep them apart. In the Berne and Prague papers there is no record of a male attacking young though there are several instances of mothers destroying and eating their own young, particularly if the litter size was large. Pitt also believed the sire helped kill for the family, like a dog fox. Several times Syl placed some of his meat near Cleo's gate. I have been unable to find any authentic record of a tom killing kits in the wild. If it happens it is probably aberrant individual behaviour, or due to accidental meeting with a hungry tom or kits later competing on the same territory.

ENEMIES

An occasional large fox may be cunning enough to take a kitten when they first begin to wander away from the mother on brief independent outings from the age of two months but such predation would be insignificant. (Foxes several times came near my wildcat litters when normally they never approached the cottage in summer.) And most adult wildcats could easily repel a fox, or escape, their reactions being much faster. The golden eagle probably has a slight effect on populations. Wildcat kits have been recorded in eyries but it is extremely rare. MacNally described an encounter when an eagle was seen to swoop down on a wildcat in the open some half-dozen times but the cat retaliated, swiping out with its claws, until the eagle retired. Kinns was given an eye-witness account of a wildcat springing on to an eagle's back after it had snatched one of its kittens, both being shot in the air by a watching keeper. The great Seton Gordon also described a fight between the two in his *Book on the Golden Eagle,* when the cat was killed after its severe injuries caused it to run round in circles, and the eagle was also later found dead. But the wildcat's main enemy has always been man.

DISTRIBUTION

Today found in the Scottish Highlands, France, Spain, Germany, most of south and central Europe (but not Scandinavia or Finland) including Rumania—its European strongholds in more remote mountainous country—then across west and south Russia into Asia.

STATUS PAST AND FUTURE OF THE WILDCAT IN BRITAIN

Wildcats formerly lived all over England, Wales and Scotland, though they were never natives of Ireland, and they co-existed with the mammoth, cave lion and bear, the reindeer and wolf for thousands of years before the domestic cat was introduced to western Europe around 1200 B.C. Their fossil remains have been found in up to two-million-year-old Pleistocene deposits at Gray's Thurrock, Essex, the Bleadon caves of the Mendips, Cresswell Crags in Derbyshire, Ravenscliff in Glamorgan and rocks of the Weald at Ightham in Kent. The Scottish wildcat is generally believed to be one of the seven sub-species of European wildcat which probably evolved in Europe and Asia from the extinct ancestral species, *Felis lunensis*. Wildcats, known variously as the Wood Cat, Cat of the Mountains, the British Tiger, or Bore Cat, were very common in England and Wales up to the end of the fifteenth century, and in 1127 their skins were being used for lining clothes. King John, Richard II and Edward II and III granted licences for hunting wolves, foxes, martens and wildcats in many English counties. But increasing human population and the thinning, felling and burning of forest cover from the Iron Age to the nineteenth century for timber and grazing land, the extermination of wolves and the driving out of bandits and rebels drove the wildcat north to its final fastnesses in Scotland—a migration that had first begun with the retreating glaciers of the Ice Age towards the end of the Pleistocene and start of the Holocene era over 10,000 years ago.

Hamilton records that some parts of the wildcat were used as medical aids, the flesh being "helpful to the gout." Its fat was "hot, dry, emolient, discursive and anodyne," and "mixed with palm oil and oil of aniseed, it dissolves tumours, eases pain, prevails against nodes on the skin and the cold gout." As if that wasn't enough, "certain excrements made into a powder and mixed with mustard seed, juice of onions and bear's grease enough to form an ointment, cures baldness and the alopaecia." Its independence and ferocity were well known and even Shakespeare in 1606, playing on the word "Cat," in *The Taming of the Shrew*, had Petruchio say to Katharine "Thou must be married to no man but me for I am he and born to tame you Kate. And bring you from a wildcat to a Kate, conformable as other household Kates."

After its extinction in England and Wales, the industrial rich of the nineteenth century went north on the new railways to pursue the sports of hunting grouse, deer, rabbits and hares. The many new estates employed thousands of gamekeepers who regarded all predators as vermin—the final and direct persecution of the wildcat had begun. They were trapped, snared and shot in huge numbers. Keepers, taking all vermin as their own "perks," could get a sovereign a time for a wildcat in taxidermist shops. Later it was also persecuted for alleged depredations on lambs and occasional raids on unhoused poultry—for which it is still shot today.

By the turn of the century naturalists were predicting its extinction in Britain. Summarizing Hamilton, Ritchie, Harper and Millais (who quotes Harvie Brown) the picture in 1904 was as follows:

England: wildcats were extinct in Northampton by 1712, considerably diminished in Cumberland by 1790, last one killed near Loweswater in the Lake District in 1843, and extinct in the Hambledon Hills, Yorkshire, by 1881.

Wales: almost extinct by 1826 but one trapped in Montgomeryshire in 1864.

Scotland: Aberdeen—surviving Glen Tanar until 1875 but almost extinct in county by 1891; Angus (Forfar)—almost extinct by 1850; Argyll—last of the race killed at Loch Awe in 1864, one appeared Glen Orchy in 1899, but still rarely found around Ardnamurchan, Sunart, Ardgour and Morvern. Virtually extinct in south Argyll by 1864. Banff—almost extinct by 1850; Berwick—last border wildcat killed near old Cambus in 1849; Dumfries—extinct by 1832; Dumbarton—extinct by 1857; Elgin—practically extinct by 1850; Inverness-shire—last wildcats killed at Glenmore in 1873 and by 1882 it was very rare but not extinct in south and central areas though the north and west, with western Ross, was its main stronghold in Scotland; in Kincardine—a pair killed at Glen Dye in 1850 by which time practically extinct; Kirkcudbright—extinct by 1832; Moray—one killed 1860 near Forres but a few still existing; Nairn—almost extinct by 1850 (one killed at Cawdor [undated] measured three feet, nine inches); Perthshire—last killed at Atholl 1857, Ben More 1864 and believed extinct in south by 1870. A wildcat killed twelve miles from Perth in 1925 was believed to have been part of a new spread south from Lochs Ericht and Laggan, Inverness-shire, where it reappeared in 1912; Ross and Cromarty—last killed in east Ross 1873, believed extremely rare, even in the west. One killed Dornoch Firth 1912; Stirling—extinct in most parishes by 1842; Sutherland—dwindling by 1880; Wigtonshire—extinct by 1832.

In 1881, Harvie Brown recorded the wildcat as then extinct south-east of a rough line from Oban, up the Brander Pass to Dalmally, along the Perth border, including Rannoch Moor, to the junction of the counties of Perth, Forfar (Angus) and Aberdeen, then north-east to Tomintoul in Banff, then north-west again to Inverness.

Such was the situation through the early 1900s, with the cat clinging on in its last remote areas in north-west Argyll, Kintyre, Stirling, west Inverness-shire and western Ross. The more intelligent land owners, such as the Earls of Seafield, realized the preservation of a fascinating but dwindling native mammal was worth the loss of a few brace of sport grouse and afforded the wildcat some protection. But the Great War was its main saviour, just as it helped other persecuted creatures like pine martens and eagles to recover, for many keepers were away after a different target.

The plantings by the new Forestry Commission gave the endangered wildcat population a further boost, for not only were they tolerated for their predation on rabbits, voles and ground birds who ate young seedlings, but the woods gave them new shelter and encouraged an increase in a large variety of prey. World War Two also provided some amnesty, as in the First War. In recent years the growth of private forestry too, has further helped. The wildcat was also tolerated in deer "forests" for its feeding on voles and rabbits who ate the grass, and hares whose sudden scatterings spoilt deer stalks. Today greater ecological knowledge among younger keepers is helping change the old die-hard attitudes.

In his excellent 1961 survey, from Aberdeen University, Dr David Jenkins received 135 full replies to 248 questionnaires he sent to Highland estates. His findings are briefly summarized here:

Aberdeen—wildcats rather uncommon but present in upper Deeside, in smaller numbers in upper Strathdon and re-appearing in Glen Muick. No increase; Angus—wildcats long been *locally* common, particularly in upper Glen Clova but rare or absent elsewhere. After 1955 began to spread into Glen Lethnot and Glen Esk and possibly Glen Prosen; Argyll—probably still rather rare but hard to tell in the new forested country; Ayrshire—no wildcats present; Banff—a few on low ground but may be fairly widespread over higher ground; Caithness—rather uncommon but six killed by one estate in 1960; Inverness-shire—widely distributed in woods and moors but no evidence of sudden change. Probably increased during World War Two but reduced again when keepers returned from service. (One estate, Glenmazeran, killed eighty-six wildcats in the years 1950, 1953, 1955, 1958 and 1960—thirty-five of them in 1958.) Generally though, quite plentiful in county; Kincardine and Kinross—probably rare or absent; Moray and Nairn —few wildcats over low ground but there had been a sudden remarkable increase on some moors and hills, around 1957 to 1959; Perthshire—fairly widely distributed over moorland but probably in low numbers. Some changes in local densities but no widespread increase; Ross and Cromarty—uncommon and little evidence of recent change; Stirling—Dr J. D. Lockie informed Jenkins there had been four sight records of wildcats and one trapped at Fintry since February 1962—a notable extension to their south-east range; Sutherland—uncommon and no evidence of recent change.

That was the information on improved wildcat status as could be best obtained up to 1961. Since then the Institute of Terrestrial Ecology in Huntingdon have conducted a survey and produced a distribution map as at spring 1977, showing that the wildcat still has a long way to go before it reaches its southern range prior to 1900 where it was known eastwards from the tip of Kintyre, Ayrshire, Renfrew, more rarely in Lanark, Dumfries and Berwick. Its strongholds between 1900 and 1959 appear to have been north Kintyre, central and north Argyll, south-west and north-east Perth, with scattered remnants widely distributed over Inverness-shire, and a few individual sightings in south-east Aberdeen, western Ross and south-east Sutherland. But where wildcats depended largely on rabbits in the north-west generally, myxomatosis in the mid 1950s almost certainly set back their recovery considerably.

Sightings from 1959 to today show an apparent spread to areas where they had been rare for well over a century. Today the strongholds are in central and north Argyll, north Stirling and south-west Perth, south Aberdeen, north Angus, south and north-east Inverness-shire, with a great increase in Moray and Banff. Ross and Cromarty have fair populations widely distributed, which spread into south and central Sutherland.

Despite this encouraging trend in recent years, a great controversy remains. To what significant extent, if any, has the Scottish wildcat interbred with feral domestic cats, of which there have long been a large number in the Highlands? And to what extent has such interbreeding affected total populations and, in particular, the purity of the original true wildcat race? Also, if it has occurred, how many of the modern sightings are of hybrids? There is a strong body of learned opinion, dating back to the late nineteenth century, that the wildcat population is heterogeneous, not homogeneous, the diverse elements being due to the admixture of domestic blood. Hence, for instance, the wildcat's proven ability to have more than one litter a year. But there is an equally strong body of opinion that such interbreeding is extremely rare, that its effect would probably be infinitesimal as it has not yet been *proved* that the hybrids are fertile.

The exact origin of the domestic cat is not known for sure but consensus indicates it originated from the African wildcat, *Felis lybica,* or the Sand cat, *Felis margarita,* or both (each has black rings on the tail) or with possible mixtures of other small wildcats found in the Middle East and much of Asia, such as *Felis ornata, cafra* and *ocreata.* It is believed such cats found small prey common near man's dwellings and were first domesticated by the Egyptians, prior to 1600 B.C., who esteemed their tame cats as being sacred to the goddess Pasht—from which the name "Puss" is said to derive. The tame cats spread in popularity through the Mediterranean area and, apart from the Phoenicians' introductions, also became popular with Romans who took them throughout their Empire. From the large number of domestic cat breeds that exist today, it is clear they evolved from a large genetic pool. Many unallied species of cats will interbreed, even two so far apart as lion and tiger, producing ligers and tigons. Given such evident interbreeding between the smaller similar-sized wildcats, and with regard to man's shooting and trapping of thousands of Scottish wildcats over the years, is it reasonable to assume that many, bereaved of their mates, would *not* breed with feral tabbies in heat they found on their grounds?

Hamilton in 1896, after a "careful examination" of many pelts reputed to be wildcats', wrote, "I found many indications of a mixture between the wild and the domestic cat. It seems the original wildcat as it existed in olden days has been almost exterminated throughout Europe. Its place has been taken by a mongrel race, the result of continual interbreeding during many centuries . . ." He claimed the offspring *were* fertile, though he does not appear to have given examples of proof, but he went so far as to dub the hybrids *Felis cattus feras!*

Wildcats *will* breed with domestics in captivity. Millais records Cocks as having bred some pretty hybrids between a male wildcat and a female domestic Persian cat in 1903, and in April 1904 with a female Abyssinian cat. But similar crosses had previously been bred by a Mr Pusey, of Pusey House, Berks. Pitt records she mated her wildcat male Satan to a domestic cat. She bred a number of hybrids which were not as fierce as their sire but "inherited a considerable measure of his untamed spirit" and were "nervous and queer tempered." She wrote: "These two cats will mate, and their offspring are fertile, but the hybrids show almost complete dominance of the wildcat type." She also stated that the offspring of the first *cross* showed "throwbacks as regards coat pattern and length of fur to both the wild and domestic grandparents." Boorer states that "there is always the possibility that a 'wildcat' which is reported is not pure-bred, but is the result of a mis-alliance between a domestic cat and a true wildcat, for the two species interbreed readily." Matthews states: "Individual animals may show evidence of crossings by small size and thinly furred tails." In 1920 Ritchie sought to establish wildcats had degenerated in size, and cited measurements of limb bones examined at Dunagoil in Bute:

	Prehistoric Wildcat	Modern Wildcat	Domestic Cat
Humerus (upper arm)	120mm (4¾ins)	106mm (4⅛ins)	90mm (3½ins)
Ulna (inner forearm bone)	140mm (5½ins)	119mm (4⅔ins)	101mm (4ins)
Femur (thigh bone)	135mm (5⅛ins)	119mm (4⅔ins)	99mm (4ins)

Stephen and Jenkins, however, in 1964 referred to the heterogeneity recorded among Scottish wildcats, and argued there is no evidence to suggest the increase in modern populations is due to more hybridizing. Citing upper Glen Esk, Angus, where wildcats have shown a marked increase, Jenkins states, "A census of domestic cats showed of 23 animals only one was partly tabby. If hybridizing had been occurring on an important scale it would be expected that the domestic population would show signs of it, and occasional multi-coloured variants might be seen among the wild ones. Since such obvious hybrids have not been seen, it is perhaps reasonable to assume that the variation recorded is characteristic of the Scottish race, although conceivably due to intermittent crossing throughout the recent history of the species."

I would like to make the point that domestic cats gone wild often become as wild as true wildcats, that hybrids often become as untamable as their wild parent (as Pitt confirms), and that therefore neither type would probably be around to show up in a census of twenty-three domestic cats. But Jenkins succinctly suggests it seems unlikely Scottish wildcats should be more likely to interbreed with domestic cats than their continental counterparts, and that as wildcats have increased recently in a few areas where there is a rich food supply, the number of their breeding seasons each year may be adapted to better environmental conditions. It would be interesting if this can be proved.

As both authors point out earlier: "The true picture of in-between cats will never be clear until someone has bred wildcat to domestic, hybrid to hybrid, and wildcat to hybrid." True, and again, it will only be really clear if this was to be done with a large number of cats over many years, so a reasonable facsimile of the genetic pool that exists in nature was achieved. It has been argued that though hybrids often become nearly as ferocious and assume a pelage similar to true wildcats (so how could one tell them at a distance in the wild anyway?), they usually have a fused tail, that the black rings fuse together, especially on the dorsal surface, and the tail usually tapers.

In an effort to try and solve these controversies, I examined some eighty-eight pelts of wildcats classified as *Felis silvestris grampia* in the British (Natural History) Museum in London, dating from 1867. I felt if Scottish wildcats *had* been hybridizing significantly during the last century and before, such differences should show up; also a possible gradual decline in size of specimens.

Omitting zoo and incomplete specimens and what were clearly immature pelts, I recorded all the head and body and tail lengths, divided the specimens into decades, from pre-1900 to the last dated specimen in the collection —October 1946. The brief results below are interesting. (To nearest mm, with some measurements made on dry skins):

Average pre 1900 (7 specimens)
Head and body: 639mm (25ins); *Tail:* 310mm (12¼ins)

Remarks: One silvery cat. One 1886 Dumfries cat with light *brown* pelage with second tail ring fused on dorsal surface into the black tail tip.

Average 1900 to 1910 (10 specimens)
Head and body: 566mm (22¼ins); *Tail:* 279mm (11ins)

Remarks: One 1901 Ardgour, Argyll, cat, with little buff between tail rings, the first two fused on dorsal surface.

One large 1910 cat from Loch Carron, with sandy-orange pelage, with blotched tail and light extreme tip. All other features correct.

Average 1910 to 1920 (9 specimens)
Head and body: 561mm (22ins); *Tail:* 324mm (12¾ins)

Remarks: Eight of the specimens are from 1914 inclusive, seven taken during World War One.

One dark 1916 female from Dundonnell, Ross, with third and fourth tail rings fused together.

Average 1920 to 1930 (10 specimens)
Head and body: 578mm (22¾ins); *Tail:* 287mm (11⅜ins)

Remarks: One small 1928 male from Glenshee, Perth, with sandy pelage and scrawny tapering tail, though rings clear.

One 1930 female from Dundonnell, Ross, with thin tail, though rings clear.

Average 1930 to 1940 (42 specimens)
Head and body: 573mm (22½ins); *Tail:* 293mm (11½ins)

Remarks: There appears a decline in head and body length from the early 1930s to the late 1930s, but such variation would not be necessarily representative of the Scottish wildcat race as a whole.

Heaviest recorded in collection is fifteen-pound ten-ounce 1934 male from

Ardgay, Ross, with a 625mm (24⅝ins) head and body and 360mm (14ins) tail.

One unsexed 1937 cat from Ardnamurchan, Argyll, with light sandy pelage. Its dorsal stripe split into three.

One 1933 female with tail rings all fused together.

One sandy 1938 female from Pitlochry, Perth, with three fully fused tail rings.

One 1939 male from Pitlochry with scrawny *pointed* (undamaged) tail.

Average 1940 to 1950 (4 specimens)

Head and body: 546mm (21½ins); *Tail:* 285mm (11¼ins)

Remarks: One large, 622mm-317mm (24¼ins-12½ins) unsexed, unplaced 1945 cat with sandy pelage and extreme end hairs of tail white. Usual black tip after that but first two rings are split unevenly.

One 1946 female from Spean Bridge, Inverness-shire, with scrawny tapering tail but long black tip and good rings.

While from these eighty-two specimens it appears, overall, that there has been a slight decline in size between 1867 to 1946, the lack of more specimens in the last section makes the examination on this point inconclusive. A far greater range of skins, possibly divided into areas, and including samples from 1946 to the *present day*, needs to be examined for a value judgment. What is conclusive, however, is the considerable variety (within defined limits) of pelage, the proportions of tail to body length, and the weight of wildcats. Although the Ardgay male is the heaviest recorded at fifteen pounds, ten ounces, there are several *longer* cats, most of whose weights are not recorded: a 1925 male from Spean Bridge (768mm-343mm [30⅓ins-13⅓ins]) with a total length of 1,111mm (43⅔ins); a 1933 Inverness-shire male (761mm-317mm [29¾ins-12½ins]) total 1,078mm (42¼ins); a 1909 female from Glenmoriston, Inverness-shire (746mm-318mm [29½ins-12½ins]) total 1,064mm (42ins); and a 1900 male (723mm-330mm [28⅓ins-12¾ins]) total 1,053mm (41⅛ins), who weighed twelve pounds, eight ounces. All from over forty years ago. *Recorded* weights of adult wildcats in the British Museum collection vary from: males—five pounds, fourteen ounces, and one of six pounds, to fifteen pounds, ten ounces; females—5½ pounds to 9¾ pounds (but there are several larger females whose weights, if recorded, would probably have exceeded this).

Although the wildcat is usually described as short-tailed, there are fifty-one specimens whose tails well exceed half their head and body length, the longer tails mostly occurring in the pelts dating from more recent years—a slight, though not complete, indication of an influence from possible interbreeding with the longer-tailed domestic cat. Almost universally, the wildcat is described as having a thick bushy blunt-tipped tail with well separated rings, but there are eight specimens, mainly females, with fused tail rings, plus five specimens with thin tapering tails which, as all other pelage aspects are correct, don't appear to have been wrongly classified. Details below:

Fused tails

1886 One unsexed cat
1901 One female
1910 One unsexed cat
1916 One female
1933 One female
1938 One female
1939 One female
1945 One female

Tapering tails

1928 One male
1930 One female
1935 One female
1939 One male
1946 One female

If these features *are* a sign of the influence of interbreeding with domestic cats, then Hamilton's statement that it has been occurring for centuries appears to have some validity, but much more work on a far wider range of specimens, plus a long term breeding project, would have to be completed before definite conclusions can be drawn.

It is worth noting that a fusing of the inner two of the four nape lines into a black patch, which is a feature of six of the larger males (from different areas), is not found in the specimens after 1938.

Measurements sent to me by John B. Murray of eleven pelts in the Royal Scottish Museum, Edinburgh, all taken between March 1957 and May 1959 in the Pitlochry region of Perthshire, show average lengths: head and body 566mm, tail 319mm. These averages contrast with those of the first eleven specimens which appear from this area in the British Museum collections, taken between March 1938 and February 1939, which show average lengths: head and body 577mm, tail 301mm. Again, the slight decrease in body size and increase in tail length over roughly twenty years is at least interesting, if not conclusive.

My opinion, and it is only an opinion, is that interbreeding with domestic cats *has* occurred and has had an effect on the Scottish wildcat race but that the pure breed most certainly still exists, especially on higher ground, in densest woodland and in its most remote retreats, where feral domestic cats have not yet penetrated, but that it is still a relatively rare animal, especially when viewing the British Isles as a whole.

The Scottish Highlands are not only the last real wilderness area with a magnificent fauna in Britain, but one of the last and finest in western Europe. Spain, Germany and Czechoslovakia now protect their wildcats completely. It surely can no longer be questioned that these last wild members of the cat family in Britain are today worthy of special protection laws too.

HB7H